Japanese Language in Use

Also available from Continuum:

Japanese Linguistics: An Introduction
Toshiko Yamaguchi

Japanese Language in Use

An Introduction

Toshiko Yamaguchi

continuum
LONDON • NEW YORK

Continuum

The Tower Building　　　　80 Maiden Lane
11 York Road　　　　　　　Suite 704, New York
London SE1 7NX　　　　　　NY 10038

First published 2007

British Library Cataloguing-in-Publication Data
A catalogue record for this book is available from the British Library.

ISBN: 0–8264–9351–3 (hardback)
　　　　9–780–8264–9352–1
　　　　0–8264–9352–1 (paperback)
　　　　9–780–8264–9351–4

Library of Congress Cataloging-in-Publication Data
A catalog record for this book is available from the Library of Congress.

Typeset by RefineCatch Limited, Bungay, Suffolk

Contents

Preface   ix
Acknowledgements   xi
How to use this book   xiii

Chapter 1   Pragmatics I   1

        1.1 Explanation   2
             1.1.1 のだ/んだ   2
             1.1.2 わけだ   8
             1.1.3 ものだ/もんだ   9
             1.1.4 ことだ   12
        1.2 Judgement   14
             1.2.1 Confirmation   14
             1.2.2 Expectation   15
             1.2.3 Assumption   16
             1.2.4 Regret   17
             1.2.5 Opinion   18
             1.2.6 Speculation   19
             1.2.7 Uncertainty   21
        1.3 Order and request   25
             1.3.1 Imperative forms   27
             1.3.2 な-form   28
             1.3.3 なさい   29
             1.3.4 て-form   31
             1.3.5 てください/ください   34
             1.3.6 いけません   35
             1.3.7 だめ   35
             1.3.8 んだよ   36
             1.3.9 の   37
             1.3.10 Addition of よ   37

Chapter 2		**Pragmatics II**	**39**
	2.1	Reference	40
		2.1.1 General	40
		2.1.2 Physical reference	41
		2.1.3 Intratextural reference	43
		2.1.4 Psychological reference	45
	2.2	Co-text	50
	2.3	Context	54
	2.4	Implicatures	61
		2.4.1 Conventional implicature	62
		2.4.2 Conversational implicature	63
	2.5	Figure of speech	70
		2.5.1 Metaphor	70
		2.5.2 Simile	71
		2.5.3 Personification	71
		2.5.4 Metonymy	72
Chapter 3		**Discourse**	**76**
	3.1	Coherence	76
	3.2	Cohesion	80
	3.3	Conjunctions	84
	3.4	Clausal linkage: て versus *Renyō*	87
	3.5	は and が	93
		3.5.1 Old versus new information	93
		3.5.2 Main protagonist	94
		3.5.3 Proper nouns	96
		3.5.4 Discourse theme	97
		3.5.5 New episode	97
		3.5.6 Self-contained fact	98
		3.5.7 Suspense	99
		3.5.8 Contrast	102
	3.6	Sentence-final forms	105
		3.6.1 Elaboration	106
		3.6.2 States and views	108
		3.6.3 Tied up with the protagonist	110
	3.7	Ellipsis	113
		3.7.1 What is ellipsis?	113
		3.7.2 When わたし becomes overt?	117

Chapter 4		Language and culture	121
	4.1	Gender	121
		4.1.1 Personal pronouns	121
		4.1.2 Lexical and prefixed words	126
		4.1.3 Particles	127
	4.2	In-groups and out-groups	139
		4.2.1 Family	139
		4.2.2 Company	145
	4.3	Politeness	150
	4.4	Honorifics	153
		4.4.1 Respect honorifics	153
		4.4.2 Humble honorifics	155
	4.5	Young people	160
		4.5.1 Clipping	160
		4.5.2 Affixation	161
		4.5.3 Reduplication	162
		4.5.4 Meaning extension	163
		4.5.5 Indirectness	163
		4.5.6 New grammar	165
Chapter 5		Radio talk	169
	5.1	Opening a talk	170
	5.2	Closing a talk	172
	5.3	Maintaining a talk	175
		5.3.1 Statement and reply	175
		5.3.2 Question and answer	177
		5.3.3 Request and answer	182
	5.4	Conversational strategies	183
		5.4.1 Backchannels	184
		5.4.2 Hedges	189
		5.4.3 Hesitations	190
		5.4.4 Interruptions	191
		5.4.5 Repetitions	192
		5.4.6 Laughs	193
	5.5	Talk II	194
	5.6	Transcribed Talk I	199
		References	217
		English Index	223
		Japanese Index	229

Preface

Japanese Language in Use: An Introduction is a follow-up to an earlier book entitled *Japanese Linguistics: An Introduction* (abbreviated as JL in the main text) published in February 2007. Similar to JL, the main purpose of the present book is to introduce linguistic notions relevant to the analysis of authentic texts extracted from various written and spoken sources. While the first book is concerned with language structure, this book is about language use. It selects relevant topics from the areas of pragmatics, discourse, sociolinguistics and Japanese conversation, and targets students who desire to acquire a specialist knowledge of the Japanese language. A significant difference between the two books is that the final chapter of this book is dedicated to spoken discourse, introducing the rudiments of Japanese conversation, while the focus of the other chapters is on written discourse. Readers who are already familiar with the notions explained in JL or have a specific interest in the use of Japanese language should start with this book.

Like JL, this book is structured in a way that promotes the active commitment of students to language learning. Students are encouraged to read the book attentively and carefully; and to be active participants, tackling the tasks in the activities of each chapter. The book contains 149 texts in total. The main task is to observe the linguistic facts or strategies critically displayed in these texts and to practise explicating the uses of the language. Since most activities are followed by commentaries that discuss the main subject matter, these can serve as a place where my own projections are compared with those of the readers. In other words, the commentaries are not to be taken as model answers that students have to follow or learn by heart, but instead are open to criticism. Through a combination of explanation, activity and commentary, I hope that students develop their own strategies to work effectively on the authentic texts based on their newly acquired knowledge of linguistic concepts.

The presentation of the texts used in this book differs according to their level of difficulty and their significance to the task in each activity. Some texts are given a full English translation, accompanied by a Japanese transliteration. Others are given one or the other, while still others are provided with neither translation nor transliteration. When some features of a language are considered from more than one perspective, they are cross-referenced across sections and chapters throughout the two books.

The two books were originally designed to be one single volume when I started writing in 2003. The project resulted in two independent books in 2007. These books are both 'lead-ins' to Japanese linguistics because of their emphasis on language description and understanding. In my view, students who have learned Japanese as a foreign/second language should ideally have a good grip on the 'natural language' before looking at it from theoretical perspectives. My strong hope is therefore that the knowledge acquired from these companion volumes will enable students to approach advanced language studies. Getting students to understand authentic language, either written or spoken, at an early stage of their study through a reasonable number of linguistic notions and their definitions is key to successfully educating individuals to become independent, knowledgeable specialists in Japanese studies or in Japanese linguistics. It is my heartfelt wish that the books will be useful guides for students of Japanese as well as Japanese language teachers or teachers of Japanese linguistics, and will be able to meet their demands with regard to learning and teaching.

No single book can be without shortcomings. I wholeheartedly welcome any criticisms and comments from readers and users.

TY
March 2007

Acknowledgements

The author and the publisher would like to thank the following copyright holders for permission to reprint their material:

'Calling You', from *Ushinawareru Monogatari*, first published in Japan by Kadokawa Shoten Ltd, 2003. Copyright © Otsu, Ichi. With kind permission of Kadokawa Shoten Ltd.

'Danchi Tomō', first published in Japan by *Weekly Spirits* 9 May, 2005 pp. 351–362. Copyright © Oda, Tobira. With kind permission of Shogakukan Ltd.

Denaoshitoide!, first published in Japan by Kodansha Ltd. Copyright © Isshiki, Makoto. With kind permission of Kodansha Ltd.

Doraemon: Nobita Grafity, first published in Japan by Shogakukan Ltd, 2002. Copyright © Fujiko Production.

Doraemon: Kandō-hen, first published in Japan by Shogakukan Ltd, 1995. Copyright © Fujiko Production.

Fuzoroi no Ringo-tachi III, first published in Japan by Magazine House Ltd, 1991. Copyright © Yamada, Taichi.

Hagoromo, first published in Japan by Shinchosha Ltd, 2003. Copyright © Yoshimoto, Banana.

Hiatari Ryōkō, first published in Japan by Shogakukan Ltd, 1996. Copyright © Adachi, Mitsuru. With kind permission of Shogakukan Ltd.

Itsumo Misora, first published in Japan by Shogakukan Ltd, 2001. Copyright © Adachi, Mitsuru. With kind permission of Shogakukan Ltd.

Kuma no Ko Ūfu, first published in Japan by Popular Ltd, 1977. Copyright © Kanzawa, Toshiko & Inoue, Yosuke. With kind permission of Poplar Ltd.

Kuruma no Iro wa Sora no Iro, first published in Japan by Popular Ltd, 1977. Copyright © Aman, Kimiko. With kind permission of Poplar Ltd.

Madogiwa no Totto-chan, first published in Japan by Kodansha Ltd, 1984. Copyright © Kuroyanagi, Tetsuko.

Nihon no Rekishi, vols 13 and 18, first published in Japan by Shueisha Ltd, 1982. Copyright © Shueisha.

'Te o Nigiru Dorobō no Monogatari', from *Ushinawareru Monogatari*, first published in Japan by Kadokawa Shoten Ltd, 2003. Copyright © Otsu, Ichi. With kind permission of Kadokawa Shoten Ltd.

'Tsumetai te', from *Sabishigari*, first published in Japan by Kodansha Ltd, 2002. Copyright © Tōdō, Shizuko.

The extracts from *Asahi.com*, first appeared in Japan by Asahi Newspaper Ltd, 2003–2005. Copyright © Asahi Newspaper Ltd.

The extracts from *Asahi Newspaper*, first published in Japan by Asahi Newspaper Ltd, 1940, 1985, 2002–2005. Copyright © Asahi Newspaper Ltd.

The extracts from *Yomiuri Newspaper*, first published in Japan by Yomiuri Newspaper Ltd, 2004. Copyright © Yomiuri Newspaper Ltd.

Two extracts from *Welcome to the Studio*, first broadcast in Singapore by the International Channel, 2006. Copyright © FM96.3.

Publisher's Note: Every effort has been made to contact copyright holders; however, we would welcome correspondence from copyright holders whom we have been unable to locate.

How to use this book

Presentation of Japanese words, sentences and authentic texts

1. Japanese words in the main text are romanized in italics and given an English translation.

   > When we say 小泉首相 *Koizumi shushō* 'Prime Minister Koizumi', we refer to the prime minister of Japan. We can also refer to a book that we hold in our hand by saying これ *kore* 'this'. (Chapter 2, section 2.1.1)

2. Romanization is normally expressed in small letters, but the first letter of a romanized word is capitalized when the word belongs to any of the following categories:

   > Personal name: 愛子 *Aiko*, トットちゃん *Totto-chan*
   > Place name: 東京 *Tōkyō*, 金沢 *Kanazawa*
   > Book title: ふぞろいの林檎たち *Fuzoroi no Ringo-tachi*
   > Example sentence: 日本語は難しいです。
   > *Nihongo wa muzukashī desu*
   > (Chapter 3, Example (1))

3. The English translation is not always given, particularly when the word is merely functional.

   > In this section we deal with four types of explanation, のだ *noda*, わけだ *wakeda*, ものだ *monoda* and ことだ *kotoda*, all of which contain a copula だ *da* preceded by の, わけ, もの or こと. (Chapter 1, section 1.1)

4. When the same Japanese word is used a second time in the same paragraph, it appears without romanization or an English translation. In the text below, ドラえもん and のび太 (in the third and fourth lines) appear alone because they are mentioned for the second time.

   > Try to explain what information のび太 *Nobita* and ドラえもん *Doraemon* share in this drawing and why they use んだ *nda* here. ドラえもん possesses a magic mirror with which のび太 can see more than what is visible to the naked eye. (Chapter 1, Activity 2)

5. Example sentences are presented with their romanization in the second line and their English translation in the third line.

ごはんの上にきゅうりをのせます。
Gohan no ue ni kyūri o nosemasu
Place pieces of the cucumbers on the rice.
(Chapter 4, Example (59))

6. When a word or phrase is emphasized in an example, it is presented in boldface in the Japanese example and, where adequate, its romanization or English translation.

   これはあんパンです。 (Chapter 2, Example (1))
   Kore *wa anpan desu*
   This is a red bean bun.

7. × means that the example is unacceptable.

   ×佐藤さんが私から本をもらった。
   (Chapter 7, Example (36) in JL)

8. △ means that although the example is not completely unacceptable, an alternative given in the text is more appropriate.

   △ ぼくははな夫をころされた。
   (Chapter 7, Example (22) in JL)

9. Authentic texts are presented in a box (Text 5.25 in Chapter 5 is an exception), the majority of which are transliterated in *hiragana*. Some texts are translated into English. Authentic texts are accompanied by their source (e.g., © year copyright holder / title (page), name of the publisher).

   ┌─────────────────────────────────────┐
   「とにかく自分のスイングをするだけだった。結果が

   出たのは何より？その通り。」試合後、片岡はぽつり、

   ぽつりと口を開いた。笑顔は見せなかった。
   └─────────────────────────────────────┘

(Chapter 3, Text 23)

Methods of romanization

10. The Hepburn system has been adopted. This system was devised by James Curtis Hepburn (1815–1911), an American missionary who arrived in Japan in 1859, and it is nowadays the most widely used method to transcribe Japanese into the Roman alphabet. The table below compiles basic and palatalized sounds. It reads in horizontal rows from left to right. One row consists of one,

two, three or five sounds. Each sound is presented in the Roman alphabet (the first column) and *hiragana* (the second column). These two presentations are separated by a dotted line. Shaded rows indicate voiced sounds as opposed to their voiceless alternatives.

Basic sounds										Palatalized sounds					
a	あ	i	い	u	う	e	え	o	お						
ka	か	ki	き	ku	く	ke	け	ko	こ	kya	きゃ	kyu	きゅ	kyo	きょ
ga	が	gi	ぎ	gu	ぐ	ge	げ	go	ご	gya	ぎゃ	gyu	ぎゅ	gyo	ぎょ
sa	さ	shi	し	su	す	se	せ	so	そ	sha	しゃ	shu	しゅ	sho	しょ
za	ざ	ji	じ	zu	ず	ze	ぜ	zo	ぞ	ja	じゃ	ju	じゅ	jo	じょ
ta	た	chi	ち	tsu	つ	te	て	to	と	cha	ちゃ	chu	ちゅ	cho	ちょ
da	だ	ji	ぢ	zu	づ	de	で	do	ど						
na	な	ni	に	nu	ぬ	ne	ね	no	の	nya	にゃ	nyu	にゅ	nyo	にょ
ha	は	hi	ひ	fu	ふ	he	へ	ho	ほ	hya	ひゃ	hyu	ひゅ	hyo	ひょ
pa	ぱ	pi	ぴ	pu	ぷ	pe	ぺ	po	ぽ	pya	ぴゃ	pyu	ぴゅ	pyo	ぴょ
ba	ば	bi	び	bu	ぶ	be	べ	bo	ぼ	bya	びゃ	byu	びゅ	byo	びょ
ma	ま	mi	み	mu	む	me	め	mo	も	mya	みゃ	myu	みゅ	myo	みょ
ya	や			yu	ゆ			yo	よ						
ra	ら	ri	り	ru	る	re	れ	ro	ろ	rya	りゃ	ryu	りゅ	ryo	りょ
wa	わ							o	を						
n	ん														

11. Special attention should be paid to the following sounds: し, じ, ち, つ, しゃ, しゅ, しょ, じゃ, じゅ, じょ, ちゃ, ちゅ and ちょ are presented as 'shi', 'ji', 'chi', 'tsu', 'sha', 'shu', 'sho', 'ja', 'ju', 'jo', 'cha', 'chu' and 'cho', respectively.

12. When a small っ is romanized, the consonant following it is doubled; for example, 真っ赤 as 'makka' and ちょっと as 'chotto'. When the doubled consonant contains 'shi', 'chi', 'shu' or 'sho', the doubling is presented as 'sshi', 'tchi', 'sshu' or 'ssho'. For example, キッチン is given as 'kitchin' and キャッシュ as 'kyasshu'.

13. Long vowels are presented by a macron placed immediately above the prolonged vowel. For example, 重要 is given as 'jūyō' and シーズン as 'sīzun'.

14. Long vowels are not indicated with macrons in English text. For example, くまの子ウーフ is presented as 'Kuma no Ko Ūfu' in Japanese text, but is given as 'A Bear Cub Uf' when it appears in English text (Chapter 1, Activity 1, p. 4). Similarly, the conventional romanization of Kōdansha or Tōkyō is Kodansha or Tokyo without a macron in English text.

15. When a special consonant ん is followed by a vowel or the consonant /n/, it is separated from the vowel/consonant by a hyphen to avoid the mispronunciation of the two independent sounds. For example, 館内 is given as 'kan-nai' (Chapter 2, Text 8) or そんな as 'son-na' (Chapter 3, Text 4).

Presentation of complex expressions

16. When compound words are a composite of two or more smaller compound words, they are separated by a hyphen. For example, 親子電話 is given as 'oyako-denwa'.

17. When compound words are a composite of a compound word and a single word, they are separated by a hyphen. For example, 腕時計 is given as 'ude-dokei'.

18. When compound words are a composite of a compound word and a character, they are separated by a hyphen according to the meaningful units they consist of. For example, 日記帳 is given as 'nikki-chō' and 決勝戦 as 'kesshō-sen'. When the compound word has an idiosyncratic meaning as a whole, it is not separated by a hyphen. For example, 春一番 'the first storm in the spring' is given as 'haruichiban'.

19. When compound words consist of two characters, they are not separated by a hyphen. For example, 着陸 is given as 'chakuriku' and 花畑 as 'hanabatake'.

20. When grammatical markers are attached to a word, they are represented as part of the word. For example, while 書いた (containing the past tense marker 'ta') is presented as 'kaita', 殺された (containing the passive marker 'are' and the past tense marker 'ta') is presented as 'korosareta'.

21. When complex predicates (containing a connective て) are romanized, they are presented as being attached to the verb but separated from what follows it.

> 先生：今日は、たくさんの学生が遅れていますね。
> *Sensē: Kyō wa takusan no gakusē ga okurete imasu ne*
> (Chapter 1, Example (2))

22. When complex predicates do not appear as parts of an

independent example but are referred to in the main text, they may be presented as a single unit.

> いってしまいました *itteshimaimashita*
> (Chapter 4, Activity 1)

23. Particles are presented as separate units. The first example below contains から, は and ぜ. Copulas are treated in the same way. The second example below contains a copula だ.

> 明日から、酒はやめるぜ。 (Chapter 4, Example (36))
> *Ashita kara, sake wa yameru ze*
> I will stop drinking beginning tomorrow.

> これはうそのような話だ。 (Chapter 2, Example (12))
> *Kore wa uso no yōna hanashi da*
> This is like an incredible story.

24. When a grammatical marker (e.g., copula だ) appears in a meaningful unit, it is represented as part of the previous element.

> それで今日はあくびばかりしてるわけだ。
> *Sorede kyō wa akubi bakari shiteru wakeda*
> That's the reason why you are yawning all the time today.
> (Chapter 1, Example (4))

Notes on romanization and phonetic and phonological transcriptions

25. Romanization is not identical to phonological or phonetic transcription (see Chapter 1, Table 1.1 in JL), although they occasionally resemble each other. The former provides the hands-on pronunciation of words based on English phonography, while the latter adopts IPA (the International Phonetic Alphabet) and is used to describe the sounds. The examples below are presented in the following order: (i) romanization, (ii) phonological transcription, and (iii) phonetic transcription:

> 布団 'Japanese-style bed quilt'
> (i) *futon*　　(ii) /huton/　　(iii) [ɸɯ̟ton]
> 月 'moon'
> (i) *tsuki*　　(ii) /tuki/　　(iii) [tsɯ̟ki̥]

Abbreviations

26. The following abbreviations are employed in the book:

| JL | *Japanese Linguistics* | Chapter 1 to Chapter 5 |
| A | Anaphoric | Chapter 2, Activity 1 (Table 2.2) |

C	Cataphoric	Chapter 2, Activity 1
		(Table 2.2)
S1	Sentence 1	Chapter 3, sections 3.3 and 3.4
		(Table 3.1)
S2	Sentence 2	Chapter 3, sections 3.3 and 3.4
		(Table 3.1)
Aux	Auxiliary	Chapter 3, section 3.6.3
		(Table 3.5)
C	Customer	Chapter 3, section 3.7.1
S	Shop assistant	Chapter 3, section 3.7.1
M	Male	Chapter 4, section 4.1.3
F	Female	Chapter 4, section 4.1.3
INFORM	Informal	Chapter 4, section 4.1.3
		(Table 4.2)
T	Text	Chapter 4, section 4.1.3
		(Table 4.3)
P	Person	Chapter 4, section 4.2.1
H	Host	Chapter 5, the whole text
G	Guest	Chapter 5, the whole text

Index

27. Indexes, English and Japanese, are provided at the end of the book. Key concepts are in boldface both in the main text and the index to draw the reader's special attention.

1 Pragmatics I

Pragmatics is the study of the ways in which language is used. 語用論 *goyōron*, which means 'the study of language use', is the general term for pragmatics in Japanese linguistics. Broadly speaking, pragmatics centres on two perspectives. First, language exists with its user (e.g., speaker versus hearer and writer versus reader). Second, language use is an embodiment of human communication. Language and communication are inextricably linked because humans use language, written or spoken, to embody their intentional activity (Searle 1969: 16–21, cited in Mey 2001: 94); in other words, any utterance we make results not from a mere collection of forms but rather articulates the user's communicative intentions or 'forces'. One method of articulating the user's intention is to express it explicitly. 'Explicit' is meant as an overt linguistic form of the user's intention.

How does the speaker express his or her intentions explicitly while speaking or writing? Two linguistic notions are in order here; one is **modality** and the other is **speech act**. Modality determines the factual status of the proposition described by the sentence. The speaker makes more explicit the truth-value of the sentence by adding a degree of certainty about what is said (Palmer 2001: 24ff.). For example, when I say 'It's possible that he will come tomorrow', I elaborate on his coming based on my knowledge that his coming is likely to happen. By contrast, speech act is concerned with the **performative** attitude of the speaker towards the proposition described by the sentence. When someone performs an act, he or she carries out an action deliberately. For Austin (1962: 79), 'apologize' is performative, while 'being sorry' is descriptive, the reason being that we can say 'I am willing to apologize', but we cannot say 'I am willing to be sorry' (ibid.: 80). The speaker performs an act to make explicit how he or she is involved in the denoted action. When I say 'I promise that he will come tomorrow', I express my attitude towards his coming through my act of promising; that is, I am 'performing an act' on his coming.

The concept of 'speech act' goes back to John Austin's influential book *How To Do Things With Words* (1962), which argues that a language user does not simply describe the states of affairs but also performs an act on them. When I say 'I will come tomorrow', this utterance can be ambiguous from the perspective of speech act. It can be my desire ('I want to come tomorrow') or it can also be my offer ('I offer to come tomorrow'). According to Austin, sentences are categorized as 'descriptive' (or

1

alternatively 'constative') and 'performative'. Descriptive sentences let the speaker describe the fact, while performative sentences let the speaker act on the fact. The use of performative verbs (e.g., *promise* and *offer*) enables the speaker to integrate his performance with regard to what is stated in the utterance. The systematization of performative acts or more technically **illocutionary acts** has been the central theme among speech act theorists (see Hancher 1979 as an example of an earlier study).

Japanese has quite a few expressions that play a role in verbalizing the speaker's intentions. However, it is not easy to draw a clear-cut line between modality and speech act in authentic texts, since in a number of cases the degree of certainty and the act of performance coalesce. This chapter has therefore chosen three theoretically neutral concepts to look more closely at the nature of a speaker's intended meanings (explanation (1.1), judgement (1.2) and order and request (1.3)).

1.1 Explanation

Japanese possesses expressions used for **explanation**. Explanation means that the speaker gives reasons for, or details about, the existence of a situation under discussion. For example, instead of simply saying 'The bus was delayed', Japanese will often say '*I explain to you* that the bus was delayed' or '*The reason is* that the bus was delayed'. In this section we deal with four types of explanation, のだ *noda*, わけだ *wakeda*, ものだ *monoda* and ことだ *kotoda*, all of which contain a copula だ *da* preceded by の, わけ, もの or こと. When these forms are used in colloquial speech, /no/ is normally reduced to /N/, a special consonant (see Chapter 2, section 2.1 in JL), resulting in んだ /Nda/ and もんだ /moNda/, respectively. The uses of these four variables for explanation differ, depending on the aspects of the background speech settings in which the utterance is embedded. In other words, the speaker 'explains', to add his opinions about the fact described by the main clause. As Rubin remarks (1998: 86), these forms often function as rhetorical devices. They are used even if there is nothing specific to 'explain', but by using the form of explanation the speaker succeeds in being effective or persuasive in his communication.

1.1.1 のだ/んだ

のだ has two functions. One is to give a reason for the fact shared by both speaker and addressee, and the other is to emphasize the speaker's statement. The latter is often accompanied by the specific emotions of an individual. Consider (1), in which a student gives a reason why he was late for class.

2

(1) a. 先生: 加藤君、１０分遅刻ですよ。
     Sensē: Katō-kun, juppun chikoku desu yo
   b. 学生 1. 大雪でバスがなかなか来なかった**んです**。
     *Gakusē 1: Ōyuki de basu ga nakanaka konakatta**ndesu***
   a. Teacher: Mr Kato, you're 10 minutes late.
   b. Student 1. The bus didn't come on time due to heavy snowfall.

When the teacher notes that many other students have not arrived for her class, one student may tell her that the reason is the delay of the bus due to heavy snowfall. In this context, からです *karadesu* instead of んです *ndesu* can be used (2). Since the student who answered is not delayed, 'being late for class' is not his own problem. The use of からです leads the teacher and student to talk about the students' delay objectively. It is awkward to replace (1) with からだ, showing that the reason the student provides in (1) concerns his own delay. The contrast between (1) and (2) suggests that んです functions as an explanation in the interlocutor's personal domain (see Sakairi et al. 1991: 155–156).

(2) a. 先生 : 今日は、たくさんの学生が遅れていますね。
     Sensē: Kyō wa takusan no gakusē ga okurete imasu ne
   b. 学生2 ：大雪でバスが遅れている**からです**。
     *Gakusē 2: Ōyuki de basu ga okurete iru **karadesu***
   a. Teacher: There are many students late for class.
   b. Student 2: Because the bus is delayed due to heavy snowfall.

Let us look at the second function of んです. When and how does the speaker actually emphasize his statement? As Makino and Tsutsui state (1986: 327), 'emphasis' comes into play when the speaker emotively accentuates his idea with or imposes it upon the addressee. A typical situation with the speaker emphasizing his explanation might take place in a doctor's office. The conversation, such as in (3), is what normally happens between a doctor and a patient. Here the conversation would be unnatural if んです were not present. The patient must explain his bodily conditions as explicitly as possible, hence the use of んです. Interestingly, (1) could be paraphrased as 大雪でバスが来ませんでした 'The bus didn't come due to heavy snowfall' in a simple declarative, suggesting that (1) is less emphatic than (3b). A paraphrase of (3b) in English translation could be '*I assure you that* I have a headache' or '*I assure you* that I suffer from nausea'. The possibility of adding a performative verb makes it clear that the speaker is acting performatively in the given speech situation. As mentioned earlier, an emphatic expression of this kind is a rhetorical device to persuade the doctor.

(3) a. 医者 : どうしましたか。
     Isha: Dōshimashitaka
   b. 患者 ：頭が痛い**んです**。吐き気がする**んです**。
     *Kanja: Atama ga ita**ndesu**. Hakike ga suru**ndesu***

3

    a. Doctor: What can I do for you?
            (literally: What happened to you?)
    b. Patient: I have a headache. I suffer from nausea.

It is important to note that のだ *noda* further functions as a rhetorical device in an interrogative. In this case the issue is not really an explanation. Text 1.1 illustrates a scene from ドラえもん *Doraemon,* in which フーコ *Fūko,* a small typhoon, leaves のび太's *Nobita's* house in order to fight against a big typhoon that has caused lots of rain in the area. With a closer look, we notice that an interrogative どこへ行くんだ *Doko e ikunda* 'where are you going?' is not simply a query about where she goes but is, more importantly, a warning: she should stay at home (because it would be dangerous). When the rain finally stops, フーコ does not come back to the house, indicating her death.

Text 1.1   どこへ行くんだ

© Fujiko Production / *Doraemon*: *Kandō-hen* (p. 47), Shogakukan

Activity 1

Narrative texts often contain many んだ *nda-*forms to emphasize the protagonist's mental condition. Those who have read JL may recall a text extracted from a children's book くまの子ウーフ *Kuma no Ko Ūfu* 'A Bear Cub Ufu' in Activity 7 in Chapter 3. In this text you were asked to examine mimetic words. This time you will isolate sentences with んだ and explain why んだ is used in the story. んだ certainly serves to make the conversation between a bear cub ウーフ and those he encounters more 'vivid', 'realistic' and 'exciting' for the reader. This passage contains not only んだ but also のです *nodesu,* its politeness counterpart. Before you continue, think about why のです is used in line 17 instead of んだ. The answer may be that the sentences in which it occurs are not uttered by ウーフ but instead are parts of the narration of the story, or more precisely, the third-person narrator's descriptions of the happenings on the scene. Text 1.2 is a combination of dialogue and narration. When ウーフ converses with those he encounters, んだ is used constantly.

4

Text 1.2 くまの子ウーフ

1	ぶなの木の下で、ひるねをしていたくまの子ウーフは、目をさまして、木をみあげました。ぶなの木は、みどりの葉をつけて、さもきもちよさそうに風にふかれていました。「木はいいなあ。木になりたいなあ。」と、ウーフは思いました。
5	「こんなもしゃもしゃの毛皮のかわりに、みどりの葉っぱをつけて、すずしそうに立っているんだ。そしてさ、じっとたっていたら、みつばちがきて、すをつくるかもしれないね。そしたら、ぼく、きのぼりしなくてもはちみつがなめられるよ。だって、ぼくが木なんだもの。」ウーフははちみつのことをかんがえて、ごくんとつばをのみこみま
10	した。それから、 「でも ...」と、くびをふりました。 「木は、はちみつをなめないのかな。そんならぼくは、みつばちになろう。そしたら、すごいぞ。ぼくのうちにはいつだって、はちみつがいっぱいあるんだ。」ウーフは、たまらなくなりました。けれど、い
15	ったい、どうやったら、みつばちになれるのでしょう。ウーフは両手をひろげました。みつばちはいつだって、こんなふうにして、ぶーんととんでくるのです。[...] 水をばしゃばしゃさせて、やっとおきあがったときです。 「おう、くまこう、なにしにきたんだ。」
20	川の中からふなが、かおをつきだしました。 「おまえ、わしたちをつかまえにきたな。」 「ちがうよ、ちがうよ。」 ウーフは、びっくりしていいました。 「ぼく、さかなになりたいの。ねえ、さかなは手も足もないくせに、
25	どうして泳げるの。」

すると、ふなは目玉をぎょろっとさせて、いばりました。

「わしらは生まれたときから泳げるんだ。おまえもさかなになり

たけりゃ、そのけむくじゃらな手と足をすてちゃいな。」

「えっ？」

30 「そいつはろくなことをしない。たたいたり、すくったり、口へもっ

ていったりな。」

ふなは小さなからだの、どこからでるかと思うような大声でどなり

ました。

「おう、あんまりちかづくなよ。くまこう。」

35 「うー。ぼくはただ、どうしたらさかなになれるかきいているんだ。」

「ほ？おまえ、ほんきかい。そんなら教えてやってもいいがな。さか

なになるには、つらいしゅぎょうがいるんだぞ。」

「そのつらいしゅぎょうって、なに。」

「つまりだな、その、ふゆになって、川にこおりがぎちぎちはってき

40 ても、おまえさんみたいな毛皮にくるまっちゃおれんのだ。はだかで

川のそこにすわっていられかな。」

© 1977 Kanzawa, Toshiko / *Kuma no Ko Ūfu* (pp. 6–12), Poplar

Commentary

Table 1.1 (p. 7) summarizes the occurrence of のだ, んだ or のです in Text 1.2.

It is important to note that three のだ forms (①, ② and ③) express ウーフ's imaginations, while others (⑥, ⑦, ⑧, ⑨ and ⑩) refer to the real situation. Each sentence of the first three describes ウーフ's dream of becoming a tree, succeeding in drawing the reader's attention to what ウーフ says in his utterance. If he became a tree, bees would start building nests around him, and this would enable him to eat honey without climbing the tree. The use of んだ here serves to emphasize a statement; the story writer succeeds in representing ウーフ's enthusiasm for being listened to – he is eager to give details about his dreams. ④ and ⑤ are part of the narration. のです is used as the narrator shares the information about ウーフ's dreams and comments on them. ⑥ なにしにきたんだ 'Why did

Table 1.1 *Summary of the occurrence of* のだ, んだ *or* のです *in Text 1.2*

No.	Line	Examples	Translations
①	6	すずしそうにたっている**んだ**	I would be standing calmly.
②	8	木な**んだ**もの	I would be a tree.
③	13–14	はちみつがいっぱいある**んだ**	There would be lots of honey.
④	15	どうやったら、みつばちになれる**のでしょう**	How on earth can he become a bee?
⑤	17	ぶーんととんでくる**のです**	Bees would be flying over here.
⑥	19	なにしにきた**んだ**	Why did you come here?
⑦	27	泳げる**んだ**	We can swim.
⑧	35	きいている**んだ**	I'm asking you.
⑨	37	しゅぎょうがいる**んだ**ぞ	You will need training.
⑩	40	毛皮にくるまっちゃおれん**のだ**	We can't be wrapped up in a fur.

you come here?', uttered by a carp, asks for an explanation from ウーフ, who is, to his surprise, on the riverside. ⑦ and ⑧ also contain んだ. The former gives an explanation of ウーフ's question of why carps can swim. The latter also gives an account of the carp's question of why ウーフ came close to him. In the last two instances (⑨ and ⑩), the carp warns ウーフ that he has to undergo tough training in order to become a fish, indicating that during the training he would not be wrapped up in fur but instead remain naked in the water, even if the river were frozen. The instances of のだ in this passage clearly show that the protagonists make use of the forms of explanation to facilitate their communication.

Activity 2

This activity is not accompanied by a commentary.

One crucial property of のだ is that the participants in the conversation share certain information that enables them to use explanation. Try to explain what information のび太 *Nobita* and ドラえもん *Doraemon* share in this drawing and why they use んだ here. ドラえもん possesses a magic mirror with which のび太 can see more than what is visible to the naked eye. のび太 finds an ant on the floor of his house and wants to look more carefully at it in the mirror (see Text 1.36, p. 31). The mirror shows a large number of flying ants. At this moment, のび太 and ドラえもん look outside the house and find a great number of ants flying in the sky (Text 1.3), exclaiming that a prince and a princess have been born and that they are now setting off to create a new country. The picture on the mirror is a reflection of the reality outside the house.

Text 1.3 うまれたんだ／旅だつんだよ

© Fujiko Production / *Doraemon*: *Kandō-hen* (pp. 176–177), Shogakukan

1.1.2 わけだ

わけ *wake* literally means 'reason', and わけだ *wakeda* is used to give a reason or an explanation for a previous context. Contrary to のだ *noda*, the meaning of explanation comes directly from the original meaning of わけ. Both のだ and わけだ function as explanatory devices, though the way they give the explanation differs. Recall that のだ is used to signal an emphatic explanation by the speaker. わけだ is, in contrast, used to give a **logical explanation** for, or a logical consequence of, an event. In (4) student B explains A's constant yawning by the fact that he stayed awake late the night before. One can see a logical relationship between staying awake till three o'clock in the morning and yawning during the day.

(4)　学生 A: 昨夜 3 時まで友達と話してたよ。
　　gakusē A: *Sakuya sanji made tomodachi to hanashiteta yo*
　　Student A: I talked with my friends till three o'clock this morning.
　　学生 B: それで今日はあくびばかりしてる**わけだ**ね。
　　gakusē B: *Sorede kyō wa akubi bakari shiteru **wakeda** ne*
　　Student B: That's the reason why you are yawning all the time today.

Note that the examples with のだ／んだin (1) and (3) cannot be replaced by わけだ. Clearly the reason is that they do not deal with logical explanation.

Activity 3

In narrative, logical explanation is represented as a combination of 'cause' and 'effect'. Example (4) demonstrates that the わけ *wake* clause expresses 'effect', while cause is mentioned in the previous utterance. In Text 1.4, extracted from Asahi.com, わけだ *wakeda* likewise represents 'effect'. Read the passage carefully and determine which part of it serves as cause.

Text 1.4 わけだ

> エルサレムからバスで揺られること２時間ほどで、左手にアクア・ブル
>
> ーの湖が現れた。岸と青い水の境目を、まるでソルティドッグのグラスの
>
> ように真っ白い塩がふちどる。あたりは摂氏４０度を超える砂漠で、ヨル
>
> ダン川から流れ込む水よりも蒸発する水分量のほうが多く、塩分が高い湖
>
> ができたという**わけだ**。

© 2005 *Asahi.com* 14 March

Translation:
After we took a bus trip for about two hours from Jerusalem, the lake in aqua blue caught our sight. The border between the shore and the blue water is fringed by pure white salt that resembles a glass of Salty Dog. The adjacent area is a desert with the temperature more than 40 degrees centigrade. The water that evaporates is higher in amount than the water that flows into the sea from the Jordan River. **These explain** how the lake with a high containment of salt came into existence.

Commentary

わけだ refers to the consequence of the event(s) previously mentioned. In Text 1.4 the journalist reports on the Dead Sea in Israel. The Sea contains an excessive amount of salt. This passage explains how such a sea came into existence. The journalist first reports that the temperature in the desert that surrounds the sea is over 40 degrees centigrade, and because of this high temperature, the amount of water that evaporates is much higher than that of the water that flows into the sea. The high evaporation of water is reported as the cause of the creation of the Sea. This article neatly demonstrates the structure of cause and effect by using わけだ.

1.1.3 ものだ／もんだ

もの *mono* literally means a 'thing' that is tangible. もの in a sentence like おいしい**もの**がたべたい *oishī mono ga tabetai* 'I would like to eat something delicious' refers to a tangible thing that is delicious. When もの is combined with the copula だ, it serves to provide an explanation in two different ways. In one situation, ものだ provides an explanation based on the speaker's personal experience, whereby a sense of emotion or

9

empathy can be aroused. In the other it provides an explanation based on a general opinion or fact shared by most (if not all) people. Let us look at Text 7.3 in Chapter 7 (p. 164) in JL once again. Here you find an expression 道順をたずねられる**ものだ**から *michijun o tazunerareru **monoda** kara* 'As we are asked the way to (the restaurant)'. Here the journalist gives an explanation as to why subway station personnel and liquor store clerks wanted to check the exact location of the restaurant. We can rephrase the sentence as 道順をたずねられるから by removing ものだ, but this paraphrase cannot represent the author's appreciation of the fact that many people talk about this restaurant. Now consider (5). ものだ here 'explains' the correlation between being away from Japan and the process of acculturation. Imagine a context in which Mr X, who has been living outside of Japan for thirty years, recalls his experience abroad. What he says in (5) does not express his appreciation or emotion but rather refers to a general phenomenon that Japanese people living abroad may encounter. While people's concern about the location of the restaurant is a temporal, short-lived phenomenon, the acculturation phenomenon can be seen as a universal fact that can affect most people. Thus, the use of ものだ in (5) functions as an explanation based on a general opinion.

> (5) 外国に長くいると、日本文化から遠のく**ものだ**。
> *Gaikoku ni nagaku iru to, nihon-bunka kara tōnoku **monoda***
> When we stay in a foreign country for a long time, we tend to be estranged from Japanese culture.

Activity 4

Text 1.5 is taken from a leading article (社説 *shasetsu*) in Asahi Newspaper. You have learned that ものだ has two functions. Try to identify which function is more appropriate for ものだ in this article and explain why.

Text 1.5 税金を払っているようなものだ

米経済のかじ取り役である連邦準備制度理事会 (FRB) も「最近の景気

減速は石油価格の大幅な上昇による」と認めている。今後、物価

の上昇が目立ってくれば、各国の中央銀行は利上げへの不安から

株安の連鎖を起こしかねない。今の石油価格のうち、1 バレルあたり

5〜10ドル分はイラク情勢やテロの不安などの危険要因による上乗せ分(リスクプレミアム)と見られている。消費国は産油国に税金を払っているようなものだ。

Vocabulary:
かじ取り役 *kajitori-yaku*　leader
連邦準備制度理事会 *renpō junbi sēdo rijikai*　Federal Reserve Board
景気減速 *kēki-gensoku*　business decrease
石油価格 *sekiyu-kakaku*　oil price
大幅な上層 *ōhaba na jōsō*　large increase
物価 *bukka*　prices
目立つ *medatsu*　prominent
各国 *kakkoku*　each country
中央銀行 *chūō-ginkō*　central bank
利上げ *riage*　rise in rate of interest
株安 *kabu-yasu*　a fall in shares
連鎖 *rensa*　chain
起こす *okosu*　to cause, trigger
情勢 *jōsē*　the state of affairs, conditions, situations
危険要因 *kiken-yōin*　dangerous primary factors
上乗せ分 *uwanose-bun*　a sum added to an ordinary price, risk premium
消費国 *shōhi-koku*　consumer country
産油国 *sanyu-koku*　oil producing country
ような This functions as a simile (see Chapter 2, section 2.5.2). The author states that since the current oil price includes a risk premium, it looks as if consumer countries are paying a tax to oil-producing countries.

Commentary

By using ものだ, the journalist demonstrates the general point of view shared by many nations that consumer countries like Japan are paying a 'tax' to the oil-producing countries. Tax, as used here, corresponds to the amount of money resulting from the rise of the oil price. The journalist states that the increase of the oil price may run parallel to the additional amount triggered by 'dangerous primary factors' such as the war in Iraq and terrorism. A sum of US$5 to $10 per barrel may be used to pay off these factors, and this can be called a 'risk premium' (リスクプレミウム). From this context, there is no sign that the journalist is presenting his personal point of view with ものだ.

A word of caution is in order. もんだ *monda* (a colloquial form of ものだ) frequently occurs when the speaker is reflecting upon a past event of his or hers. Text 1.6 is a drawing extracted from ドラえもん *Doraemon*, depicting のび太 *Nobita* back in the lumberyard where he used to play as a little boy. Using もんだ expresses a sense of yearning. Although this form does not have an explanatory component to the same extent as ものだ in Text 1.5, his recalling his favourite place to play explains a strong attachment to the past.

Text 1.6　遊んだもんだ

© Fujiko Production / *Doraemon: Nobita-Grafity* (p. 46), Shogakukan

1.1.4　ことだ

こと *koto* literally means 'thing'. Unlike もの, it refers to an intangible or abstract thing. It also serves to form a nominal element out of a verbal element. For example, ぼくは音楽をきく**こと**が趣味だ *boku wa ongaku o kiku koto ga shumi da* means that my hobby is to listen to music, whereby 'to listen' is a nominalized verb. One can say どういう**こと**ですか *dō yū koto desu ka* in much the same way as どういうわけですか *dō yū wake desuka* 'What does it mean?' to seek an explanation from one's speech partner. Note, however, that ことだ *kotoda* is not used in exactly the same way as other expressions of explanation. When こと is combined with だ, it gives an account of the previous context. That is, ことだ 'explains' the topic previously mentioned by giving an account of it. Consider Texts 1.7 and 1.8, which exemplify two cases. Text 1.7 explains that the completion of big apartment buildings (topic) means that people who move in will become new residents in the area (account). Text 1.8 explains that a common characteristic shared by Hungary and the Akita prefecture in Japan (topic) is the high rate of suicide by aged people (account). By using ことだ, the author elaborates on or adds more details to the content of the topic mentioned.

Text 1.7

> ある街に、大規模マンションが突然出現する。それは、数千人の人が
>
> 突然その街に引っ越してきて新住民になる**ことだ**。(slightly modified by
>
> the author)

© 2005 *Asahi.com* 25 February

Translation:
Large-scaled apartment buildings suddenly come into existence in a certain district. **This means** that a few thousand people will suddenly move in and become new residents.

Text 1.8

> 高い自殺率が続くハンガリーには、秋田県と共通した特徴がうかがえる。
>
> 高齢者の自殺が多い**ことだ**。

© 2004 *Asahi.com* 27 September

Translation:
One can see a common characteristic between Hungary, which continuously marks a high rate of suicide, and the Akita prefecture. **That is**, aged people commit suicide.

Recall Text 1.4, where you find わけだ as a tool of explanation. In this passage, ことだ can be used instead if the sentences are reordered in such a way that the topic (the creation of a salty lake) is mentioned first, followed by two accounts that explain why this happens. This syntactic reversion enables the author to describe the same fact in a different way, as shown in Text 1.9. The addition of 理由 *riyū* 'reason' into the first sentence makes the logical link between the topic and the accounts clearer.

Text 1.9

> 塩分が高い湖ができる**理由**が二つある。あたりが摂氏４０度を超える砂
>
> 漠である**こと**、ヨルダン川から流れ込む水よりも蒸発する水分量のほう
>
> が多い**ことだ**。

Translation:
There are two **reasons** for the creation of the lake that contains a high quantity of salt. **One is that** the lake is located adjacent to the desert where the temperature is more than 40 degrees centigrade, and **the other is that** the water that evaporates from the lake is greater in quantity than the water that flows in from the Jordan River.

1.2 Judgement

When a speaker uses language, he often makes a **judgement** about the state of affairs represented by a sentence. The speaker makes use of various linguistic forms to express, or explicate, his judgement. The concept of judgement can be treated within various mental, emotional or epistemological domains depending on how the speaker judges, or forms an opinion about, the situation he participates in. Traditionally, judgement has been studied in the field of epistemic modality (Palmer 2001: Chapter 2), a grammatical category concerned with the speaker's knowledge. That is to say, the speaker makes judgements regarding the truth value or factuality of the proposition described by the sentence. This section does not present an exhaustive list of expressions of judgement; instead, its main purpose is to demonstrate how judgement is utilized in colloquial settings as depicted in ドラえもん *Doraemon*, since this popular comic strip neatly demonstrates various subconcepts of judgement and gives insight into their communicative importance in authentic text.

1.2.1 Confirmation

In Text 1.10, のび太's *Nobita*'s father is at the hospital where his wife has just given birth to a baby boy, whose name is のび太. The father is puzzled because he was expecting the boy's grandmother to be there. This expectation is verbalized by だろ *daro*, which is the marker to seek his wife's **confirmation** ('Where is your mother?' 'I guess/assume she was with you' [or alternatively, 'she might have been with you']). His wife's mother was at the hospital but went back home to report the birth of a new baby to her ancestors, while his wife, still lying in bed in the hospital, assumes that they must have passed each other on the way. だろ is a casual form, shortened from だろう *darō*, expressing that the speaker asks for confirmation of or agreement with his utterance. The expression of だろ is pronounced with a rising intonation. The important point is that だろう or だろ is used mainly by men in colloquial speech, while its equivalent for women is でしょう *deshō* or its shortened form でしょ *desho*. Confirmation does not simply arise out of the blue. のび太's father asks for confirmation based on his firm expectation that his mother-in-law must have been at the hospital.

14

Because of this relatively strong self-confidence, だろ and でしょ are not used for people whose social status is higher than the speaker's (e.g., company president, section chief, school teacher, medical doctor, lawyer or professor).

Text 1.10   つきそっていたんだろ

© Fujiko Production / *Doraemon*: *Nobita-Grafity* (p. 130), Shogakukan

1.2.2   Expectation

By using はずだ *hazuda*, the speaker expresses his **expectation**. The expectation arises as a result of the logical outcome of a current state of affairs. In Text 1.11, the officer presumes that animals would also sacrifice their lives for the country. This expectation arises from the fact that thousands of soldiers fight in the war and sacrifice their lives. The death of animals is, in his opinion, a logical consequence of the truth of war. The form はずだ is a male register and makes the utterance assertive. If the officer were a woman, she would probably use はずです in the same context.

In a less assertive speech situation, as in Text 1.12, another form, はずよ with an interactional particle よ *yo* (see Chapter 4, section 4.1.3 for the notion 'interactional particle), may be used more frequently. しずか's *Shizuka*'s mother anticipates that her daughter is likely to be back soon. This judgement is based on her assumption that her daughter is not far away from the house. In the story, however, しずか does not come back despite のび太 *Nobita* and ドラえもん's *Doraemon*'s long wait. In this regard, the use of はず may express the mother's politeness to the guests by providing her positive anticipation.

Text 1.11　死んでくれるはずだ　　**Text 1.12**　すぐもどるはずよ

© Fujiko Production / *Doraemon*:
Kandō-hen (p. 24), Shogakukan

© Fujiko Production / *Doraemon*:
Nobita-Grafity (p. 168), Shogakukan

1.2.3 Assumption

In the literature on Japanese grammar, たがる *tagaru* is understood as an expression of desire on the part of a third person – the person whom I or you talk about. This expression is composed of たい *tai*, an expression of desire for the first person (i.e., I), and a verbal suffix がる *garu* (い *i* is deleted). This suffix describes the third person's inner feelings and is therefore rarely used for the first or second person. For example, こわ**がる** *kowagaru* 'to be afraid of', うれし**がる** *ureshigaru* 'to be happy', 悲し**がる** *kanashigaru* 'to feel sad, sorrowful', さびし**がる** *sabishigaru* 'to feel lonely', and 強**がる** *tsuyogaru* 'to pretend to be strong' are expressions describing the third person's inner feelings.

In Text 1.13, のび太 *Nobita* meets ノビスケ *Nobisuke*, his future son. Because のび太 had already witnessed that ノビスケ intended to go out but was stopped by his mother, のび太 now knows, as shown in the first drawing, what ノビスケ wanted (and still wants) to do. Here たがる is used to describe the second person's (ノビスケ's) desire. As shown in the second drawing, ノビスケ confesses that there is a concert that night. Rather than merely expressing the second person's desire, たがる here serves to express のび太's **assumption** about what ノビスケ actually wants to do. Since the conversation takes place between two people, the availability of たがる is contradictory. The point, therefore, is that たがる can be used when the speaker not only describes the addressee's desire but also makes an 'assumptive' statement about it.

Text 1.13　遊びにいきたがってたね

© Fujiko Production / *Doraemon*: *Nobita-Grafity* (p. 212), Shogakukan

1.2.4 Regret

しまう *shimau* literally means 'to put something away', as in 子供が箱におもちゃを**しまう** *Kodomo ga hako ni omocha o shimau* 'The child puts the toys away in the box'. When てしまう *teshimau* is attached to another verb, it expresses a feeling of 'regret' on the part of the speaker. In Text 1.14, ドラえもん *Doraemon* is talking with a tree who came to Earth to move away all the plants because humans are not taking good care of them. てしまう is uttered by ドラえもん to emphasize that Earth would become a dead planet without plants. By expressing **regret**, the actual message here is that the plants should not be taken away from Earth. The situation referred to with てしまう can be considered hypothetical, that is, the speaker's statement is a premise: if all the plants were taken away, Earth would be a dead planet. Recall that another meaning of てしまう is to express the finality of a situation (see Chapter 7, section 7.4.2.4 in JL).

As shown in Text 1.15, てしまう has ちゃう *chau* as a contracted form. This form is used more frequently between members of the same **in-group** (see Chapter 4, section 4.2 for the term 'in-group'). Note that ドラえもん uses てしまう in Text 1.14 with the tree, whom he meets for the first time, and ちゃう with のび太, his in-group member.

Text 1.14　死の星になってしまう　　**Text 1.15**
団地になっちゃうんだよね

© Fujiko Production / *Doraemon*:
Kandō-hen (p. 212), Shogakukan

© Fujiko Production /
Doraemon: *Kandō-hen*
(p. 206), Shogakukan

The use of the contracted form ちゃう is not restricted only to
てしまう. Similar contracted forms ちゃ *cha* and じゃ *ja* replace ては
tewa and its voiced alternative では *dewa*, as shown in (6) and (7). The
alteration of the first consonant /t/ and /d/ to /tʃ/ and /dʒ/ is given rise to by
palatalizing the original sound (see Table 1.1 in Chapter 1 in JL).

(6) 行かなく**ては**いけない → 行かなく**ちゃ**いけない。
*Ikanaku **tewa** ikenai*　　*Ikanaku **cha** ikenai*
(7) 帰ってくるわけ**では**ない → 帰ってくるわけ**じゃ**ない。
*Kaette kuruwake **dewa** nai*　　*Kaette kuruwake **ja** nai*

In a more casual speech situation (when interlocutors know each
other quite well), てしまう becomes ちまう *chimau*. Speakers who use this
expression must be older than のび太, who is about ten years old (in the
fourth grade in elementary school) and ドラえもん, who is a creature of
the future (born in 2112). The expression ちまう will be demonstrated in
Text 4.4 (lines 22, 29) in Chapter 4 (pp. 134–135), in which the speaker is a
young company employee.

1.2.5 Opinion

When Japanese people express their **personal opinions**, they often attach
と思う *to omou* 'I think that', a combination of the quotative と and the
verb 思う. The addition of と思う serves to soften the assertiveness of the
opinion (see also McClure 2000: 145–147). In Text 1.16, のび太's *Nobita*'s
mother expresses the sentiment that no one in the world is more manly and
trustworthy than her husband. Interestingly, と思う is also used when a

young woman tells her close friend that she loves her husband (see Text 4.5 (line 21) in Chapter 4, pp. 135–136).

Text 1.16　この世にいないと思うわ

© Fujiko Production / *Doraemon: Nobita-Grafity* (p. 86), Shogakukan

1.2.6 Speculation

When the speaker **speculates** about a situation, he bases it on some accessible evidence, whether it be firsthand, auditory, perceptive or deductive. To use a technical term, we refer to **evidentiality**, one subarea of modality (Palmer 2001). This section introduces expressions such as らしい *rashī*, みたい *mitai* and そうだ *sōda*, which are not always interchangeable. In Text 1.17, のび太 *Nobita* speculates that ノンちゃん *Non-chan* (his female friend) could be ill because he has not seen her since the happening of an incident he now recalls with much regret – having been tricked by his bad friends, he destroyed the dinner table at which they were playing with each other. His speculation is based on the fact that he no longer sees her. In reality, her absence is not caused by her illness but by her sudden departure abroad. Speculation with らしい can also be based on what the speaker sees or observes with his own eyes. In Text 1.18, the child elephant meets his mother for the first time in many years. Although he does not remember her clearly at first, he gradually draws closer to her, signalling his recognition of her. At this moment, のび太 utters 思い出したらしい *omoidashita rashī* 'It looks like he remembers her'. Texts 1.17 and 18 show that the main property of らしい is the presence of deductive thoughts in the speaker's mind based on observable evidence; he or she reaches a conclusion from evidence already known to him or her, although there is no direct evidence for this deduction.

Text 1.17　病気になったらしい　　**Text 1.18**　思い出したらしい

© Fujiko Production / *Doraemon*:
Nobita-Grafity (p. 73), Shogakukan

© Fujiko Production / *Doraemon*:
Kando-hen (p. 192), Shogakukan

Another way of expressing speculation is to use みたい *mitai*. As shown in Text 1.19, the speaker makes a speculation based on use of one of the five senses (sight, smell, hearing, taste and touch). Here there is no presence of deductive thoughts. のび太 and his friends arrive at the ant's house and witness how the ants are taking care of the larva. Based on their firsthand personal experience using their sight, they formulate their speculation.

Text 1.19　かわいがっているみたい　　**Text 1.20**
ふってきたみたい

© Fujiko Production / *Doraemon*:
Kandō-hen (p. 173), Shogakukan

© Fujiko Production /
Doraemon: *Kandō-hen*
(p. 200), Shogakukan

In Text 1.20, のび太's mother uses みたい *mitai* because she has heard raindrops. Similar to Text 1.19, there are no deductive thoughts here; her speculation about the likelihood of rain is based on her firsthand

20

experience, that is, audition. Although the difference in meaning between らしい *rashī* and みたい is subtle, のび太 and his friends in Text 1.19 cannot say かわいがっているらしい *kawaigatte iru rashī* on the ground that the act of 'caring about something' is a judgement based directly on the scene that the speakers have witnessed; no inference is involved. In contrast, it is possible to say 思いだしたみたい *omoidashita mitai* in Text 1.18, if we emphasize that this utterance relies solely on のび太's actual visual perception (e.g., both elephants look happy). According to McClure (2000: 141–142), the confidence level of みたい is higher than らしい because the judgement is often based on observed evidence.

Text 1.21   おいしそうだ

© Fujiko Production / *Doraemon*: *Nobita-Grafity* (p. 116), Shogakukan

Another expression, そうだ *sōda*, underlines firsthand visual evidence to make a speculation. On a tropical island, のび太 stops at a palm tree with coconuts. Because they look big and fresh, he speculates that they should be delicious, as shown in Text 1.21. Unlike みたい, the use of そうだ here depends solely on visual evidence directly attainable by the speaker. そうだ with this meaning accepts the *renyo*-form of a verb or an adjective. When it accepts a dictionary form (e.g., おいしいそうだ), it carries the meaning of hearsay.

1.2.7 Uncertainty

Uncertainty is expressed when a speaker is not confident of a situation he participates in. While there are several expressions such as かもしれない *kamoshirenai* 'may, might', だろう *darō* 'will probably' (man's register), でしょう *deshō* 'will probably' (woman's register), all of which express the speaker's uncertainty about a situation, this section focuses on かしら *kashira*, which occurs frequently in ドラえもん *Doraemon*. (だろう and でしょう have two contrasting meanings (see section 1.2.1).) With かしら, the speaker expresses not only uncertainty but also emotions, such as

21

surprise or astonishment, that arise from unexpectedness. Both Texts 1.22 and 23 demonstrate an unexpected event. Because of this surprising situation, the feeling of uncertainty is evoked accordingly. In Text 1.22, のび太's *Nobita*'s mother is astonished at his sitting at the desk and studying, and she therefore wonders if he has a fever. Text 1.23 mentions two boys who are astonished at a violent man (whose nickname is キョーボー *kyōbō* 'an atrocious man') because he is suddenly behaving mildly. This man constantly mistreated his dog ペソ *peso*. But のび太, having heard this sad story, had switched the dog with its owner. Later on, the two boys, playing baseball, hit the ball by mistake into a garden. When they meet the garden's owner, to their astonishment he not only returns the ball but even asks to join the game. 本気かしら *honki kashira* expresses uncertainty derived from their feeling of great surprise.

Text 1.22　熱でもあるんじゃないかしら

© Fujiko Production / *Doraemon*: *Kandō-hen* (p. 100), Shogakukan

Text 1.23　本気かしら

© Fujiko Production / *Doraemon*: *Kandō-hen* (p. 91), Shogakukan

As shown in 1.24, かしら is not always accompanied by surprise or astonishment. It may simply express the speaker's uncertainty: のび太's mother is uncertain about the location of her wallet, that is, she wonders where she put her wallet.

Text 1.24　としのせいかしら

© Fujiko Production / *Doraemon: Nobita-Grafity* (p. 38), Shogakukan

かしら can also express a sense of expectation in some situations. Text 1.25 depicts the moment at which のび太's family is expecting a newborn baby (who is actually のび太 himself). のび太, his father and ドラえもん are at the hospital. ドラえもん utters どんな子かしら *Don-na ko kashira* 'What does he look like?' because he looks forward to meeting のび太 when he was a baby. This utterance expresses 'uncertainty' in the sense that the baby has not yet been delivered and people do not know what the baby is like.

Text 1.25　どんな子かしら

© Fujiko Production / *Doraemon: Nobita-Grafity* (p. 11), Shogakukan

In the literature, it is considered that かしら is used mainly by women, but in this story it is used also by men.

Activity 5

There is no commentary for this activity.

There are three expressions (marked in boldface) used for judgement in the following extract from a short story, 冷たい手 *Tsumetai te* 'Cold

Hands'. Explain why the protagonists employ these expressions in the story. This extract describes a scene that takes place in 秋子's *Akiko*'s new house. Her old female friend, 比呂子 *Hiroko*, visits her to celebrate her recent move to a new house. 比呂子, now married to a man twenty years older than she, was a lover of 秋子's present husband. She intentionally came to their new house during his absence.

Text 1.26

1　秋子がキッチンからコーヒーカップをのせた盆を手にあらわれた。

　クッキーを盛った愛らしい藤の器もその横に置かれている。

　「コーヒーでよかった**かしら** 」

　「ええ、ありがとう」

5　「このクッキーも召し上がってみて。私の手作りなの。下の子が、い

　くつかアトピーがかった体質なものだから、おやつもできるだけ手作

　りにして、無添加の材料を使うようにしているの」ベランダを背にし

　てソファにすわっている比呂子の斜め前、キッチンに近い肘掛け

　椅子に秋子は浅く腰かけた。

10　あらためて顔を見合わせ、秋子は口もとをほころばせる。

　「本当によくきてくれたわ。比呂子さん。少しも変わらないのねえ。

　うらわましいわ。きっとご主人に大切にされているからなのね」

　三十八歳の比呂子と武村はちょうど二十の開きがあった。[…]

　「ぶしつけだけど、これ、ささやかな新築祝い。何かよさ**そう**な品を、

15　と考えたのだけれど、住まいにちぐはぐなものになり**そう**で。もっと

　早くおわたししなくてはならなかったのに、ごめんなさいね。」

　「こっちこそ、かえって気をつかわせ**てしまって**」

> そう言ってから秋子は独身の頃の癖そのままに、目をくるりと大きく
>
> させ、両肩をすくませた。

Exercise

Try to find texts (e.g., novels, short stories, fairy tales or newspaper articles) that contain expressions embedding the language user's judgement and explain their pragmatic functions. It is also a good idea to work on the extracts in this textbook in their original text and examine them in a wider scope.

1.3 Order and request

When we communicate with each other, we not only explain things (section 1.1) or judge things (section 1.2), but also ask our interlocutors to do things. When we want to get someone to take some action, we generally have two ways at our disposal: one is to **give an order** and the other is to **make a request**. The former is stronger than the latter. When we order someone to do something, we expect the addressee to comply with our order. But when we make a request, the addressee may not necessarily comply with it. Japanese has specific speech act verbs, such as 命じる *mējiru* (to do something) or 禁じる *kinjiru* (not to do something), to form an order, as shown in (8) and (9), though these verbs are rarely used in everyday conversation.

(8) ただちに出発することを**命じる**。
     *Tadachini shuppatsu-suru koto o **mējiru***
     We order you to leave immediately.
(9) この川で泳ぐことを**禁じる**。
     *Kono kawa de oyogu koto o **kinjiru***
     We forbid you to swim in this river.

Order expressions are formed in three ways. First, the imperative suffixes *-e* or *-ro* may be attached to the verb stem. These two inflections are differentiated depending on whether the verb root ends with a consonant (e.g., 読め /yom-e/ 'Read') or vowel (e.g., 見ろ /mi-ro/ 'Look'). One exception is the irregular verb 来い 'come', which receives the inflection *-i* /ko-i/ (see Text 1.30). Second, なさい may be attached to the verb stem (e.g., 読みなさい /yomi-nasai/ 'Please read', 見なさい /mi-nasai/ 'Please look'). Third, the particle な may be attached to the verb stem to form a positive or negative order form. When な is attached to the *renyo*-form of

25

the verb, it forms a positive order (e.g., 読みな/yomi-na/ 'Read', 見な/mi-na/ 'Look'). When it is attached to the dictionary-form of the verb, it forms a negative order (e.g., 読むな /yomu-na/ 'Don't read', 見るな/miru-na/ 'Don't look').

Request expressions are created by attaching て or で to the verb stem (e.g., 読んで /yon-de/ 'Read', 見て /mi-te/ 'Look'). The simplest request form is the addition of て only (Text 1.36), but て is often accompanied by a morphologically complex form such as てください (Text 1.42), てくれ (Text 1.38), ておくれ (Text 1.37), or てごらん (Text 1.39).

Bear in mind that these different order/request forms are used adequately only when the speaker takes different degrees of **register** into consideration (see also Activity 5, Chapter 2, p. 57). As Mey puts it (2001: 41), register refers to 'the linguistic resources that speakers have at their disposal to mark their attitude towards their interlocutors'. In functional grammar (see Chapter 3 in Halliday and Hasan 1985), register is determined by the 'context of a situation', or more precisely, the configurations of three components: (i) field (situations in which the text is located), (ii) tenor (particulars of the participants), and (iii) mode (tasks the text aims at). When an order/request is made in a Japanese spoken context, their usage is highly dependent on the following dimensions: (i) formal and informal speech levels, (ii) male and female speech styles, and (iii) social status of the interlocutors. When a robber robs a bank, he orders the bank employees to raise their hands: he would say 手を上げろ *Te o agero* 'Hand(s) up!'. The register of this utterance falls under a vulgar style. A mother would say to her child 手をあげなさい *Te o agenasai* 'raise your hand' when they cross a road. The crucial factor in deciding the register of this speech is that なさい signals the mother-and-child relationship. This form embodies a social relationship that holds between senior and junior persons in a less formal speech setting (e.g., a family). A teacher may encourage her pupils to raise their hand in the classroom when they have questions. She would say 手を上げてください *Te o agete kudasai* 'Raise your hand', indicating that the utterance is in the formal register because the teacher-and-pupil relationship still maintains social distance. If ろ or なさい were used here, it would sound coercive and inappropriate. These three variations of 'Raise your hand' mirror three different social activities that interact with the choice of a language form.

In what follows we continue examining ドラえもん *Doraemon* (1995, 2002) and look more closely at how and what order/request forms are in use in a spoken context. It will become clear that order/request forms say more than their literal, imperative meanings when they are employed in different social situations.

1.3.1 Imperative forms

As briefly mentioned above, order forms are created by adding -*e*, -*ro* or -*i* to the verb stem. These forms are frequently employed by men, particularly when the conversation takes place among close friends in a colloquial setting. These forms express a strong authority and hence strong compliance. Text 1.27 depicts everyone running away from a location. The same form is used when someone gets angry, as shown in Text 1.28. 勉強しろ *Benkyō shiro* 'Study' does not necessarily convey its literal meaning of ordering のび太 *Nobita* to study, but because のび太 secretly used ドラえもん's *Doraemon's* money, this imperative form connotes that のび太 should do something sensible rather than filching someone else's money.

Text 1.27 にげろ　　　　　　　　　**Text 1.28** 勉強しろ

© Fujiko Production / *Doraemon*: *Kandō-hen* (p. 174), Shogakukan

© Fujiko Production / *Doraemon*: *Nobita-Grafity* (p. 62), Shogakukan

When people support a person who is competing with someone else, the imperative form is in order. As demonstrated in Text 1.29, のび太 and ドラえもん are encouraging フー子 *Fūko*, who fights against the big typhoon. In this speech situation, the form is used regardless of whom it is directed to; that is, the same form (まけるな *Makeruna* 'Do not lose', がんばれ *Ganbare* 'Fight') can be used for their father or even their teacher if they are fighting in the same way. Text 1.29 depicts two boys (ドラえもん is a male cat), but girls could also use the same form in the same situation.

We mentioned in Text 1.28 that する takes しろ as an order form. Another irregular verb is 来る *kuru* 'to come', which becomes 来い *koi* 'come' as an order form. As depicted by Text 1.30, this form is used by men towards their close friends, animals or animal-like creatures. のび太 talks with a wind called フー子 *Fūko*.

Text 1.29 がんばれ

© Fujiko Production /
Doraemon: *Kandō-hen*
(p. 47), Shogakukan

Text 1.30 とってこい

© Fujiko Production / *Doraemon*:
Kandō-hen (p. 44), Shogakukan

1.3.2 な-form

With the particle な *na*, one can construe two different order forms, positive and negative. These forms are used among people who know each other and occur in informal situations. The positive form serves to show a sense of intimacy, as shown in Text 1.31. のび太 *Nobita* has made friends with a dog called イチ *Ichi* 'one', who was found abandoned near his house. Since his mother dislikes keeping animals at home, he decides to leave the dog in an ancient world with a machine that produces food. When he bids イチ farewell, のび太 says to him のびのびと生きな *Nob-inobi to ikina* 'Live well'. The adverb のびのびと indicates a situation in which one leads a life without constraints.

Text 1.31 生きな

© Fujiko Production / *Doraemon*: *Kandō-hen* (p. 154), Shogakukan

Text 1.32 むちゃくちゃいうな

© Fujiko Production / *Doraemon*: *Kandō-hen* (p. 181), Shogakukan

Text 1.32 shows a negative order form. むちゃくちゃ *muchakucha* is an abstract noun indicating 'disorder' or 'confusion'. While のび太 wishes to keep animals (e.g., lions or elephants) at home, ドラえもん tries to get him to realize that what he says is unrealistic and unreasonable. な-forms are uttered more commonly by men, but it may be possible for women to use them.

1.3.3 なさい

なさい *nasai* is an order form derived from the honorific verb なさる *nasaru* 'to do' by changing *-ru* to *-i* at the end. This form is attached to the *renyo-* form (し in する 'to do' and ね in ねる 'to sleep') and is often used by parents talking to their children. All three examples in Texts 1.33, 34 and 35 represent the parent–child relationship. Note, however, that the exact meaning of なさい differs slightly depending on the speech situation in which the form is employed. In Text 1.33, its use is considered as the mother's encouragement to her son, while in Text 1.34 it is a mild order to her son to go to bed. In Text 1.35, のび太's *Nobita*'s father is not in a good mood and gives のび太 a strong command to look up his questions in an encyclopedia by himself (although he ends up struggling to find an 'answer' to his homework). This last order form implies strong compli-ance, while the father maintains his parental relationship to his son by not using the short imperative form (i.e., しらべろ 'Look in').

Text 1.33 元気だしなさい

© Fujiko Production / *Doraemon*: *Kandō-hen* (p. 154), Shogakukan

Text 1.34 ねなさい

© Fujiko Production / *Doraemon*: *Kandō-hen* (p. 181), Shogakukan

Text 1.35 しらべなさい

© Fujiko Production / *Doraemon*: *Nobita-Grafity* (p. 147), Shogakukan

1.3.4　て-form

As we mentioned at the outset of this section, the simplest request form is to add て *te* to the verb stem. Because it is a request form, it sounds much less authoritarian than short forms. In Text 1.36, のび太 *Nobita* asks ドラえもん *Doraemon* to lend him a magic mirror, since he has found an ant in the house (see Text 1.3, p. 8). In this situation a short form (かせ 'Lend me') would be too rude, and another alternative かしな *kashina* sounds odd, as these forms fail to express a sense of 'asking'.

Text 1.36　かして

© Fujiko Production / *Doraemon*: *Kandō-hen* (p. 176), Shogakukan

　て-forms are often combined with auxiliary verbs such as おくれ *okure*, くれ *kure* or ごらん *goran*, as seen in Texts 1.37 to 1.39, to add some extra meaning. These forms are not used by all members of Japanese society, and their occurrence depends on the social status of the speaker and addressee.

　ておくれ is used by older people, particularly parents or grandparents, to their in-group members in informal settings. Young people do not use this form. When おくれ is attached, it expresses the speaker's wish. In Text 1.37, のび太's grandmother expresses her wishes for her grandson that he will grow vigorously in the future.

　てくれ is a request form used most commonly by men, as in Text 1.38. くれ is another irregular imperative form of the verb くれる, meaning 'to give' (see Chapter 7, section 7.3.5 in JL). てつだってくれ *tetsudatte kure* literally means 'Give me your help'.

31

Text 1.37 そだっておくれ

© Fujiko Production / *Doraemon*: *Nobita-Grafity* (p. 50), Shogakukan

Text 1.38 てつだってくれ

© Fujiko Production / *Doraemon*: *Kandō-hen* (p. 61), Shogakukan

Text 1.39 contains て ごらん *te goran*. This is originally an honorific expression and is written as ご覧 (see Table 4.8, p. 154 in Chapter 4), meaning 'to look at, watch'. When it co-occurs with て, it means 'to make a try'. It is used by both genders directed towards an addressee who has the same or lower social status than the speaker's. のび太 *Nobita* is talking to a male tree whose name is キー坊 *Kībō*. This tree is considered to have a lower status than his, since のび太 is older and can teach him how to read letters.

Text 1.39　おぼえてごらん

© Fujiko Production / *Doraemon*: *Kandō-hen* (p. 198), Shogakukan

　　When someone becomes angry, てらっしゃい *terasshai* can be used to mark his or her high degree of anger. らっしゃい is shortened from いらっしゃい, and the latter is formed by replacing *-ru* in いらっしゃる with *-i*. Note that いらっしゃる is an honorific expression for 行く *iku* 'to go', 来る *kuru* 'to come' and いる 'to be' (see Table 4.8, p. 154 in Chapter 4). For example, we say with honour 先生がいらっしゃいました *Sensē ga irasshai mashita* 'The teacher is coming/has arrived'. When combined with て, ていらっしゃる serves as an honorific form of the aspectual ている *te iru*. Thus, 先生は私をおぼえている *sensē wa watashi o oboete iru* 'The teacher remembers me' becomes 先生は私をおぼえていらっしゃる in an honorific form. The actual message conveyed in Text 1.40 goes beyond a request; のび太's mother has firmly determined not to give up her search until she finds him (who is hiding inside the big snail shell). It is possible to say おぼえていなさい *oboeteinasai*, but the use of an honorific form has a stronger impact on the mother's determination.

Text 1.40　おぼえてらっしゃい

© Fujiko Production / *Doraemon*: *Kandō-hen* (p. 78), Shogakukan

　　When the て-form is presented by the negative ない, it can be used by the speaker to soothe his addressee. In Text 1.41, ドラえもん tries to encourage のび太, who is emotionally excited. It is true that ドラえもん is asking のび太 not to get excited, but the real message conveyed might be his attempt to calm him down.

Text 1.41　こうふんしないで

© Fujiko Production / *Doraemon*: *Nobita-Grafity* (p. 36), Shogakukan

1.3.5　てください/ください

A small tree called キー坊 *Kībō* is talking to a tree whom she has met for the first time. They are talking about the plants on Earth. In a formal speech situation like this, an order form is too rude to be used; instead a request form such as てください is preferred, as shown in Text 1.42.

As in Text 1.43, ください *kudasai* can appear alone without て *te*, since it is a main verb meaning 'to give'. It is derived from a respect honorific form くださる *kudasaru* for くれる *kureru* 'to give'. ください is formed by replacing る with い. Due to the formal situation, ください takes precedence over other informal expressions such as くれ or ちょうだい *chōdai* (a shortened humble honorific form for もらう *morau* 'to receive').

Text 1.42　やめてください

© Fujiko Production / *Doraemon*: *Kandō-hen* (p. 213), Shogakukan

Text 1.43　時間をください

© Fujiko Production / *Doraemon*: *Kandō-hen* (p. 215), Shogakukan

1.3.6　いけません

When a senior person prohibits a junior person from taking some action, negative order forms are used. While young people may use な-forms among one another, parents are more likely to use ません *masen*, as shown in Text 1.44. In the mother-and-son speech situation depicted here, the な-form (植えるな *Ueruna* 'Don't plant!') would be too strong, since the mother is teaching her children the right way to handle the trees in the garden. いけません *ikemasen* is preceded by a contracted form ちゃ *cha*, whose full form is ては *tewa*.

Text 1.44　植えちゃいけません

© Fujiko Production / *Doraemon*: *Kandō-hen* (p. 196), Shogakukan

1.3.7　だめ

だめ *dame* 'no, nothing' is used in an informal situation in which the speaker prohibits someone from taking a particular action. It is preceded by the contracted form ちゃ *cha* (whose full form is ては *tewa*) and can be used regardless of the social status of the interlocutors. In Text 1.45, のび太's *Nobita*'s grandmother has got up and come to the living room. Knowing that she is ill, のび太 warns her to go back to bed. His utterance

35

is translatable as 'You must not get up and come here' or 'You should stay in bed'. It is grammatically possible to paraphrase the imperative in Text 1.44 with 植えちゃだめ *Uechadame*, whereby the mother's didactic tone may disappear.

Text 1.45　おきてきちゃだめ

© Fujiko Production / *Doraemon*: *Nobita-Grafity* (p. 66), Shogakukan

1.3.8　んだよ

Requests can be expressed without using request forms. For example, んだよ *ndayo* (combination of んだ [section 1.1.1 above] and an inter-actional particle よ [Chapter 4, section 4.1.3]) can be used to make a request. のび太 *Nobita* has taken a child elephant from Africa and made friends with him. ドラえもん *Doraemon* asks him to return it to Africa the following morning. The use of んだよ sounds less authoritarian and, in this regard, ドラえもん plays a didactic role in giving のび太 a moral instruction.

Text 1.46　帰すんだよ

© Fujiko Production / *Doraemon*: *Kandō-hen* (p. 186), Shogakukan

1.3.9　の

Similarly to Text 1.46, orders can be expressed without using a specific order form. As seen in Text 1.47, using a negative interrogative きけないの *kikenaino* 'Don't you listen to me?', the mother gives her son のび太 *Nobita* a strong command. She is angry because he has taken animals to the house again. The actual message she is conveying is not that he does not listen to her but that he must listen to her words (いうこと *yūkoto*, literally: 'what one says'). By articulating two messages (one is のび太's failure to listen to his mother and the other is the mother's order to listen to her) in one form, きけないの sounds more authoritarian than ききなさい 'Listen', which is commonly used between the mother and her son/daughter (see section 1.3.3). As an exclamation mark indicates, the utterance serves as a rhetorical question in the sense that it does not expect an answer and makes a strong assertion (see also Wales 2001: 346).

Text 1.47　きけないの

© Fujiko Production / *Doraemon*: *Kandō-hen* (p. 78), Shogakulan

1.3.10　Addition of よ

There is a tendency for some order forms to be accompanied by an assertive particle よ *yo* (see also Backhouse 1993: 136). A pragmatic characteristic of よ is to put forward or emphasize the speaker's assertions or opinions to the addressee. This characteristic of よ goes well with the nature of order and request. Some examples, which we have seen above, are compatible with よ: まてよ *mateyo* 'Wait', しろよ *shiroyo* 'Do it', だめよ *dameyo* 'Not good'. Men's forms such as まて *mate* and しろ *shiro* strengthen their assertiveness when accompanied by よ, while だめ creates a women's register. Its male register would be だめだよ *damedayo* (see Chapter 4, section 4.1.3 for the use of particles).

Activity 6

Try to complete Table 1.2, which summarizes the order/request forms dealt with above. Pay special attention to the following three questions: (i) Is the speech situation formal or informal? (ii) Who uses the form to whom? and (iii) In which speech setting does the conversation take place? If none of the columns is relevant, leave it blank. Try to complete the activity without looking back at the explanations in section 1.3.

Table 1.2 *Summary of order/request forms*

No.	Examples	Formality	Speaker	Addressee	Speech acts
1	勉強しろ	informal	male	male/female	order
2	がんばれ		male/female		
3	生きな				
4	むちゃくちゃいうな				order
5	しらべなさい		parent		
6	かして				
7	そだっておくれ			child	
8	おぼえてごらん				
9	おぼえてらっしゃい		mother		
10	こうふんしないで				
11	やめてください	formal	first encounter	first encounter	request
12	植えちゃいけません				
13	おきてきちゃだめ				negative request
14	帰すんだよ				
15	さけないの	informal	female		
16	だめよ				negative order

Exercise

Most of the conversations we have examined in section 1.3 take place either between young boys or between parents and their sons. Find *manga* that handle female protagonists and list, following Table 1.2, the order and request forms used by women.

38

2 Pragmatics II

Chapter 1 has examined linguistic forms that convey the speaker's message directly. This chapter, too, deals with the speaker's message, but here our focus is on the message that is conveyed indirectly, that is, the message is implicit since it is interpretable in accordance with covert conditions. Chapter 2 presents five areas of pragmatics that play a role in interpreting the indirect message: (i) reference (2.1) (how does the speaker link the linguistic form to its reference in the real world?), (ii) co-text (2.2) (what roles does the linguistic environment play?), (iii) context (2.3) (how relevant is the speech setting?), (iv) implicature (2.4) (what does the speaker tacitly mean when he speaks?), and (v) figure of speech (2.5) (how does the speaker expand the literal meaning of a linguistic form?).

As shown in Chapter 1, when the speaker uses language, his concern is not only the grammaticality of a sentence, but also its appropriateness as an utterance in a given speech situation. To put it differently, utterances may 'implicate' different scenarios depending on how they are to be taken in a given speech situation. 'John is eating a cake' literally means that he puts the cake into his mouth, chews it and swallows it, but if this is uttered in a situation in which the cake is mouldy, it can convey the speaker's embarrassment. The linguistic form 'John is eating a cake' is *used* to express the speaker's unstated emotions. This example reveals that pragmatics is the study of 'speaker meaning' (see also Yule 1996: 3). When someone utters a sentence, it often carries an implicit meaning aside from its invariant literal meaning. When someone says 'It's hot', its literal meaning is a statement mentioning a high temperature (see also Chapter 6, pp. 133 and 152–153 in JL for the meaning of 'hot'). This statement can function as an indirect request when a guest utters it in a running taxi; the taxi driver may immediately switch on the air conditioner. A communicative meaning arises when the speaker means or the addressee understands more than what the linguistic form literally says. Communicative meaning is thus anchored to the context: if the context is perceived differently, the interlocutors will also consider the same fact differently. 'John is eating a cake' can refer to the speaker's relief, not embarrassment, when John, who had been ill a long time, finally has an appetite for eating.

Otto Jespersen (1992 [1924]: 309–312) remarks that three things are to be distinguished in speech activity: expression, suppression and impression. Expression is what the speaker gives, while suppression is what the speaker does not give. Impression is what the addressee receives. What is noteworthy in his observation is that impression is often produced by what is suppressed, and this production is more effective than by expression. Expressing details is thus redundant and often blatant. This effectiveness happens because suppression leaves room for the addressee to be imaginative or to think over what is not expressed. Jespersen also discusses Japanese drawings in which contours are not completely filled in. This incompleteness, he argues, becomes a resource for an artistic effect. The same line of thinking can be applied to language use: the less the speaker says, the greater the effect is.

2.1 Reference

2.1.1 General

Reference is an act in which the user of a language makes use of linguistic forms to refer to entities in the real or imagined world.[1] When we say 小泉首相 *Koizumi shushō* 'Prime Minister Koizumi', we refer to the prime minister of Japan. We can also refer to a book that we hold in our hand by saying これ *kore* 'this'. In the first case, we have a 'proper' reference because the act of reference is direct. Nouns such as 小泉首相 are therefore called **proper nouns** or 固有名詞 *koyū-meshi*. In the second case we do not have a proper reference, as これ stands for a particular book in the speaker's speech environment. Words such as これ are called **demonstratives** or 指示詞 *shijishi* or 指示代名詞 *shiji-daimēshi*, because they point out or direct a referent in relation to the language user. Unlike proper nouns, reference through demonstratives in Japanese is made by means of how the speaker/addressee is located physically, psychologically or socially. In this regard, personal pronouns, or 人称代名詞 *ninshō-daimēshi*, behave similarly. For example, the reference to 'I' differs depending on how the speaker is regarded socially in a given speech situation. If 'I' is a man talking to his friends, he can refer to himself as 僕 *boku* or 俺 *ore*, while he would refer to himself as 私 *watashi* or 私 *watakushi* when he delivers a formal speech in front of an audience (see Chapter 4, section 4.1.1).

In this section we draw our attention to different types of demonstratives whose usage is sensitive to how the speaker views the referent in terms of physical, textual and psychological distance. Table 2.1 demonstrates six different types of demonstratives. All words in each row share the first *hiragana* (in boldface), and all words in a column are differentiated by the first *hiragana* that corresponds to the distance of a referent.

Table 2.1 *Demonstratives*

	① **Pronoun**	② **Determiner**	③ **Locative noun**	④ **Directive noun**	⑤ **Manner adjective**	⑥ **Manner adverb**
Proximate	これ	この	ここ	こちら	こんな	こう
Intermediate	それ	その	そこ	そちら	そんな	そう
Distal	あれ	あの	あそこ	あちら	あんな	ああ

2.1.2 Physical reference

Demonstratives in (1) function as pronouns (standing for a noun) and in (2) as determiners (preceding a noun). In both cases, the speaker points to a red bean bun; the way it is pointed to depends on the distance of the speaker to the bun. これ/この is employed when the red bean bun is close to the speaker, while あれ/あの is used when the bun is far away from the speaker. その is used in two ways: when an entity is away from the speaker but close to the addressee, and when an entity is a little away (but not as far as the distance encoded in あれ/あの) from both the speaker and the addressee.

(1) **これ/それ/あれ**はあんパンです。
   Kore/Sore/Are *wa anpan desu*
   This/That is a red bean bun.

(2) **この/その/あの**パンはあんパンです。
   Kono/Sono/Ano *pan wa anpan desu*
   This/That bun is a red bean bun.

Because the meaning of the demonstratives is determined relative to the location of the speaker/addressee, they are often subsumed under the notion, **deixis** (originally from Greek *deiknumi* 'to show'). Look at Texts 2.1 to 2.3, excerpted from いつも美空 *Itsumo Misora* 'Always Misora (personal name)'. In Text 2.1, a boy finds a coin at the beach and says こんなところ *konna tokoro* 'here' (literally, 'this place') because the place the coin is found is close to him. A manner adjective こんな modifies a noun ところ 'place'. In Text 2.2, 公太 *Kōta* notices an injury to 美空's knee when she enters the room he is in. Because he points to something that is close to his addressee, he uses a determiner その 'that'. In Text 2.3, 美空 is present with her mother in a room. The mother tells her that they have the same liking or taste. あっち *acchi* refers to a place far from where 美空 and her mother are. Because 美空 is involved in watching a video, the use of あっち implies that she does not want to attend to what her mother says. A directive noun あっち is a spoken variant of あちら '(over) there'.

41

Text 2.1　こんなとこ

© 2001 Adachi, Mitsuru / *Itsumo Misora* (p. 72), Shogakukan

Text 2.2　そのキズ

© 2001 Adachi, Mitsuru / *Itsumo Misora* (p. 29), Shogakukan

Text 2.3　あっち行ってて

© 2001 Adachi, Mitsuru / *Itsumo Misora* (p. 134), Shogakukan

2.1.3 Intratextual reference

The use of demonstratives does not always depend on the physical location of the speaker/addressee. In Text 2.4, と も お *Tomō* visits 根津ゆきお's *Nezu Yukio*'s house. Because the atmosphere is awkward, と も お (on the right) suggests doing something interesting to break the silence. ゆ き お (on the left) replies that he does not feel like it (literally: 'I can't be in that mood'). そ ん な *son-na* points to と も お's word, that is, the previous utterance in discourse.

Text 2.4 そ ん な 気

© 2005 Oda, Tobira / *Danchi Tomō* (p. 353), Shogakukan

Because と も お's and ゆ き お's utterances cut across the text, this reference is termed **intratextual**. Intratextual reference is divided into **anaphoric** and **cataphoric** relations depending on whether the referring element (the element the speaker is referring to) appears before or after the demonstrative. In Text 2.4, そ ん な 気 *son-na ki* 'such a mood' refers back to と も お's suggestion, its textual function being anaphoric.

Text 2.5 is the beginning of a children's book that demonstrates an example of the anaphoric use of そ の *sono*. そ の in the second sentence refers to the taxi mentioned in the first sentence.

Text 2.5 Anaphoric その

空いろのぴかぴかの**タクシー**が、一台、とまっていました。**その**うしろに
しゃがみこんで、さっきから、ねっしんにタイヤをしらべているのは、こ
の車のうんてんしゅ――、松井五郎さんです。まるいはなの上に、つぶつぶ
のあせがひかっています。

© 1977 Aman, Kimiko / *Kuruma no Iro wa Sora no Iro* (p. 6), Poplar

Translation:
A freshly washed taxi in the colour of blue sky was kept parked. Mr Goro Matsui, the driver of this car, was sitting behind **it** (the taxi) and examining the tyres seriously. Sweat on his round nose was shining.

Text 2.6 is an extract from a story 窓ぎわのトットちゃん *Madogiwa no Totto-chan* 'Totto-chan at the Window'. The first sentence contains a demonstrative こう *kō* 'this way', which is used cataphorically, referring to the teacher's utterance mentioned in the next sentence.

Text 2.6 Cataphoric こう

つい先週のことだった。ママはトットちゃんの担任の先生に呼ばれて、は
っきり、**こう**いわれた。「おたくのお嬢さんがいると、クラス中の迷惑に
なります。よその学校にお連れください！」
若くて美しい女の先生は、ため息をつきながら、くり返した。
「本当に困っているんです！」

© 1984 Kuroyanagi, Tetsuko / *Madogiwa no Totto-chan* (p. 14), Kodansha

Translation:
It had happened only a week ago. Mother had been sent for by Totto-chan's homeroom* teacher, who came straight to the point.
'Your daughter disrupts my whole class. I must ask you to take her to another school.' The pretty young teacher sighed. 'I'm really at the end of my tether.'

(*Totto-chan. The Little Girl at the Window*.
Translated by Dorothy Britton. 1982: 11).

---

* The homeroom teacher in the translation refers to what is called a form tutor in Britain. In Japan, pupils in primary schools, as in the setting depicted in Text 2.6, are assigned to a class and each class has a form tutor. This tutor is concerned with ethical matters of the pupils in addition to his or her own teaching. So a form tutor might visit a pupil's home or discuss the pupil's general performance at school with the parents.

2.1.4 Psychological reference

When proximate demonstratives are used intratextually, their function is not only to indicate intratextual reference but also to express the speaker's **psychological closeness** to the referent. Look at Text 2.6 once again. When こう *kō* is used, what it refers to (the teacher's utterance) is treated as psychologically close to the protagonist (Totto-chan's mother). The narrator describes a scene in which the mother was sent for to see the home-room teacher because of her daughter's bad performance. By referring to the teacher's utterance with a manner adverb こう, the narrator establishes a close relationship between the teacher and the mother. It is interesting to see that the English translation does not contain the demonstrative *this* but the definite article *the*. Consider Text 2.5 once again. When この *kono* replaces その *sono*, this emphasizes that the taxi is the deictic centre in the driver's mind.

Examples (3) and (4) below illustrate the same point as the texts above. Imagine that these examples appear in a diary. They represent the same story (or proposition): X has met a woman called よう子 *Yōko*, and X finds her an interesting person. Both demonstratives, この *kono* and その *sono,* refer to よう子 mentioned in the first sentence. When この is used, X draws special attention to よう子. When その is used, the description of よう子 is anaphoric; that is, X is not emotionally committed to the description of よう子.

(3) よう子さんという女の人に会った。**この**人は見かけによらずおもしろい人だ。
Yōko-san to yū on-na no hito ni atta. Kono hito wa mikake ni yorazu omoshiroi hito da
I met a woman called Yoko. **This** person is an interesting person in spite of her outlook.

(4) よう子さんという女の人に会った。**その**人は見かけによらずおもしろい人だ。
Yōko-san to yū on-na no hito ni atta. Sono hito wa mikake ni yorazu omoshiroi hito da
I met a woman called Yoko. **That** person is an interesting person in spite of her outlook.

In conversation, あの *ano* has a special psychological function as well. When both speakers share knowledge about the referring entity (i.e., よう子さん), あの is used, as in (5). In contrast, その is used, as in (6), when the addressee obtains no knowledge about it. In other words, その here is anaphoric only, in much the same way as in (4).

(5) A: 昨日、よう子さんという女の人に会いました。
Kinō, Yōko-san to yū on-na no hito ni aimashita
I met a woman called Yoko yesterday.

45

B: ああ、そうですか。**あの** (△その) 人はよく知っています。

Ā, sō desuka. Ano hito wa yoku shitte imasu

Oh, did you. I know **the woman** very well.

(6) A: 昨日、よう子さんという女の人に会いました。

Kinō, Yōko-san to yū on-na no hito ni aimashita

B: **その** (×あの) 人は知りません。めがねをかけていましたか。

Sono hito wa shirimasen. Megane o kakete imashitaka

I don't know her. Did **the woman** wear glasses?

In summary, この and あの function as a **psychological reference** in a text, while その mainly remains anaphoric. In Text 4.5 in Chapter 4 (pp. 135–136), a female protagonist 綾子 *Ayako* refers to her husband by saying あの人 *ano hito* (line 21) in a conversation with her male friend 良雄 *Yoshio*. As he knows that 綾子 is married, the use of the demonstrative あの makes sense in that both 綾子 and 良雄 know who the referring person is (see also Kuno 1973, Chapter 24).

In Text 2.7, ともお *Tomō* is on his way back home with his classmates. He says that he has not seen 根津 *Nezu*, his classmate who was absent from school that day. Another classmate in the group wonders if ともお knows that 根津's leg is seriously injured as the result of an accident. In this accident, he fell badly against a ball kicked by ともお. The reason ともお's classmate uses あいつ *aitsu* is that everyone knows who 根津 is, although he is not present in the conversation.

Text 2.7   あいつの足

© 2005 Oda, Tobira / *Danchi*
Tomō (p. 352), Shogakukan

© 2005 Oda, Tobira / *Danchi*
Tomō (p. 353), Shogakukan

Activity 1

Demonstratives are marked in boldface. Based on your acquired knowledge of the reference system in Japanese, state what they refer to and what functions they have in the following story narrated by わたし *watashi* 'I'. わたし is a female high school student who feels isolated from her classmates. Because of this isolation, she has developed a habit of imagining things such as a mobile telephone, which she has never possessed before.

Text 2.8

1 「①その髪形、いいね」

小学生の時、髪を短くしたわたしに向かって、ある女の子が言った。

わたしは幸福な気持ちになり、②それから二年間、同じ髪形を選んだ。

しかし、彼女の言葉がお世辞にすぎなかったのだと気づいたのは、

5 中学生になってからのことだ。学校の廊下を歩いていると、数人の

友達を引き連れた彼女にすれちがった。一瞬、わたしの顔を見て、

彼女は友達に耳打ちした。

「③あの子、少し前から④あの髪形なんだけど、似合っていないよね」

舞い上がっていた自分がばかみたいだ。⑤そういった経験が数多く積

10 み重なり、わたしはだれかと話をする時、ひどく緊張するようになっ

た。春に⑥この高校に入学してからというもの、だれとも親しくなる

ことができないでいた。[...]

昼休みになると、よく図書館を訪れた。教室には居場所がなかっ

たし、学校内でわたしを受け入れてくれる場所は⑦そこだけだった。

15 館内は静かで、空調の設備が整っている。壁際にあるヒーターから、

暖かい空気が出ていた。すぐ風邪をひくわたしにとってはありがたい。

47

⑧その日、突っ伏して目を閉じると携帯電話のことを考えた。もし、自分に⑨それを持つ権利があるとしたらどんなのがいいだろう。

最近よく、⑩そのことを考える。想像するだけならだれにも迷惑をかけない。失敗をすることもないし、思い通りにできる。色は白がいい。触った感じは、つるつるがいい。いつしか自分だけの携帯電話を想像するのが楽しくなる。わたしには⑪この、想像をするという行為が重要だった。

© 2003 Otsu, Ichi / *Calling You* (pp. 7–9), Kadokawa Shoten

Commentary

The anaphoric (abbreviated as A) use of demonstrative pronouns is most frequent in this extract (see Table 2.2). The narrator of the novel, わたし 'I', is not physically located in the school at the time of narration, but her mind is connected with the school since she is currently a student at the school. This is why she uses この in ⑥; by using この, the narrator's psychological closeness to the school is justified. When an anaphoric その replaces この, 高校 'high school', to which その would refer, has to be mentioned in the previous discourse, since その, as we have seen in section 2.1.4, serves mainly as an anaphor in a text. The use of この in ⑪ may have both anaphoric and cataphoric relations, since it refers back to what has already been said and at the same time refers forward to the rest of the sentence – a partial repetition of the previous sentence. The repetition might enhance the degree of importance of the act of imagining a mobile telephone. Because of the emotions associated with この, it may also be categorized as a psychological reference. Since 想像する *sōzō suru* 'to imagine' appears in the previous sentence, one may be tempted to say that この is simply anaphoric. But then how do we explain why 想像する has to be repeated, since it is possible to say わたしにはこの行為が重要だった *Watashi niwa kono kōi ga jūyō datta* without having 想像をする 'to imagine' overtly? In addition, we may also be unable to explain why その cannot replace この, if この is merely anaphoric. In this passage, the act of imagination is the deictic centre of わたし's mental world, and this fact seems to reinforce our solution that psychological reference is also at work.

It is important to note that reference is not always made by use of demonstratives. In line 12 we find the expression 館内 *kan-nai* 'inside the building'. This lexical word refers to the inside of the library (図書館 *toshokan* 'library'), which appears in line 11.

Table 2.2 References and functions of demonstrations in Text 2.8

	Physical	Intratextual		Psychological	Functions
		A	**C**		
①	○				closer to わたし
②		○			referring to the previous discourse – the time when her classmate said that わたし's hairstyle is nice
③	○				far from classmates who talk about わたし's hairstyle
④	○				far from classmates who talk about わたし's hairstyle
⑤		○			referring to the previous discourse describing わたし's bitter experience with classmates
⑥			○		the speaker refers to the school where わたし is a student
⑦		○			referring to the library mentioned in the previous discourse
⑧		○			referring to the previous discourse describing the day when わたし visited the library
⑨		○			referring to 携帯電話 in the previous discourse
⑩		○			referring to the previous discourse in which わたし often thinks about the mobile telephone
⑪		○	○	○	referring to 携帯電話を想像する and 想像するという行為

2.2 Co-text

Co-text refers to the linguistic materials in a text. Co-text limits the range of interpretations of the referring expressions in a sentence. In other words, co-textual information helps the language user decide what/whom a linguistic form is referring to. When we refer to 小泉首相 *Koizumi shushō* as the prime minister of Japan, we know there is only one referent in the world. By contrast, an expression such as 先生 *sensē* 'teacher' can have more than one referent. Consider the examples in (7) below. (7a) refers to

49

the teacher as an individual, while (7b) refers to the teacher as a profession. Note that the decisive factor that differentiates (7a) and (7b) is the different implications imparted by each predicate. The verb 帰りました 'went back home' in (7a) connotes that the subject must be a person, while 大変な仕事 'a hard job' in (7b) does not refer to the person but to the job the teacher is assigned to. The speaker who utters a sentence in (7) and the addressee who hears it are committed to the pragmatic act of assigning an appropriate referent to a linguistic item.

(7) a. 先生は帰りました。
       Sensē wa kaerimashita
       The teacher went home.
     b. 先生は大変な仕事です。
       Sensē wa taihen na shigoto desu
       Being a teacher is a tough job.

Activity 2

Look at the following sentences, which contain 飛行機 *hikōki* 'airplane, aircraft'. You may notice that 飛行機 does not always have exactly the same meaning, though these meanings are still related to the basic sense of 飛行機 – a vehicle with wings and engines that enable it to fly through the air. Analyse the predicate for each sentence and relate its meaning to the use of 飛行機. Each sentence has a different predicate.

(8) a. 飛行機が今着陸します。
       Hikōki ga ima chakuriku shimasu
       The airplane is now landing.
     b. シンガポールから成田まで飛行機で約6時間30分かかります。
       Singapōru kara narita made hikōki de yaku rokujikan-sanjuppun kakarimasu
       It takes about six and half hours from Singapore to Narita by plane.
     c. 飛行機は新幹線より高いです。
       Hikōki wa shinkansen yori takai desu
       Travelling by plane is more expensive than by Shinkansen.
     d. 飛行機は快適です。
       Hikōki wa kaiteki desu
       Airplanes are comfortable.
(9)   私は飛行機で帰りました。
       Watashi wa hikōki de kaerimashita
       I went home by plane.

Commentary

(8a) refers to a vehicle that flies, as is suggested by the predicate 'to land' (着陸します). In (8b) to (8d), 飛行機 does not refer to a flying machine but is used in its extended senses. In (8b), 飛行機 serves as an instrument with which to gauge the flight time from Singapore to Narita, Japan. In (8c), 飛行機 refers to the cost of a trip when flying by air in comparison to travelling by *Shinkansen* (bullet train). In (8d), 飛行機 stands for the atmosphere in the airplane when we are on board (see section 2.5.4 below for metonymy). All these extended senses of airplane are motivated or limited by the particular co-textual information of each predicate. When you compare (8b) and (9), you may notice that both sentences contain the same postpositional phrase 飛行機で, but because of the predicate 帰りました 'went home' in (9), the phrase 飛行機で 'by airplane' can refer to a vehicle (which I boarded) in addition to the instrument (that brings passengers from one place to another). (8b) does not necessarily contain the first meaning.

Activity 3

This activity is not accompanied by a commentary.

In Text 2.9, a female narrator わたし *watashi* 'I' is on the way to the airport to meet シンヤ *Shinya*. Her bus is delayed. Even after she arrives at the meeting point (a nearby bus stop outside the airport building), he is, to her surprise, not there yet. 飛行機 *hikōki* 'airplane, aircraft' is mentioned five times in this passage. Explain whether the use of 飛行機 has the same referent or not.

Text 2.9　飛行機

1　時刻は十二時十三分。彼の乗った①飛行機が到着する時刻までに、

飛行場へはたどり着けそうにない。そのことを、頭の奥に向かって伝え

た。十二時二十分。予定では、シンヤの乗った②飛行機はすでに着陸

しているはずだ。膝の上に載せた小さなバッグの取っ手につけたキー

5　ホルダーをいじりながら、わたしは、わたしたちのことをぼんやり考

えていた。これまでに交わしてきた会話を、一つ一つ思い出していた。

その多くは愉快なもので、顔に笑みが広がるのを抑えられなかった。

それから、小学生や中学生の時の辛かったこと、悲しかったことま

でなぜか思い出した。冷えた窓ガラスに額を押しつけて外を見ると、

10 すでにバスが飛行場のそばまできていることを知った。③**飛行機**を

降りて到着ロビーを歩いているところだろうか。もしかすると、

空港を出てバス停へ向かっているかもしれない。[...]

あらかた乗客がいなくなると、ようやくわたしは立ち上がり、

財布を取り出しながら出口へ向かった。お金を払い、ステップを降

15 りると、冷たい風が額を打ち、寒さに弱いわたしは体を震わせた。

④**飛行機**の轟音が上から聞こえ、ひょっとして風というものはジャン

ボ機が通り過ぎた時に発生するのだろうか、とぼんやり思った。では、

⑤**飛行機**のない時代に風は存在しなかったのだろうか。そして、

シンヤはバス停まで迎えにきてくれているだろうか。時間を見ると、

20 微妙なところだった。まだ飛行場の中かもしれない。

© 2003 Otsu, Ichi / *Calling You* (pp. 32–34), Kadokawa

Activity 4

Look at the following excerpts from newspaper articles. These excerpts contain the synonymous words ランチ *ranchi* 'lunch' and 昼食 *chūshoku* 'lunch', which are used interchangeably (see Chapter 3, Text 3.2, p. 56 in JL). Explain how these two words differ in meaning on the basis of co-textual information.

Text 2.10

都路村古道の小高い丘に建つペンションで９２年に営業開始。和室と洋室が２部屋ずつあり、15人程度利用できる。１泊２食付きで１人１万円 (税、サービス料込み)。日中は正午から午後１時半まで、①**ランチ**サービス (1050 円)もしている。宴会なども受け付けている。予約は 0247 ・ 75 ・ 3329 へ。

© 2004 *Asahi.com* 7 January

Text 2.11

手料理を持ち寄って仲良し親子で②**ランチ**パーティーをするのが好きです。下の子がまだ３カ月で、あまり手の込んだものは作れません。下準備が楽でウケそうな、しゃれた一品を教えてください。

© 2003 *Asahi.com* 29 September

Text 2.12

今年１０月に始めた左京区の修学院中。③**昼食**の時間になると、当番の生徒が配膳室へやってくる。委託された業者が配送した弁当形式の給食は、ご飯は温蔵庫で、おかずは保冷庫で保管される。取材した日、空き教室を活用した「いきいき交流ルーム」(④**ランチ**ルーム) では、３年７組 36 人が⑤**昼食**を食べていた。

© 2004 *Asahi.com* 15 October

Text 2.13

私たちの会では２０００年７月から、金沢市増泉の地域生活支援センターで、予約制の「コミュニティレストラン　カモンミール」の名前で⑥**昼食**サービスを始めた。地域生活支援センターは、精神障害者の社会復帰施設として９６年度から国が始めた事業。[...]１食 300 円。週２回で始まった⑦**昼食**サービスは現在、特別メニューで開かれる日以外は、毎週木曜日にオープンしている。

© 2003 *Asahi.com* 25 February

Commentary

ランチ *ranchi* as used in ① refers to a special menu (normally a set menu) served around midday in restaurants. This explanation is cued by サービス *sābisu* 'service' with which ランチ forms a compound (see Chapter 5, sections 5.4 and 5.5 for the term 'compound' in JL). As in ② and ④, however, ランチ does not directly refer to the meal (although it implies it). While ② refers to the time in the middle of the day at which people go in a party to have lunch, ④ points to the room used by pupils for having lunch.

昼食 *chūshoku* 'lunch' is a more general word among Japanese people referring to the meal around midday. When you have 昼食, you can have lunch in any place. It can take place at home or school, in the work place or in a restaurant. ③ and ⑤ refer to lunch at school. 昼食 in ⑥ and ⑦ is used in the context of 昼食サービス 'lunch service'. From what is reported in Text 2.13, the meaning of 昼食サービス approaches that of ①ランチサービス in Text 2.10 in the sense that the meal is served in a particular place outside the home. But it differs in that the service is not oriented toward profit-making – the restaurant is located in the so-called Local Life Support Centre (or 地域生活支援センター *chīki sēkatsu shien sentā*) in Kanazawa City as part of a governmental welfare project. ランチサービス as used in Text 2.10 connotes that the restaurant aims at profit-making.

As you may have noticed, co-textual information is not entirely sufficient to infer the exact meaning of a linguistic form in a text. For instance, both ランチサービス and 昼食サービス in Texts 2.10 and 2.13 stand in a similar co-text on the grounds that both predicates, している and 始めた, express the activity of serving the meal. In other words, these predicates are interchangeable. Moreover, ランチ and 昼食 can both co-occur with the same predicate (e.g., 食べる *taberu* 'to eat' (see ⑤) or 注文する *chūmon suru* 'to order'), indicating that they can have the same co-text. Without reference to the context in which the linguistic forms are actually used, it is difficult to comprehend what exactly referring expressions mean. It follows that, apart from the co-textual information available, the interpretation of ランチ and 昼食 needs to refer to a **context** or a real speech setting, to which we shall now attend.

2.3 Context

While co-text concerns the linguistic environment that helps the language user to search the appropriate referent, **context** (コンテクスト in Japanese pragmatics) is the speech environment in which the utterance is actually realized. The identification of the context helps the user to assign the appropriate referent to a linguistic form. Recall the sentence 'John is eating a cake'. Apart from its literal meaning, the interpretation of this sentence depends on different contexts. If John were eating a rotten cake, the speaker's attitude would not be positive. If John had been ill, the eating of a cake would be a positive sign. When we are in a room in Southeast Asia and someone says that it is cold, it might imply that we should reduce the strength of the air-conditioning. The same sentence will not convey the same message when it is uttered on a wintry day in Northern Europe. The context of this utterance implies putting more clothes on. Context or, more precisely, speech environment is composed of various situational elements. In order to work out how exactly context influences the making of a text, we need to identify at least the following elements in a text: (i) what happened or what is happening, (ii) who is involved and how they are involved, (iii) what exists and how it exists, (iv) what the speaker means by what he or she says, (v) what the addressee means by what he or she says, and (vi) how speaker and addressee cooperate. In Activities 5 and 6, you will look at different types of contexts and how they determine the meaning of the utterance.

Activity 5

お前 *omae* or おまえ *omae* is a second person pronoun used mainly by men in informal speech (see Chapter 4, Table 4.1). When the pronoun appears alone, we may have difficulty identifying who has said it to whom. Only the context can tell us its proper referent. Try to find the meaning of お前 and おまえ in Texts 2.14 and 2.15.

Text 2.14　お前

> 1　綾子「お父ちゃん」
>
> 　　実「なんだよ？」
>
> 　　綾子「（部屋の方から微笑して現れ）結局、うちが一番幸せね」
>
> 　　実「幸せ？」
>
> 5　綾子「岩田さんとこもあまりうまく行ってないみたいだし、陽子さん
>
> 　　も仲手川さんも独身だし、晴江さんは自殺さわぎだし」
>
> 　　実「人生ってもんは、そんなもんよ」
>
> 　　綾子「うまく行ってるの、うちだけじゃない」
>
> 　　実「**お前**も楽太郎だねぇ」

10　綾子「浮気してる？」

　　実「し、してるもんか」

© 1991 Yamada, Taichi / *Fuzoroi no Ringo-tachi* (p. 24), Magazine House

Text 2.15　おまえ

1　何か真剣な顔で話をしている一群がそばにいたので、耳をすます。彼

　　女の出演していたテレビドラマの最終回についてどう思うか、という

　　議論がされていた。俺は場違いなところに来ている気がして、内山君

　　に聞いた。

5　「外で煙草を吸ってきてもいいかな」

　　すると、周囲にいた人たちから同時に視線を向けられる。いずれも俺

　　を非難するようなまなざしだった。

　　「**おまえ**、煙草を吸った手で握手するつもりか」

　　内山君は怒ったように言った。

© 2003 Otsu, Ichi / *Te o Nigiru Dorobō no Monogatari* (p. 158), Kadokawa

Commentary

お前 *omae* in Text 2.14 is uttered by 実 *Minoru* to his wife 綾子 *Ayako*. This marital relationship can be inferred by expressions uttered by 綾子, such as お父ちゃん *otōchan* 'father' (address form by in-group members) (line 1), うち *uchi* 'home' (line 3) and 浮気してる？ 'Do you have a secret lover?' (line 10). The conversation between the two persons creates a context that helps us recognize that 実 is 綾子's husband. This relationship allows 実 to address his wife as お前.

What could explain the use of おまえ in Text 2.15? Can we say that the conversation here is conducted by a couple? If the utterance stood alone, it would be difficult to make a definitive judgement here, but from the context of this passage, you should infer that 俺 *ore* 'I' is talking with his male colleague 内山君 *Uchiyama-kun* 'Mr Uchiyama'. 俺 feels alienated because of discussions by a group of people nearby (lines 1–3). When 俺 asks 内山君 to go out briefly for a cigarette to avoid the feeling of oddness, people around him immediately look at him critically. At this moment, 内山君 uses おまえ as a reply with a somewhat angry tone; this use of おまえ may be understood as the speaker's resentment or reproach.

In this context, おまえ belongs to the offensive register (see Chapter 4, Table 4.1). Note that 内山君 does not always use おまえ when he talks to 俺. Text 2.16 demonstrates such an example in which 内山君 uses きみ *kimi* 'you' to 俺 shortly after the conversation in Text 2.15:

Text 2.16　きみ

「**きみ**がデザインした腕時計がなぜ最近、急に売り上げを伸ばしているか というとだね。例の映画のラストシーンで、そっくりの腕時計を彼女がは めているからなんだ。」そのために、映画を見た女の子たちが買っていっ てくれるのだという、デザインがいいと、買ってくれた人は満足している らしい。しかし購入する動機は、あきらかに映画だった。

© 2003 Otsu, Ichi / *Te o Nigiru Dorobō no Monogatari* (pp. 159–160), Kadokawa

When we inspect a speech situation, it is important to understand the speaker's intention encoded systematically in an utterance. Assigning the right meaning of お前 or おまえ into a given conversation makes the actual message more revealing. As we have seen in the texts above, social or situational relations among the interlocutors in a given speech appear to play a role in deciding the meaning of the form used. This aspect of language use falls under **register** (see Chapter 1, section 1.3, p. 26). When language is being used, however, other factors such as the speaker's or addressee's emotions embedded into a given spoken discourse also come into play. In Activity 6 we look at how emotions are encoded in the expression ばか *baka* in Japanese.

Activity 6

Text 2.17 is taken from 陽あたり良好 *Hiatari Ryōkō* 'Full of Sunshine'. 高杉君 *Takasugi-kun* 'Mr Takasugi' and かすみ *Kasumi* are talking about horoscopes. かすみ is interested in 高杉君's horoscope. He finds out that the woman who is well-matched for him has the initial K. After wondering whose name it could be, he arrives at かすみ's name, which indeed has an initial K. At the moment 高杉君 mentions かすみ's name, she utters バカみたい *baka-mitai* 'You fool' (literally: 'You look like a fool'). In addition to the literal meaning of ばか, consider carefully the expression in the drawing and explain what emotions, if any, かすみ expresses.

Text 2.17 バカみたい

© 1996 Adachi, Mitsuru / *Hiatari Ryōkō* (p. 81), Shogakukan

Commentary

ばか *baka* is used as a basic insult, and it generally means 'fool', 'idiot' or 'dumb'. It often refers to someone who has done a foolish, stupid or disrespectful thing, but, unlike swear words such as 'bastard' in English, it does not carry an offensive meaning directed at the other party. As mentioned in Mangajin's *Basic Japanese* (1998: 66), ばか as an expression of insult sounds pretty mild to the Western ear. In Text 2.17, ばか does not indeed bear the strong sense of insult. It is used to comment on 高杉君's *Takasugi-kun*'s mention that かすみ *Kasumi* has K as its initial and she could be a well-matched woman for him. This may astound or even embarrass her. The use of バカみたい *baka-mitai* 'You fool' may serve to conceal her emotions. The question she asks (i.e., 星占いなんか信じるの？ *Hoshi-uranai nanka shinjiruno* 'Do you believe in things like a horoscope?') may not count as a genuine question (as it does not seek an answer); instead it makes an indirect statement that he should not believe what the horoscope says. In this regard, バカみたい may also be meant as an emphatic expression to re-convey this indirect message (see chapter 1, section 1.3.9 for the notion 'rhetorical question').

When you look at the ninth line of Text 2.8 above, you find a similar expression ばかみたい (舞い上がっていた自分が**ばかみたいだ** 'It was silly of me to be enraptured'). The narrator of this story finds herself foolish to have been in raptures over a superficial praise, but the sense of embarrassment or surprise may not be present here.

うそ *uso* is another word that we often encounter in *manga*. It literally means a lie, but it does not always contain a sense of disapproval or reproach as does the English word *lie*. When the information is false or untrue, うそ is often used in informal speech, as shown in Text 2.18. Here

ウソォ (with an emphasis on the final sound by repeating a vowel /o/) is uttered by かすみ's male friend, 有山君 *Ariyama-kun* 'Mr Ariyama', because he believes that the fish (which they talk about in the scene) cannot be a carp. The discussion concerns the category of the fish. かすみ *Kasumi* believes that it is こい *koi* 'carp', while 有山君 considers it to be ふな *funa* 'crucian carp'. By saying ウソォ, he shows that he has a different opinion. It can be paraphrased as 'I don't think so' or 'I don't agree' rather than 'It is a lie' or 'It is untrue'.

Text 2.18 ウソォ

© 1996 Adachi, Mitsuru / *Hiatari Ryōkō* (p. 323), Shogakukan

Activity 7

We have so far examined word-level expressions whose actual meaning is made clearer by the context. In this activity we look at expressions longer than words. Read carefully Text 2.19, an extract from 手を握る泥棒の物語 *Te o Nigiru Dorobō no Monogatari* 'A Story about a Thief who Holds Your Hands' and find ONE sentence-level expression whose true meaning is inferred from the given context. The extract is a conversation between 俺 *ore* 'I' and his colleague 内山君 *Uchiyama-kun* 'Mr Uchiyama'. A decent company they have established sold a type of watch half a year ago and is now planning to sell a new watch with a different design. 俺 *ore* 'I' is the one who worked on the design of both the old and new watches. It is unfortunate that the old watch did not sell well. Text 2.19 begins with a scene in which 俺 meets 内山君 in the office after visiting his aunt, who is temporarily residing in the city.

Text 2.19

内山君の家でもあり会社でもある二階建てのみすぼらしい建物の駐車場に
車を停め、事務所の入り口を開ける。社長である内山君は背が低く、

鼠に似ている。俺が出社してきたのを見ると、彼はコーヒーを用意しな

がら視線をそむけた。そのタイミングが絶妙だったため、不審なものを

感じた。

「叔母さんはどうだったんだい？」

内山君はコーヒーの入ったカップを俺の机に置いた。

「元気だったよ」

そう答えて、しばらく俺たちは、それぞれ無言で机のまわりを片付けて

いた。やがて片付けるものもなくなると、彼は口を開いた。

「ところで......。今度発売を予定していたきみのデザインした腕時計、

作らないことにした」

ほう。俺はうなづいた。

「すぐれたジョークだ」

© 2003 Otsu, Ichi / *Te o Nigiru Dorobō no Monogatari* (p. 129), Kadokawa

Translation:
I parked the car in the parking lot – in the shabby, two-storied building that is Mr Uchiyama's house and company. The company boss, Mr Uchiyama, is short and looks like a mouse. When he noticed I had arrived at the office, he averted his eyes and prepared his coffee. As the timing was perfect, I felt something suspicious.

'How was your aunt?' Mr Uchiyama put the cup filled with the coffee on the desk.

'She was fine,' I answered.

We were both silent for a while tidying up the desk. When he had nothing else to tidy up, he opened his mouth.

'By the way, . . . We were planning to sell the watch you designed, but we have decided not to produce it.'

'I see,' I gave a nod.

'That's an excellent joke!'

Commentary

The expression we are concerned with is すぐれたジョークだ *sugureta jōku da* 'That's an excellent joke' uttered by 俺 *ore* 'I' (final line). Since the new watch has already been designed and awaits its production, the utterance by his boss must have been a real shock for 俺. 俺 does not mean that it is a joke in its literal sense; instead he is being **ironic** by saying the opposite (see Chandler 2002: 134–135; Hebron 2004: 151; Knowles and Moon 2006: 122 and Matthews 1997: 187, for the notion of 'irony'). Jokes are normally told to amuse the hearer, but by using the word *joke*, 俺 conveys his true message such that what 内山君 *Uchiyama-kun* has just said (cancellation of producing the new watch) is nothing to be amused about. The use of irony, or meaning the opposite, intensifies the speaker's emotions (e.g., surprise, disappointment or shock). In particular, 俺's use of an adjective すぐれた 'excellent' to modify a joke readily indicates that he is affected greatly (see also Chapter 4, section 4.1.2, pp. 126–127 for the notion of 'irony').[2]

2.4 Implicatures

Implicature (含意 *gan-i* in Japanese pragmatics) is a term developed by the philosopher Paul Grice in the 1960s. His major ideas were presented in a book *Studies in the Way of Words* (1989) towards the end of his life. Implicature is the unstated meaning a speaker attaches to an utterance within discourse. If the utterance corresponds exactly to the distinct meaning (i.e., entailment) of the sentence, we do not need to talk about implicature. Implicatures can be understood in two ways, that is, conventionally or conversationally.

    Conventional implicature refers to the meaning attached to an utterance reflecting the language users' conventions. The term 'conventional' means that the implicit meaning associated with the utterance is understood uniformly by a group of language users. When someone asks you 'Do you know what time it is?', your answer will normally be, in an English-speaking circumstance, 'It's X o'clock' instead of saying 'Yes, I do' or 'No, I don't'. According to Huddleston (2002: 861–862), the reason we naturally choose 'It's X o'clock' as the correct answer is that the addressee conventionally knows that the **primary force** in this interrogative is the question of what time it is. When we make an utterance, be it a statement, question or directive, it often has such a force that is not always made verbally explicit. Similarly, when a wife who cannot drive asks her husband, 'Do you think you could drive me to the bus stop?', the conventional force of this question is a request: 'Please drive me'. Because the husband is a cooperative addressee, he understands the speaker's unstated intention immediately. The different uses of お前/おまえ 'you' in Texts 2.14 and 2.15 (pp. 55–56) pertain to conventional implicature, as the use of these expressions reflects conventionalized social relationships in Japan.

Conversational implicature refers to the implicit meaning attached to an utterance in a conversation. An understanding of this meaning is influenced largely by the conversational context, or more precisely, inter-actions between individuals who participate in a conversation. To the question 'How are you today?', I may answer 'I went to bed late last night' to implicate that I am not well today. Although this answer is, grammat-ically speaking, not a correct answer, it is relevant pragmatically: it informs my interlocutor of my unhealthiness indirectly. One important property of conversational implicature is that its interpretation depends on the unstated information available in a given conversation. Another friend of mine who has just heard my interaction and also joined the same party the previous night may say that 'You went to bed early!'. This friend has the opinion that the time I went to bed is still early. This kind of interaction happens because she has failed to understand what I meant by what I said. The interpretation of conversational implicature often relies on the inter-locutor's experience in everyday life. Eleven p.m. (the time I actually went to bed) can be late for some people and early for others.

Although both conventional and conversational implicatures are the implied (that is, inferred) meanings, they can be distinguished in terms of their naturalness (see Grundy 2000: 85). Conventional implicature conveys 'natural meaning' in the sense that it does not depend on an ongoing conversational context, whereas conversational implicature conveys 'non-natural meaning' as it is derived from the conversational context – it varies in accordance with the interlocutors' knowledge, experience, conversational settings and so on. Because of the non-naturalness of con-versational implicature, misunderstandings (like the above) may occur frequently (see Mey 2001: 45). For Leech (1983: 30–32), the utterance interpretation is a form of problem-solving strategy.

When inspecting actual texts carefully, we notice that these two types of implicatures often co-exist or interact with each other. In other words, despite the distinction between the two, the choice of a conventional meaning can depend on the message being conveyed conversationally.

2.4.1 Conventional implicature

Look at Text 2.20, which shows a future setting in which ノビ太 *Nobita* is married to しずか *Shizuka*. しずか forms an interrogative (あなた今何時だと思ってるの？ 'What time do you think it is?'). As ノビ太 has come home drunk, the force of this utterance is not a question about the time; instead it is understood conventionally as an exclamatory statement – he has come home very late. The implicature is conventional because Japanese people infer the implicated meaning if uttered in this particular speech setting. In a different speech setting in which a mother directs a similar question to her child who is still awake at midnight, the primary force is a directive, neither the question nor the exclamatory statement being the correct inference. Considering the fact that it is already midnight, the child immediately realizes that he has to go to bed. What these examples tell us is that utterances have a force conventionally agreed upon by language users.

Text 2.20　今何時だと思ってるの？

© Fujiko Production / *Doraemon: Nobita-Grafity* (p. 213), Shogakukan

2.4.2 Conversational implicature

Text 2.21 is an extract from a novel ハゴロモ *Hagoromo*. A female protagonist ほたる *Hotaru* meets the daughter of a woman who is her father's lover. This daughter's name is るみ *Rumi*. What attracts ほたる's attention is not the fact that るみ is the daughter of the woman (as she will become her future sister upon her father's remarriage) but the unique manner in which るみ behaves herself (lines 1–3). るみ quickly notices that ほたる is fascinated by her, and she smiles at ほたる (line 4). What is intriguing in this text is that it demonstrates the co-existence of both conventional and conversational implicatures.

Text 2.21

1　ナプキンで口を拭う仕草、フォークで口に運ぶ仕草、水を飲んで、ち
　　ょっと遠くを見る感じ。全てが他の人にはできないような、彼女だけ

の、もう他にはないひとつだけの動きであり、やり方だった。私は
つい見とれてしまい、彼女はそれに気づいて私にちょっと笑いかけた。

5 「私たちだけでその辺を歩かない？」

とるみちゃんは言った。彼女の声は不思議に低く、甘く懐かしい感
じだった。

「作戦会議ね。」

とるみちゃんのお母さんは言った。父は苦笑いしていた。

10 そして私たちは公園を歩き始めた。

「名前はなんだっけ？」

「ほたる。」

「私は、るみよ。」

「あの二人、結婚するかしら。」

15 私は言った。春先で、公園の緑はにぶく光り、もわっとした感じに
あたたまっていた。光が並木道に射して、柔らかい影をつくって
いた。

「ウ～ン、どうかなあ。私のお父さん、今別居中だけど、けっこう
しつこいからなあ。ほたるちゃんちのお父さんがあせって離婚を

20 せかさなければ案外結婚までいくかも。」

るみちゃんは言った。

池にさしかかったとき、さらにるみちゃんは言った。

「この池ってカッパはいるの？」

「さ、さあ．．．．．．。」

25 私は当惑して答えた。

「私は見たことない。」

するとるみちゃんは言った。

「私はよく見たよ、山奥の池で。でも最近は見なくなった。日本ではもう絶滅してしまったのかなあ。」

30 「緑色で甲羅があるの？」

「うん。それで小さいの。」

「それ、亀じゃない？」

「違うよ、立って歩いたもん。ひとりでいると、近くまできたんだけれど。」

35 「カッパと友達か......。」

「友達まではいかなかったのよ。残念なことに。」

るみちゃんは言った。

© 2003 Yoshimoto, Banana / *Hagoromo* (pp. 35–36), Shinchosha

るみ *Rumi* suggests ほたる *Hotaru* take a walk in the vicinity (line 5). The **negative interrogative question** (歩かない？ 'Shan't we take a walk?') (line 5) ensures that ほたる will agree with it (see Huddleston 2002: 883). This pragmatic interpretation is essential to the meaning of the construction, and it should be categorized as conventional implicature. Aside from this conventional force, the expectation of a positive answer that ほたる is ready to go for a walk is inferable from the conversational context: (i) ほたる is fascinated by るみ (lines 1–4), and (ii) ほたる feels comfortable with るみ's voice (lines 6–7). As a matter of fact, ほたる could refuse るみ's proposal if the conversational and conventional context is not taken into account.

As they walk along the pond, るみ again asks ほたる a question (line 23), but this time she asks a **positive interrogative question** – whether a *kappa* 'river monster' lives in this pond. ほたる is perplexed by this question because it is abrupt and she does not know the answer (lines 24 and 26). It appears that るみ is not actually asking a question here, nor is she expecting an answer. From the fact that るみ had already seen a *kappa* in another pond (line 28), the interrogative (line 23) has a conversational implicature that reveals るみ's internal mind: she begins to 'wonder' about the *kappa* she had seen before. ほたる is cooperative enough to attend to her question (lines 24 and 26) and gets involved in her interest. After this exchange, the conversation revolves around the topic of *kappa* (lines 28–36). Note that if the question were substituted by a negative interrogative (この池ってカッパ**いないの**? '**Isn't** there a kappa in this pond?') (line 23), it would sound as if るみ expects the presence of a *kappa* in the pond. But this is not what るみ is expecting, and it is indeed very unlikely that a river monster exists in the real world, as it is an imaginary animal. Thus, the interrogative in line 23 discloses the unique nature of the protagonist るみ.

るみ's mother uses the expression 作戦会議 *sakusen-kaigi* 'assembly for operational plans' (line 8) when the two girls are about to go for a walk. It literally means a meeting at which tactics are elaborated to win forthcoming battles or competitions, but in this conversational context it implies that they want to be on their own away from their parent and talk about private things. The fact that ほたる's father smiles wryly in response to the mother's utterance (line 9) may indicate that he has understood the conversational implicature attached to the expression.

Activity 8

Text 2.22 is taken from 窓際のトットちゃん *Madogiwa no Totto-chan* '*Totto-chan at the Window*'. トットちゃん has dropped her purse, which she has preciously kept, in the toilet. At the time トットちゃん is living (in the 1940s before the end of World War II), the toilet is not a flush-type but old-fashioned. トットちゃん tries to find the purse in the tank by using a ladle to scoop up the soil. At the moment she is absorbed in this dirty search, the schoolmaster passes by and asked a question, 'What are you doing?' (line 1). Explain the conversational implicature encoded in the interaction between the schoolmaster (lines 1 and 10) and トットちゃん (line 4).

Text 2.22

1　「なにしてんだい？」
トットちゃんは、手を休める時間もおしいから、ひしゃくを、つっこみながら答えた。
「お財布、落としたの」
5　「そうかい」
そういうと、校長先生は、手を、体のうしろに組んだ、いつもの散歩の格好で、どっかに行ってしまった。それから、また、しばらくの時

> が立った。お財布は、まだ見つからない。山は、どんどん、大きくなる。
>
> そのころ、また校長先生が通りかかって聞いた。
>
> 10　「あったかい？」

© 1984 Kuroyanagi, Tetsuko / *Madogiwa no Totto-chan* (pp. 69–70), Kodansha

Translation:
'**What are you doing**?' he asked Totto-chan.

'**I dropped my purse**,' she replied, as she went on ladling, not wanting to waste a moment.

'I see,' said the headmaster, and walked away, his hands clasped behind his back as was his habit when he went for a stroll.

Time went by and she still hadn't found the purse. The foul-smelling pile was getting higher and higher. The headmaster came by again. '**Have you found it**?' he inquired.

(*Totto-chan: The Little Girl at the Window*,
translated by Dorothy Britton, 1982:45)

Commentary

When we observe トットちゃん's response (line 4) grammatically, it is not the right answer to the schoolmaster's question (line 1). To his question 'what are you doing?', her grammatical answer would be 'I'm looking for my purse'. However, her response is to tell him that she has lost her purse – giving the reason she is ladling in the toilet. The reason she answers this way is that the schoolmaster's question carries a conversational implicature for her, that is, 'Why are you doing that?' The schoolmaster serves as a cooperative addressee and understands her reaction. This is proven by his second question (line 10) 'Have you found it?'. Thus, the real message 'I am looking for my purse' is indirectly carried over with her response (line 4). Since the schoolmaster is on the spot, it must be easy for him to realize what she is doing (but it is not necessarily clear why she is doing it). This contextual information should make the response conversationally relevant in such a way that telling what happened is more reasonable than describing the existing fact. One could also interpret the schoolmaster's question (line 1) as surprise or perplexity ('What on earth are you doing!'). Because this type of question can carry a force, it carries a conventional implicature that presents the schoolmaster as an emotional recipient. トットちゃん therefore does not need to describe what she is doing but instead needs to explain why she is ladling. In our everyday life, we may also use the expression 'What are you doing!' to express embarrassment or surprise rather than actually asking a question.

Let us go a little step further. It is worthwhile looking at ハゴロモ *Hagoromo* once again, as shown in Text 2.23. Consider the dialogue (lines 1–2) in which the speaker gives more information than necessary. Text 2.23 describes a scene in a noodle shop run by a young man. ほたる *Hotaru* wants to pay for the noodles she has eaten and is about to leave the restaurant. When the young man, who had suddenly had to go downstairs, comes back out of breath, she asks whether everything is all right with him. He then mentions his mother who is ill in bed, validating his urgent need to have seen her. At this moment he asks ほたる whether she knows about the bus accident that took place the previous year (line 1). Her response (line 2) is that she knows about it (ああ *ā* 'yes'), but, what is more important, she adds a comment about it: 'It was a horrifying accident'. ほたる's answer would have been correct even if she had said no more than ああ. The narration from lines 4 to 8 describes ほたる's remembrance of the accident, indicating that she knows quite a bit about it. An additional comment (line 2) facilitates the conversation naturally, allowing the young man to explain (from line 11) his sad family story: his mother was greatly shocked at the death of his father in the accident and has been in bed since that time. The role of the interrogative (line 1) can be interpreted in two ways. First, it has a conventional implicature in that an interrogative containing a predicate 覚える *oboeru* 'remember' conventionally demands more than a yes/no answer. It has a conversational implicature in the sense that the conversational context makes the question (line 1) relevant such that it signals his willingness to talk more about his mother, and this reinforces the respondent's saying more than necessary.

Text 2.23

---

1 「昨年の、バスの事故をおぼえていますか?」

　「ああ、ものすごい事故だったって聞いた。」

　私は答えた。

　昨年、町内会の旅行があった。二つくらいの町内が合同で温泉に行

5 くというものだった。その時のバスの運転手が精神を病んでいて、

　全員を道連れにしてがけから落ちたのだ。その事実は複数の客が携帯

　で家族に連絡をとっていたことから明るみになり、たいへんな騒ぎに

　なった。

私もニュースで見て、家族や知り合いが参加していないか気をもん

10 だものだった。そして、いろいろな形で後悔をした。

「あの時、お袋は参加するはずだったんだけど、どうしても気がの

らなくておやじだけ行くことになったんです。おふくろは勘みたい

なのがあって、おやじに行くなってとめたんだけれど、親父はそう

いうの信じないから、行って、死んでしまったんです。」

15 「まあ......。」

「そのショックでずっと寝込んでいて。」

© 2003 Yoshimoto, Banana / *Hagoromo* (p. 62), Shinchosha

Translation:
> 'Do you remember the bus accident last year?'
> 'Yes. It was a horrific accident, I heard,' I replied.

A trip had been organized by a town association. Two towns were joined, and the trip was to go to a hot spring. The bus driver had a psychological problem and he fell from the cliff, taking all the passengers. This fact became obvious, as many passengers had contacted their families with a mobile telephone. This accident caused a stir. I saw a TV and also got worried about the possibility that my family members or acquaintances may have joined this bus trip. And, I felt regret in different ways.

> 'My mother was supposed to join the trip, too, but as she didn't feel like it, my father finally decided to join it alone. She had a sixth sense and recommended him not to join it. He did not believe what she said and went on the trip and died.'
> 'How sad.'
> 'She has been lying in bed out of shock.'

2.5 Figure of speech

Figure of speech, or 比喩 *hiyu,* is a use of language in which its normal use is extended or modified so that the speaker can add special meanings or effects to the original expression. For instance, 彼は芸術家だ *Kare wa gējutsu-ka da* 'He is an artist' can have two interpretations: one is that he is an artist by profession (original meaning), and the other is that he is not an artist but he is like an artist (extended meaning) because he is skilled at creating works of art (e.g., drawing, singing, writing novels). This second interpretation is **figurative** by virtue of the fact that he is considered an artist because of his possession of artistic traits. The speaker succeeds in creating a referential connection between 'he' and 'artist'.

Nakamura (1977: 10–16) states that figures of speech are used for three purposes. First, a speaker will use a figure of speech to describe something unknown to the addressee. If a father describes tigers to children who do not know what tigers are but only know what cats are, he might use a figure of speech: トラはネコの親分だ *Tora wa neko no oyabun da* 'Tigers are the masters of cats'. Second, we may use a figure of speech to emphasize something. When a tiger is extraordinarily quiet, we might use a figure of speech to emphasize this feature of the tiger: ネコみたいなトラだ 'That tiger is like a cat'. Third, we may use a figure of speech to avoid making a direct statement. For example, 彼女は古ぎつねだ *Kanojo wa furugitsune da* 'She is an old fox' means that she is a cunning, sly or deceitful person.

As readily shown above, figures of speech enrich a speaker's expressiveness. By implicitly comparing two (or more) entities, the speaker succeeds in expressing his or her worldview. Figures of speech are, in effect, an example of implicature in the sense that they allow the speaker to convey more than what is being said. Some textbooks do not use the term 'figure of speech' but instead subsume its extended meanings under the notion of 'metaphor'. In this book, metaphor is treated as one type of figurative expression (2.5.1) and is contrasted with simile (2.5.2), personification (2.5.3), and metonymy (2.5.4), respectively.

2.5.1 Metaphor

Metaphor, or 隠喩 *inyu,* is the assignment of a figurative meaning to a lexical word to which its original meaning is related in an extended sense.

(10) 人間は狼だ。
Ningen wa ōkami da
Human beings are wolves.

In this example, 狼 'wolf' serves as a metaphor, because it is used to denote the cruelty of human beings. The meaning of cruelty derives from our conventional understanding of wolves; they are wild animals who hunt in packs. Instead of blatantly using the word 'cruel', the speaker chooses to express himself indirectly by drawing attention to the figurative meaning that 狼 entails. The original meaning of 狼 (i.e., a wild animal) is not applicable here because human beings cannot be animals.

2.5.2 Simile

Simile, or 直喩 *chokuyu*, is another type of figurative language. It is often realized by the use of ようだ *yōda* (forming a predicate), ような *yōna* (forming an adjective), まるで *marude* (being attached to a noun), みたいだ *mitaida* (forming a predicate) or みたいな *mitaina* (forming an adjective) to point directly to the resemblance between the literal and figurative meanings. The meaning shared by these expressions is that 'X is like Y'; the speaker describes X by associating X with Y. Consider (10) again. (10) can be paraphrased as (11) in the form of a simile. Here, the resemblance between wolves and their figurative meaning, that is, cruelty, is mentioned more directly.

(11) 人間は狼の**ようだ**。
 Ningen wa ōkami no yō da
 Humans are like wolves.

(12) これはうその**ような**話だ。
 Kore wa uso no yōna hanashi da
 This is like an incredible story (= I can hardly believe this story).

(13) 波が高くて**まるで**津波だ。
 Nami ga takakute marude tsunami da
 The waves are so high that they look like a *tsunami*.

(14) 電気を消すと、夜**みたいだ**。
 Denki o kesuto yoru mitai da
 Switching off the light, it is like night.

(15) それは夢**みたいな**話だ。
 Sore wa yume mitaina hanashi da
 It sounds like a dreamlike (unrealistic) story.

2.5.3 Personification

Personification, or 擬人法 *gijinhō*, is another type of figurative language. Personification takes an inanimate entity and treats it as if it were an individual. In (16), we personify the tropical forest; that is, we treat it like an individual. When we stand in front of the burned trees and plants from the big fires in Sumatra, Indonesia, we may say (16) to describe our sadness and unhappiness. By using personification, the speaker succeeds in expressing the misery of the jungle.

71

(16) ジャングルが泣いている。
    Janguru ga naite iru
    The jungle is crying.

2.5.4 Metonymy

Metonymy, or 換喩 *kanyu,* is another type of figurative language. It is used when the speaker refers to an entity by naming something else associated with it. Association or **contiguity** is an important component that distinguishes metonymy from other figurative languages (Radden and Kövecses 1999: 19). In (17), the speaker refers to a person who is eating a ham sandwich without mentioning the person directly; instead, the speaker verbalizes the food that stands for the person. (18) shows a different use of metonymy because, instead of representing a different entity, it exhibits the part–whole relationship (see Chapter 6, section 6.1.6 in JL). This example is taken from the headline of an article in the *Yomiuri Newspaper* (31 December 2003). 牛丼 *gyūdon* 'beef bowls' stands for the selling of beef bowls; the company indicates that it may stop selling them if BSE (Bovine Spongiform Encephalopathy = 牛海綿状脳症 *gyū-kaimenjō-nōshō*) persists. The part–whole relationship is also referred to as **synecdoche** or 提喩 *tēyu* (see also Gibbs 1994: 11–12), but as Hebron (2004: 149) points out, because of the difficulty in conceptually demarcating metonymy from synecdoche, the word 'metonymy' is often taken to include both metonymy and synecdoche.[3]

    One effect of metonymy might be to cause a sensation, as seen in (17), since it is impossible for food to order something, and this impossibility in turn evokes interest or curiosity in the hearer/reader. (18) might be considered an economy of language, since we can easily infer that what is to be stopped is the sale of beef bowls. This is not to be interpreted as a statement that shops will be closed or employees will be made redundant. In other words, the metonymical use of language operates within the 'meaning potential of an utterance' (see Thomas 1995, cited in Cameron 2001: 70) that limits the range of possible interpretations. Metonymy is used frequently as a figure of speech in newspapers precisely because of this quality of economy.

(17) ハムサンドイッチがコーヒーを注文した。
    Hamu-sandoitchi ga kōhī o chūmon shita
    The ham sandwich ordered a coffee.
(18) 牛丼中止 *Gyūdon-chūshi*
    Stop Beef Bowls.

Activity 9

Identify and explain the type of figure of speech used in the following examples.

(19) a. 風のように走った。
b. 冬の使者がやって来た。
c. 心は沼のようだ。
d. ダイヤモンドは欲望だ。
e. 本は世界だ。
f. 本は紙だ。
g. 手を洗いたいのですが。
h. アメリカが負けた。
i. 太陽が笑っている。
j. 愛は盲目だ。

Commentary

The types of figure of speech are given below. The author shall leave it to you to discuss with your fellow students why each example is categorized the way it is and what kind of information you think the speaker is conveying by using a figure of speech. To give one example, the simile in (19a) expresses the idea that the person runs very fast. We have a conventional understanding of wind as being swift. Note that the meaning of figures of speech often differs from language to language. 'He runs like the wind' contains the same connotation in English and Japanese, while another English metaphor, 'He broke wind', does not make sense if translated literally into Japanese, because in Japanese 'wind' still maintains its literal meaning.

(20) a. simile
b. metaphor
c. simile
d. metonymy
e. metaphor and metonymy (本 'books' and 世界 'world' stand for the act of reading and the act of knowing the world, respectively)
f. metaphor
g. metonymy
h. metonymy
i. personification
j. personification and metonymy (愛 'love' stands for the act of loving)

Activity 10

You will now examine figures of speech in a newspaper article. Figures of speech are marked in boldface. Your task is to explain why they are used figuratively in the text. You should think about the information the writer intends to convey by using figures of speech. Do you think the use of figures of speech reflects our cultural attitudes? Text 2.24 describes the beauty and dynamism of nature at the South Pole. The extract is taken from the beginning and final parts of a report.

Text 2.24

```
           ひょうじょうゆた          こおり てんらんかい
        ① 表 情 豊か、② 氷の展覧会

しょうわきちしゅうへん        ひこうくう       なんきょく
昭和基地周辺をヘリで飛行空から見る南極は、③まるで氷の展覧会だ。

    もよう   かいすい    きかがくてき   なら しろ
まだら模様の海水や④幾何学的に並ぶ白いかたまり。

たいりく おお あつ すうせん              なんきょく ひょうじょう   えが だ
大陸を覆う厚さ数千メートルの氷が⑤南極の表情を⑥描き出している

⑦ようだ。[...]

  えいせいしゃしん        ひょうが うご   て と     わ     せっぴょうがく
「衛星写真⑧みたい。氷河の動きが⑨手に取る⑩ように分かる」と、雪氷学

   せんもん       たいいん
が専門のX隊員（４５）。
```

© 2004 *Asahi.com* 30 March

Commentary

The following is a general commentary.

① personifies the landscape of the South Pole. 表情 *hyōjō* 'expression' is associated with human facial expressiveness. The landscape cannot have a face, so through this personification the writer succeeds in underlining the power of nature at the South Pole.

②　and ③ convey the sense that the South Pole looks like an exhibition of ice. This draws attention to the impressive landscape of the South Pole by using 'exhibition' figuratively. ② is a metaphor, while ③ is a simile (まるで *marude*).

As shown in ④, the use of 的 *teki*, which turns the noun 幾何学 *kikagaku* 'geometry' into an adjectival, also contributes to the creation of a simile, verbalizing the manner in which lumps of ice are placed.

The sentence containing ⑤, ⑥ and ⑦ exhibits two types of figurative speech. ⑤ and ⑥ are personifications. The former personifies 南極 *nankyoku* 'the South Pole', as the South Pole cannot have a facial expression. The latter also personifies 氷 *kōri* 'ice', which is treated as an individual who pictures or represents (描き出す *egakidasu*) the landscape of the South Pole. Only humans can draw the landscape. Both personifications in ⑤ and ⑥ are embedded into a simile in ⑦. The author is saying that the thick ice covering the South Pole is so impressive that it represents the South Pole.

⑧ again serves as a simile, drawing a comparison between the landscape of the South Pole and the satellite picture of Earth (衛星写真 *ēsē-shashin*). It succeeds in describing the South Pole more emphatically and vividly.

⑨ 手に取る *te ni toru* literally means that someone holds something in his hands. When something is in a person's hand, it is considered to be under the control of that person. Since the movement of a glacier cannot be in someone's hand, ⑨ is a metaphor. By combining this expression with a simile ように *yōni*, ⑩ expresses the idea that something is easily accessible. X reports that she can observe the movements of the glacier with ease and clarity.

The cultural attitudes of the speaker can be identified in the choice of figurative expressions. It is safe to say that the contrast between original and figurative meanings reflects the collective attitudes of the people in a given society. An extended use of 展覧会 *tenran-kai* 'exhibition' in ② and ③ reveals a positive conception of an exhibition that is shared by Japanese people. Similarly, the extended use of 手 *te* 'hands' in ⑨ might reflect the way Japanese people perceive the functions of hands in the acquisition of the knowledge. That is to say, the concept of hands may be seen to create an imaginative container in which the knowledge acquired is to be stored.

Exercise

A headline such as 日本今夜ロシア戦 *Nihon konya roshia-sen* 'Japan against Russia this evening' is an instance of metonymy. We have said that, because of its conciseness, metonymy is frequently used in newspaper headlines. Consult Japanese newspapers and try to collect other instances of metonymical use, and discuss with your fellow students what the expressions you have found stand for.

Notes

1   For instance, when we refer to unicorns, they do not exist in the real world in which we live but in the imagined world.
2   Irony is one figurative mode of thought aside from metaphor and metonymy (see Gibbs 1994: 13; Hebron 2004: 151 among others).
3   Gibbs (1999: 73) defines the part–whole relationship more accurately; he examines synecdoche in terms of the relationship between a general category of an entity and its subpart(s), subtype(s) or salient attribute(s) (note that the notion of synecdoche is not used in this article). For example, the tautological expression 'boys will be boys' expresses the idea that boys (general category) tend to be unruly (salient attribute).

3 Discourse

In JL, the Japanese language is observed mainly at the level of the sentence. In Chapters 1 and 2 of this volume, we broadened our focus by considering the speaker's role at the utterance level, and we have seen that these roles can extend beyond the level of sentence to that of text. This chapter will examine the Japanese language more systematically from a textual level. This level is often referred to as **discourse** in linguistic literature. In Japanese linguistics, it is translated as 談話 *danwa*. The word *discourse* originates from the Latin *discursus*, referring to the action of running to and fro; at the end of Latinity it came to mean 'conversation'. The word initially referred to 'rehearsed forms of spoken language' where people 'run on' about a topic (Carter et al. 2001: 165). The modern meaning of discourse is a succession of sentences, spoken or written, arranged coherently. This indicates that discourse and text are related but also distinguishable to the extent that a study of discourse contributes to an explication of the ways sentences are linked or arranged, while text refers to a physical object containing instances for the study of discourse (see Johnstone 2002: 19–20). Essays, letters, email messages, stories and newspaper articles all represent different types of texts, and the task of discourse analysts is to discover and explain the structure of these texts. This chapter highlights the important characteristics of Japanese discourse. We first look at coherence (3.1) and then examine the nature of cohesion (3.2), followed by a closer look at different types of conjunctions (3.3) and clause linkage (3.4). Coherence is also achieved by the speaker's/writer's use of various discourse devices or strategies. Three sections are devoted to this topic: the functions of particles は and が (3.5), sentence-final forms (3.6) and ellipsis (3.7).

3.1 Coherence

Coherence is attained when a succession of sentences is logical (i.e., makes sense) and, hence, meaningful; in other words, sentences are not assembled at random but hang together according to some principles or patterns. One clear example of coherence is a **conversational discourse** in which participants attend to each other to realize talk. When A asks a question, B replies, which enables their speech to form a coherent text (see Chapter 5, section 5.1 for 'adjacency pairs'):

Coherence 1

    A: 今、何時ですか。
        Ima nanji desu ka
        What time is it?
    B: 7時です。
        Shichiji desu
        It's 7 o'clock.

B's answer does not have to refer to clock time, however. It can differ depending on the context of the conversation. In Malaysia or Singapore, B's reply can refer to the sunrise, because people in these regions know that the sun rises shortly after 7 a.m. throughout the year. The content of the following conversation is different from that of the above, but still constitutes a coherent text in that B attends to A's question by utilizing their shared pragmatic knowledge.

Coherence 2

    A: 今、何時ですか。
        Ima nanji desu ka
        What time is it?
    B: 太陽が昇ったところです。
        Taiyō ga nobotta tokoro desu
        The sun has just risen.

Incoherency occurs when B's answer does not match A's question. Under normal circumstances, B's utterance in the following conversation does not contribute to coherence.

Incoherence

    A: 今、何時ですか。
        Ima nanji desu ka
        What time is it?
    B: 昨日の夕食はおいしかった。
        Kinō no yūshoku wa oishikatta
        The dinner yesterday was delicious.

Activity 1

The text in the box below is a recipe for pizza toast. Unlike **narrative** texts, this type of text is called a **procedural** text, since it describes how to do things (see Dooley and Levinsohn 2001: 8). What is your opinion of the sequence of the five statements? Do you think the text is written coherently or randomly? If the latter, reorder the statements and explain your rearrangement.

Text 3.1 ピザトースト

ピザトースト

《材料》（8枚分）

フランスパン 8 枚　ベーコン 3 枚　トマト中½個　チーズ 8 枚　ピーマン

1 個　バター・練りがらし　ケチャップ

作り方

① パンの片面にバターと練りがらしを合わせたものをぬり、その上にケ
チャップをぬり、並べておきます。

② ベーコンは1枚を3等分に切り、トマトはたてに薄切り、ピーマンは
種を取って輪切りにします。

③ 250℃で予熱したオーブンで、チーズが溶けるまで約5分焼きます。

④ 準備しておいたパンの上に、ベーコン、トマト、チーズ、ピーマンの
順にのせます。

⑤ アルミホイルを敷いたオーブン皿にパンを8枚並べます。

Vocabulary:

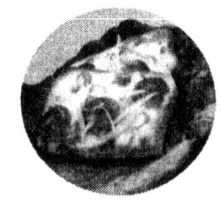

フランスパン *furansu pan*　baguette
ベーコン *bēkon*　bacon
ピーマン *pīman*　capsicum
練りがらし *nerigarashi*　mustard
片面 *katamen*　one side
ケチャップをぬる *kechappu o nuru*　to spread ketchup
3 等分に切る *santō-bun ni kiru*　to cut into three pieces
薄切りにする *usugiri ni suru*　to cut thinly
種を取る *tane o toru*　to remove the seeds (of a capsicum)
輪切りにする *wagiri ni suru*　to cut round
アルミホイルを敷く *arumihoiru o shiku*　to place tin foil
予熱する *yonetsu suru*　to warm up
溶ける *tokeru*　to melt
焼く *yaku*　to bake
準備する *junbi suru*　to prepare
パンの上に順にのせる *pan no ue ni jun ni noseru*　to put X one after
another on the (sliced) bread
パンを8枚並べる *pan o hachi-mai naraberu*　to place eight pieces of
(sliced) bread in a row

Commentary

The following is a sample answer to Activity 1. The statements are reordered in the following way.

Text 3.2　ピザトースト

---

❶　パンの片面にバターと練りがらしを合わせたものをぬり、その上にケ

　　チャップをぬり、並べておきます。①

❷　ベーコンは1枚を3等分に切り、トマトはたてに薄切り、ピーマンは

　　種を取って輪切りにします。②

❸　準備しておいたパンの上に、ベーコン、トマト、チーズ、ピーマンの

　　順にのせます。④

❹　アルミホイルを敷いたオーブン皿にパンを8枚並べます。⑤

❺　250℃で予熱したオーブンで、チーズが溶けるまで約5分焼きます。③

Coherence in Text 3.1 is achieved by discovering a **temporal sequence**. We have to think about what would be the first step in cooking the pizza toast. We share the general knowledge that we start by preparing the bread and the ingredients (that is, slices of bacon, tomato, cheese and capsicum) that we have to put on it. This gives us a clue that ❶ and ❷ come first. The order of these two is irrelevant in real time, but it would be more appropriate to have ❶ first and then ❷, as it makes sense to cut the bacon and other ingredients after we have prepared the bread. ❸ precedes ❹, as it describes a step in which ingredients are attached to the bread; this step is followed by the next in which the bread is placed in an oven. It is necessary to place tin foil on the oven tray before baking the bread. This procedure gives us a clue that ❹ precedes ❺. Note that not only the temporal sequence gives us a hint with respect to this order but so do grammatical clues. For example, we encounter the use of ておく *teoku* twice. We have learned that ておく expresses the completion of an action that is considered a preparation for a further action in the future (see Chapter 7, section 7.4.2.3 in JL). 並べておきます *narabete okimasu* in ❶ implies that preparing the bread with butter and mustard is a prerequisite for placing the ingredients in stage ❸. The noun-modifying construction 準備しておいたパン *junbi shite oita pan* in ❸ refers to the bread mentioned in ❶. It implies the readiness of the bread for the next step. ておく is employed when the next step is expected to follow. It would therefore be odd to say 焼いておきます in ❺, as there is no further step.

79

3.2 Cohesion

In the recipe above, coherence is established by putting the statements in temporal sequence. Our general knowledge about cooking helps us order this sequence appropriately. But temporal information is not the only clue for constructing a coherent text. Consider the text below, a short passage from a diary written in the first person 僕 *boku* 'I'.

Text 3.3

(I) 今日僕はデパートへ買い物に行った。(II) 両親の銀婚式のプレゼントを買うためだ。(III) **それから**、友達の家に立ち寄った。(IV) **友達は**夕食をごちそうしてくれた。(V) **Ø (=夕食は)** 奥さんの手作りのちらし寿司だった。(VI) **奥さんは**まだはたちだという。(VII) 僕はこのニュースに驚いた。

Translation:

(I)   I went to the department store to do some shopping today.
(II) This was because I intended to buy a gift for my parents' silver wedding anniversary.
(III) After that, I dropped by my friend's house.
(IV) My friend treated me to dinner.
(V)   The dinner was *chirashi-zushi* prepared by his wife.
(VI) His wife is only twenty.
(VII) I was surprised by this news.

Look at (I) and (II) in the text. These two sentences occur in parallel temporally: the narrator's going to the department store is contemporaneous with the idea that he intends to buy a gift for his parents. Upon closer look, we notice that what links these two sentences is a **cause-and-effect** relationship; that is, the reason the narrator went shopping was to buy a gift. Cause is signalled by ため *tame* in the second sentence, which expresses a reason. The diary is arranged coherently, but coherence is not achieved by a temporal sequence. Connecting words such as ため are termed cohesive devices or markers. When sentences are linked to each other by a cohesive device, we call this link **cohesion**.

In this text, cohesive devices have two functions: one is to express a cause-and-effect relationship, as already mentioned, and the other is to act as a **reference** (see Chapter 2, section 2.1.1 for the notion of 'reference'). With reference, the writer refers back to what has been mentioned in previous discourse. For example, a link between (III) and (IV) is created by referring to 友達 *tomodachi* 'friend' once again, while the link between (IV) and (V) is created by not expressing 夕食 *yūshoku* 'dinner' twice (but implying it). The link between (V) and (VI) is also established by referring to 奥さん *okusan* 'wife' once again. A demonstrative (e.g., この *kono*, その *sono*, あの *ano*) is another referring device. このニュース *kono nyūsu* (VII) refers to the previous statement (VI). それ in それから *sorekara* 'and then, after that' (III) can be seen as a **demonstrative** (see Chapter 2, Table 2.1) referring to what (II) states, but the whole expression functions as a **conjunction** that connects temporally continuous actions.

The above discussion points to the important fact in discourse study that a coherent text is not realized simply by putting sentences one after another, but by arranging them to be connected, overtly or covertly, by the **author's logical thinking**. To sum up, each sentence in Text 3.3 conveys the following information:

(I) states the fact of what the narrator did (shopping) that day.
(II) gives the *reason* why the narrator went shopping.
(III) states that the narrator dropped by his friend's *after* shopping.
(IV) informs the reader that *the narrator's friend* treated him to dinner.
(V) explains that the *dinner* (∅) was prepared by the wife of the narrator's friend
(VI) informs the reader that *the wife* is only twenty.
(VII) states that the narrator was surprised by *this* news that the wife is only twenty.

Activity 2

In the following paragraph, an editorial article in a newspaper, words that link parts of the text are marked in boldface. State whether each linking word is 'temporal', 'causal' or 'referential'. If they do not fall under any of these categories, the writer is most probably using other cohesive devices to realize the link. Write 'conjunction' for this latter case, and explain what effect it has on the previous context.

Text 3.4

> ぞっとする、①この怠慢
>
> 連休の羽田空港で、管制官が旅客機2機を工事のため閉鎖された滑走路に着陸するよう指示する失態があった。危うく大惨事になるところだった。
>
> 当時の管制官18人全員が滑走路の閉鎖を忘れていたというのだ②から、あきれてしまう。

81

みどりの日の夜のことである。滑走路灯の工事のため、３本の滑走路のうち１本が午後９時半に閉鎖された。

機長たちは閉鎖を知っていた。

帯広からの日航機は２度にわたって、③この滑走路でいいか確認を求めた。管制塔は指示を繰り返して着陸させた。

④続いて新千歳からやって来た日航機にも、管制塔は閉鎖された滑走路へ進入するよう繰り返し指示した。疑問に思った機長は「着陸できるのか」と尋ねた。管制官からの答えは驚いたことに、「⑤それはできない」だった。交代に来た同僚から閉鎖を知らされたのだ。

着陸と離陸のときは事故がいちばん多く、操縦士が最も緊張する。⑥そんなときに⑦こんな混乱した指示が来れば、どうすればよいのか。

⑧この機長は自分の判断で着陸のやり直しを告げたうえで、許可を得て別の滑走路に降りた。

滑走路の工事はまだ始まっていなかった。⑨とはいえ、実害はなかったと問題を小さく考えるのは間違いだ。

2000年に台湾の国際空港で、シンガポール航空機が工事中の滑走路から離陸しようとした。機体が工事車両らしい滑走路にあたって、炎上し、約８０人が亡くなった。工事中の滑走路での離着陸の恐ろしさがわかる。

昨年６月、新潟空港で⑩も管制官が閉鎖中の滑走路に小型旅客機を着陸させた。⑪このときの教訓は羽田に生かされなかったのか。

⑫今回のミスでは、乗員と乗客は前の便に５１人、後の便には１６１

人乗っていた。工事の準備で車両が滑走路に入っていたらと思う

⑬と、ぞっとする。

© 2005 *Asahi Newspaper* 2 May

Commentary

The functions of linking in Text 3.4 can be summarized as follows:

① referential
② causal
③ referential
④ conjunction
⑤ referential
⑥ referential
⑦ referential
⑧ referential
⑨ conjunction
⑩ referential
⑪ referential
⑫ referential
⑬ causal

①この怠慢 *kono taiman* 'this laziness' refers to the fact that air traffic controllers forgot that one runway (out of three) had been closed, and they guided two airplanes to land on this runway. Because ①この *kono*, appearing in a headline, refers forward to the content of the article, it is a cataphoric usage (see Chapter 2, section 2.1.3). The phrase headed by ②から *kara* explains why the author of this article is disappointed at this extraordinary happening in the Haneda control tower. ③この refers back to the runway, mentioned in the previous discourse, that was closed at 9.30 p.m. ④続いて *tsuzuite* is a conjunction that realizes the link between the airplane that landed on the closed runway (though no accident fortunately ensued) and the other airplane that received the same instruction but landed on another runway. ⑤それ *sore* refers to the utterance of the pilot, who reconfirmed the message from the control tower. ⑥そんな *son-na* refers back to the moment of take-off and landing, at which the pilot became most tense. ⑦こんな *kon-na* also refers back to the message from the control tower, which was confusing. ⑧この *kono* refers back to the pilot who reconfirmed the message of the control tower. ⑨とはいえ *towa-ie* 'however, nevertheless' is a conjunction enabling the author to express a concessive statement: although the construction work had not begun and no serious accident occurred, we have to take the control tower's carelessness seriously. ⑩ も *mo* is attached to the Niigata airport, where the same type of accident had occurred. The author is contrasting the two airports. ⑪ この *kono* refers back to the incident in Niigata. The author criticizes the controllers in Haneda, who had not learned a lesson from this previous incident. ⑫ 今回 *konkai* refers to the mistake that occurred this time. For expressions such as 'this time' or 'last time', Japanese has lexical words (e.g., 前回 *zenkai* 'last time'). ⑬ と *to* serves to express the causal relation between the author's imagination of the presence of other vehicles and the blood-curdling feeling it caused.

The purpose of this activity was to demonstrate that a text such as the above is constructed by different cohesive devices. What is noteworthy in this article is the frequent use of referential cohesion. In what follows, you will explore different conjunctions in a folktale. You may notice that this folktale does not use reference as a cohesive device. This means that cohesion is realized differently in different types of text.

3.3 Conjunctions

You have learned that when a speaker or writer creates a text, sentences are connected meaningfully, and the meaningful connection results in a coherent text. As we have seen in Texts 3.3 and 3.4, a coherent text is often signalled by the efficient use of cohesive devices. In this section, we will look more closely at **conjunctions** (also termed *connectives*). Conjunctions refer to words that conjoin or link sentences or clauses, thereby also indicating semantic relationships. Consider Text 3.5, which contains nine instances of conjunctions. Read through the text: さるかに合戦 *Sarukani-Gassen* 'Battles between the Monkey and the Crabs', which is the beginning of the folktale. This tale got its name because the mother crab's children avenge her, and with the support of their friends (bees, a needle and a mortar) they win in the end. The monkey is crushed to death under the heavy mortar that falls on him from the roof of the house. In the text, conjunctions are marked in boldface. Decide how they link together the various parts of the text.

Text 3.5 さるかに合戦

> 1 むかし、むかしあるところに、おなかをすかせたおかあさんがにが住
>
>   んでいました。毎日、毎日食べものをさがしていました。ある日、
>
>   大きなおにぎりをみつけました。よろこんで食べようとしたとき、い
>
>   じわるなさるがやってきて、むりやりおにぎりをうばおうとしました。

5 「やめてください。これはわたしのものよ！」かには、ひっしにおに

ぎりを守ろうとしました。**すると**、さるはかくしていたかきのたねを

取り出して言いました。

「おにぎりとこのたねをとりかえよう。これをまけば、大きなかきの

木がはえ、あまいかきが、どっさりなるぞ」

10 **そして**、むりやりおにぎりをとりあげ、すぐに食べてしまいました。

おなかをすかせたかあさんがにには、たねをじめんにまいて、

毎日水をかけてやりました。

「はやくめをだせ、かきのたね。ださぬとはさみでちょんぎるぞ。」

すると、じめんの中から、小さなめがでてきて、ずんずんのびて、大

15 きな木になりました。**やがて**、かきの木には、あまくておいしそうな

実がいっぱいなりました。**でも**、かには木にのぼれません。こまって

いると、いじわるなさるがまたやってきました。

「おれがとってやろう。」

さるは木によじのぼる**と**、かきを食べはじめました。

20 おなかをすかせたかには、「わたしにもとってください。」と声をか

けましたが、さるはあまいかきをぜんぶ食べてしまいました。

「おさるさん、ひとつくださいな。」

お母さんがにには、泣きながら願うと、さるはまだ青くてかたいかきを、

かにになげつけたのです。からだをつよく打たれたおかあさんがに

25 はとうとうしんでしまいました。

しかし、そのとき、おかあさんがにから、げんきな三びきの子がに

うまれたのです。

There is one instance of そして *soshite* in line 10. Its use tells the reader that what is to follow will 'add' further information to the previous sentence. On lines 8–10, the monkey wants to exchange the rice ball with the persimmon seed he has 'and' takes it quickly away from the crab. The conjunction しかし *shikashi*, as used here (line 26), tells the reader that what is to follow 'revises' or 're-focuses' the fact expressed by the previous sentence: the mother crab died 'but' three healthy baby crabs were born. Note that しかし is often said to express 'opposition' in a sentence like (1).

(1) 日本語は難しいです。しかし、おもしろいです。
Nihongo wa muzukashī desu. Shikashi, omoshiroi desu
Japanese is difficult, but it is interesting.

Here, the sentences contain two clear-cut opposing facts in that 'being difficult' stands complementarily to 'being easy' (see Chapter 6, section 6.1.4 in JL). In authentic texts, it appears that the exact meaning of conjunctions has much to do with the intention of the writer who composes the text. It is, of course, possible to say that しかし (line 26) connects 'sad' and 'happy' incidents, but it would be more accurate to say that the author 'revises' the sad death of a mother crab by providing a contrasting fact, that is, the birth of her children, which leads the story to a surprising end (the English translation would be: 'However, at this moment, three lively baby crabs were born from the mother crab').

Another conjunction でも *demo*, which encodes 'opposition', appears on line 16. It is possible to use しかし instead. Why would the writer prefer でも to しかし? The answer might be that でも is able to express a sense of regret concerning the mother crab. The sense of regret comes from the 'contradiction' brought about by the combination of two sentences: S1 (lines 15–16) says that the tree is now full of sweet fruits, but S2 (line 16) says that the mother crab cannot climb it despite the fact that she is starving. でも successfully expresses this conflicting situation. しかし (line 26) cannot be replaced with でも because two situations linked by しかし do not express conflicting facts.

Both すると *suruto* (lines 6, 14) and そのとき *sonotoki* (line 26) express a temporal relation between two sentences. すると concerns the sequence of two events, while そのとき refers to the specific time that one event occurs, at which time another event also occurs. やがて *yagate* (line 15) also emphasizes a temporal sequence, but it focuses more on the final stage of an event. The occurrence of と *to* (lines 17 and 19) differs significantly from other conjunctions in that it does not appear at the beginning of a sentence but rather at the end. Its function is temporal, that is, it introduces a clause that refers to the time at which one event occurs and another event immediately follows. と in line 19 specifies the completion of one event, at which moment another event happens. The moment the monkey has completed climbing up the tree, he starts to eat persimmons.

Activity 3

Here are some more conjunctions with a brief explanation for each group. You may be familiar with some of them. Read through the notes in the table and supplement it, if necessary, by adding conjunctions that you think are relevant. After you have finished, choose your favourite text and specify the types of conjunctions used. Note that some conjunctions can be placed in more than one category. Positions where conjunctions occur are either at the end of S1 or at the beginning of S2. No conjunctions occur at the beginning of S1 or at the end of S2.

Table 3.1   List of conjunctions

Relationship	Meaning	Example	
		S1	**S2**
additional	S2 adds or gives an alternative meaning to S1	と や	そして　および
oppositional	S1 opposes or contrasts with S2	が	しかし　だが
contradictory	S1 contradicts S2	のに	でも
temporal	S1 temporally follows S2	と	それから　すると　そのとき
causal	S1 causes S2	から ので	だから
exemplifying	S2 exemplifies S1		たとえば
continuation	S2 is a continuation of S1	て	ところで　つぎに
conditional	S2 occurs on the condition of S1	たら ば なら	

3.4　Clause linkage: て versus *Renyō*

Apart from conjunctions, Japanese utilizes two other grammatical forms, which are known as the て *te*-form and the *renyō*-form (連用), respectively, to connect or chain sentences or clauses. Although it is not always easy to distinguish between these two forms precisely, it has been claimed that the て-form shows 'a higher degree of continuity' than the *renyō*-form (Ono, 1990, cited in Iwasaki, 2002: 264).

    In this section we examine the use of these forms on the basis of two short stories and show that while the main function of the *renyō*-form is to juxtapose two (or sometimes more than two) events, the て-form imparts various semantic relations between two events. It seems that both forms can be employed when S2 is seen as a consequence of S1. In section 3.2, we have seen that temporality, causality and other cohesive devices contribute to the creation of a coherent text. This section will show that the manner in which actions are carried out and linked to each other is another important device in creating coherence in a text. Consider Text 3.6 taken from a short story 冷たい手 *Tsumetai te* 'Cold Hands'.

Text 3.6

1　あの頃、梅田が婚約解消を言い出せば、どちらもまるく片がついてい

　　たのか。梅田も自分も遊びなれていた。だから、地味でまっとうな

　　OLである秋子に、どこかしら引け目を①**いだき**、いっそう②**美化し**、

　　その裏側があるなど考えもしなかった。実際、現在の秋子もまっとう

5　な主婦におさまっている。室内のインテリアに心を③**くだき**、

　　アトピー性の皮膚炎を持つ子供のために手作りのおやつを④**常備し**、

　　どの部屋の掃除も⑤**ゆきとどき**、この家の設計からローン返済の計画

　　まで一手に⑥**引き受け**、多分、取りこぼしはない。だが十年前、

　　秋子にもうひとりの男性がいたことををこっそりとでも打ち開けてく

10　れていたなら......比呂子は軽いめまいをおぼえた。⑦**あわてて**口

　　走っていた。

　　「ごめんなさい。長居をしてしまったわ。もうひとつの用事をすませ

　　なくちゃならないの」

　　「あら、まだいいでしょう。じきに子供たちも帰ってくるから会っ

15　ていってやって」

　　「ええ、でも、また日を⑧**あらためて**、おじゃまさせていただ

　　くわ」[...]

　　梅田の家を⑨**辞し**、タクシーのひろえる表通りへむかいながら、

　　比呂子は無性に梅田に会いたくなった。⑩**会って**ふたりで、

20　たったいま耳にした秋子の過去の秘密について語ってみたい。[...]

　　歩きながら前方の電話ボックスが目にとびこんできた。梅田の勤務先

の電話番号は⑪そらんじていて、いまも忘れていない。電話ボックスを⑫やりすごし、表通りに⑬でて空車のタクシーがやってきても比呂子は手をあげなかった。ひたすら歩きつづけた。何代目の電話ボックスで足を

25 とめるか。それとも突然に⑭気が変わりタクシーを⑮ひろって自宅マンションの住所を告げるか、比呂子は数分先の自分の行動が予測できなかった。いまだに梅田を愛していた。絆は秋子の告白によって、ふたたび自分たちをつないだような気がした。しかし、夫の竹村もまたどのようなかたちであろうとも、哀しませたくない。哀しませては

30 ならない、と思うぐらいには好きだった。だが、切実なほどの想いを⑯ともなって、梅田の冷たく、しめった掌の感触がよみがえってきた。ベージュのバッグを握る比呂子の手もうっすらと⑰しめり、十月の暮れどきの風に⑱さらされ、その指先はつめたくなっていた。

© 2002 Tōdō, Shizuko / *Tsumetai Te* (pp. 158–160), Kodansha

A protagonist, 比呂子 *Hiroko*, visits the new house of her former lover 梅田 *Umeda*.[1] In the house, his wife 秋子 *Akiko* welcomes 比呂子 as her husband and children are out, for work and school. On this visit, 比呂子 learns for the first time that 秋子 had a lover prior to her marriage. Around that time 比呂子 had an affair with 梅田, who could not break his engagement to 秋子 despite all his attempts to be married to 比呂子. Having heard 秋子's confession, 比呂子's old passion revives particularly through her realization that she had had a real chance to become 梅田's wife. In this text, the *renyō*-form appears ten times, while the て-form appears seven times. Eight instances of the *renyō*-form (i.e., ① to ⑥, and ⑰ and ⑱) are employed when events or actions are juxtaposed; that is, the narrator enumerates different events. Because of this enumeration, the order of events can be reversed without a consequent change in the semantic relationships of the two parts. This characteristic of enumeration resembles the nature of coordination (see also Quirk et al. 1972: 551–552). For example, the order of ① and ② is reversible. This means that the order between the two situations (梅田 and 比呂子 have a guilty conscience regarding 秋子 *Akiko* and they praise 秋子 in person) is not determined temporally. It is thus possible to say:

(2) だから、地味でまっとうなOLである秋子を美化し、どこかしら引け目をいだき、その裏側があるなど考えもしなかった。

That's why we praised Akiko, who is a modest and honest office clerk and we felt, in some way, inferior. Not a single idea struck us that she had a hidden side behind her outer face.

In contrast, three other instances of the *renyō*-forms (i.e., ⑨, ⑫ and ⑭) are used to present the temporal sequence. In other words, S2 is connected to S1 by the 'and then' interpretation. For instance, ⑨ can be interpreted such that 比呂子 leaves the house 'and then' she directs herself towards the main street to catch a taxi. ⑫ can be interpreted such that 比呂子 passes alongside the telephone box 'and then' arrives at the main street.

When the て-form is used, the reverse of S1 and S2 is not possible, the reason being that the combination of two parts comes to carry a particular 'speaker meaning' (see Chapter 2) that in turn explains why two events are connected. As Table 3.2 summarizes, the て-form is employed when S1 stands in a particular semantic relationship to S2. For example, by using て, S1 in ⑦ succeeds in expressing the confusing manner in which 比呂子 speaks. By attaching て to 会う 'to meet' in ⑩, S1 serves as a prerequisite event for the realization of the talk between 比呂子 and 梅田. It appears that S2 is the main event, which S1 complements by giving further information. This supplementing function of S1 for S2 resembles certain cases of subordination, as presented by 'when', 'after' or 'because' clauses in English. The claim that the て-form shows a higher degree of continuity, as cited at the outset of this section, might pertain to this property of subordination.[2] Consider ⑮. It is possible to say:

(3) それとも突然に気が変わりタクシーを**ひろい**自宅マンションの住所を告げるか、比呂子は数分先の自分の行動が予測できなかった。

Or, alternatively, she could not decide on her action of the next few minutes, whether she suddenly changes her mind to take a taxi or tells the address of her apartment.

This sentence could imply that 比呂子 takes a taxi and tells the address of her apartment to someone else (not the taxi driver). When ひろって *hirotte* is employed, as in the text, the logical link between the two events (i.e., taking a taxi and telling the driver the passenger's address) is mandatory. When the *renyō*-form is applied, as in (3), the subordinate relationship appears to weaken; that is, both events happen without being dependent on each other.

Table 3.2 *Instances of* て *-forms in Text 3.6*

No.		Functions	Interpretations
⑦	あわてて	Manner	It expresses how 比呂子 speaks.
⑧	あらためて	Means/ Sequential	By/After choosing another day, 比呂子 suggests visiting 秋子 again.
⑩	会って	Sequential	The meeting of 梅田 will enable 比呂子 to talk with him about 秋子 having a lover before marriage.
⑪	そらんじていて	Cause	Because 比呂子 memorized 梅田's phone number, she can still remember it.
⑬	でて	Sequential	After arriving at 表通り, 比呂子 can take a taxi.
⑮	ひろって	Sequential	After catching a taxi, 比呂子 tells the driver where she lives.
⑯	ともなって	Simultaneity	While 比呂子 admits her affection to 梅田, she also recalls the feel of his cold and wet hands.

Activity 4

Identify the functions of the て *te*-forms in Text 3.7 from ジャスミンティの朝 *Jasumin tī no asa* 'Morning with Jasmine Tea'. The protagonist 朝子 *Asako* meets a man again at the swimming pool in a club. The excerpt begins with a scene in which the man enters the Jacuzzi and does not, to 朝子's disappointment, say a word. He pays no attention to her presence. At this moment, she starts a conversation with him.

Text 3.7

男は何も言わなかった。①**黙って**、強い水流を背中に当てた。朝子は、一

コースを見た。そのコースを泳いでいる者はひとりもいなかった。やはり、

このひとだ。そう②**思って**、朝子は声をかけた。

「この間は、ありがとうございました」

朝子は、ジャグジーの泡のたてる音を③**意識して**、大きな④**声をだして**礼

を言った。男は驚いたように朝子を見ると、怪訝そうに、それでも

軽く頭を下げた。

「おかげさまで、少しは泳ぎがらくになったような気がします」

朝子は風呂の中で、前に男がやっていたように⑤**腕を折って**、湯をかいて

みせた。それで男は合点がいったようだ。

© 1996 Ochiai, Keiko / *Jasumin Tī no Asa* (pp. 60–61), Kodansha

Translation:
The man did not say a word. Keeping silent, he exposed his back to a strong stream of water. Asako looked at one track. No one is swimming in that track. Yes, he is the person. She thought this way and spoke to him.

'Thank you for the last time.'

Asako expressed her gratitude in a loud voice. She was conscious of the bubbling sound of the Jacuzzi. The man looked at her in a surprising manner, was puzzled, but bowed lightly.

'I feel I can swim more easily – thanks for your help.'

Asako showed him in the Jacuzzi how to stroke the water by bending her arms – just the way he was doing shortly before. Then he seemed to understand what it meant.

Commentary

The function of each form can be summarized in the following manner. The form that the て-form corresponds to in English translation is in italics.

① Simultaneity (*the man did not say any word* and *at the same time* took a shower).

② Temporal sequence (朝子*'s recognition that she met him last time* is followed by her decision to speak to him).

③ Causality (朝子 spoke loudly *because she was conscious* of the noisiness of bubbles in the bath).

④ Manner (*in the manner/style of speaking aloud*, 朝子 expressed her gratitude to him).

⑤ Means (*by means of bending her arms*, 朝子 showed him how to stroke the water).

When temporal sequence is in question, either the て-form or *renyo*-form can be used. For instance, the て-form in ② can be replaced by the *renyo*-form (i.e., 思い *omoi*). Likewise, ④ and ⑤ can also accept the *renyo*-form (i.e., 声をだし *koe o dashi* and 腕を折り *ude o ori*, respectively), the reason being that manner and means (but not causality) might also be concerned with the temporal order and would therefore require the 'and then' interpretation (see ⑨, ⑫ and ⑭ in Text 3.6).

It is worth mentioning that the question of which form, *renyō* or て, is actually to be preferred may depend largely on the style the author has at her disposal. The enumeration of events by using the *renyō*-form in Text 3.6 (particularly in lines 1 to 10) has a thrilling effect such that the reader learns of a series of new events in a relatively short temporal span. Brief but rich descriptions of the protagonist 秋子 *Akiko* in these lines may also reflect 比呂子's *Hiroko*'s disquietude. In contrast, the frequent use of the

て-form in Text 3.7 may lead the reader to realize the author's special care with the interrelationship between the ongoing events. This linkage between events is likely to reinforce the intimacy between the reader and the content of the story.

3.5 は and が

3.5.1 Old versus new information

Connecting sentences means not only that two statements are conjoined but also that information in the two statements is 'conveyed'. Coherence in a text considers the way in which information is organized. Information can be either **old** or **new**. Old refers to information we already know because it has been mentioned in the previous discourse, while new means that the information is introduced for the first time into the discourse. The usage of は *wa* and が *ga* neatly reflects this distinction, as shown in Text 3.8, which is the beginning of a folktale (昔話 *mukashi-banashi*) called 桃太郎 *Momotarō* 'Peach Boy'.

Text 3.8 桃太郎

①昔昔、あるところにおじいさんとおばあさん**が**いました。②おじいさん**は**山へ芝刈りに行きました。③おばあさんは川で洗濯をしました。④ある日おばあさん**は**川で大きな桃を見ました。⑤おばあさん**は**その桃を家へ持って帰りました。

Translation:
Once upon a time, an old man and an old woman lived in a village (literally = in a certain place). The old man went to the mountain to collect firewood, while the old woman washed the laundry at the river. One day, she was doing the washing when a big peach came floating down the river towards her. She took the peach home.

When おじいさん *ojīsan* and おばあさん *obāsan* are introduced for the first time in ①, they are marked by が because they are treated as new information. When they are mentioned again in ② and ③ they are marked by は because they are now considered old information. This use of は and が can be seen as co-textual (see Chapter 2, section 2.2) in the sense that linguistic materials (which particle, は or が, appears where in a text) can tell us about the difference between the old and new information. In what follows, you will see that the use of は and が is not always co-textual.

3.5.2 *Main protagonist*

Sections 3.5.2 to 3.5.4 look at cases in which は conveys the idea of 'old information', where the indication that the information is old comes not from the co-textual arrangement of a text but from its **contextualization** – a process in which the writer constructs a viable context to use a form (such as は or が). For instance, as in the texts that follow, は is conceived of as the expression of different degrees of **familiarity** to the reader.

Text 3.9 is an excerpt taken from the beginning of a short story ジャスミンティの朝 *Jasumin tī no asa* 'Morning with Jasmine Tea'. In line 4, 土屋文人 *Tsuchiya Fumito* is mentioned for the first time and, hence, is marked by が. The same person is cited for a second time in line 7 and is marked by は. This use of は conforms to the principle of new and old information. However, you may have noticed that 水沢朝子 *Mizusawa Asako* in line 2 is not marked by が despite this being the first time it is mentioned. This use of は cannot be explained by reference to new and old information only; instead it can be explained when we consider that the protagonist 水沢朝子 is the central figure in the story. This organizational control of the discourse by the writer is due to contextualization; the writer constructs a mental world through which the text is interpreted. In this short story, the writer contextualizes 水沢朝子 by using は so that she becomes familiar or known to the reader. This organizational principle in discourse is especially significant to the composition of texts such as novels or short stories (see also Dooley and Levinsohn 2001: 24–25).

Text 3.9

1	「ねえ、どうして？」
	ジャスミンティの入ったポットにお湯を注ぎながら、水沢朝子**は**
	訊いた。「どうしてって？」
	土屋文人**が**、読みさしの雑誌をテーブルに置くと、顔**を**上げた。
5	そうして、訊き返す。
	「どうして花なんかかってきてくれたの？」
	小さく息を漏らしてから、きれいだったから、と文人**は**言った。

© 1996 Ochiai, Keiko / *Jasumin Tī no Asa*, Kodansha

Vocabulary and grammar:
読みさしの雑誌 *yomisashi no zasshi* (line 4) contains an aspectual suffix さし attached to the *renyō*-form of the verb. This suffix is not productive but occurs with 読む or 言う. It means that someone does not complete

what he or she has been doing. The expression thus means 'a magazine that Fumito did not finish reading'.

なんか *nanka* (line 6) is used when the speaker wants to avoid saying something explicitly. なんか is shortened from 何か 'something' (/na.ni.ka/ → /na.n.ka/). 花なんか literally means 'things like flowers' (see Chapter 5, section 5.6.2.8, p. 116 in JL).

Translation:
'Why?'
　　Asako(WA) asked while pouring jasmine tea into the pot. 'What do you mean by 'why'?'
　　After putting the newspaper he was reading on the table, Fumito(GA) raised his head and then asked again: 'Why did you buy flowers?'
　　'Because they were pretty', said Fumito(WA) with a small sigh.

Activity 5

A commentary is not provided for this activity.

Try to work out the use of が *ga* and は *wa* at the beginning of the children's book くまの子ウーフ *Kuma no Ko Ūfu* 'Bear Cub Ufu'. ウーフ is a bear cub who has various adventures in the story. Here, he makes a wish to become a tree because trees have green leaves and he could then lick honey without having to climb. Explain the use of は based on what you have learned so far. Consider the narrative parts only (ignore the conversations marked by 「　」).

Text 3.10

ぶなの木の下で、ひるねをしていたくまの子ウーフ**は**、目をさまして、

木をみあげました。ぶなの木**は**、みどりの葉をつけて、さもきもちよさそ

うに風にふかれていました。

「木はいいなあ。木になりたいなあ。」と、ウーフ**は**思いました。

「こんなもしゃもしゃの毛皮のかわりに、みどりの葉っぱをつけて、

すずしそうに立ってるんだ。そしてさ、じっと立っていたら、みつばちが

きて、すをつくるかもしれないね。ぼく、木のぼりしなくてもはちみつが

なめられるよ。だって、ぼくが木なんだもの。」

ウーフ**は**はちみつのことをかんがえて、ごっくんとつばをのみこみました。

3.5.3 Proper nouns

The use of **proper nouns** also does not conform to the principle of old and new information. In the context of newspapers, proper nouns (e.g., names of government officials and institutions, names of organizations or individuals, etc.) are often cited, and they are normally introduced with は *wa* even though they are being mentioned for the first time. We assume that these nouns are already familiar to us, in the sense that we are aware of these names conventionally. The following examples are taken from newspapers. Each sentence is the beginning of an article. Text 3.11 contains the name of the prime minister. Text 3.12 starts with the name of an official institution, while Text 3.13 contains the name of a public junior high school in Yokohama.

Text 3.11

小泉首相**は**２１日朝、春季例大祭がはじまった東京・九段北の靖国神社を参拝した。

© 2002 *Asahi Newspaper* 22 April

Translation:
The Prime Minister(WA), Koizumi, visited the Yasukuni Shrine in Kudan, Tokyo, where the annual Spring Main Festival began.

Text 3.12

文部科学省**は**９日、０３年から使う高校教科書の検定結果を発表した。

© 2002 *Asahi Newspaper* 10 April

Translation:
The Ministry of Education, Culture, Sports, Science and Technology (WA) made public on the 9th the results of the official examination of the textbook that will be used in high schools from 2003.

Text 3.13

横浜市の青葉大中学校**は**、神奈川県内の公立中学校では珍しく制服をやめている。

© 1985 *Asahi Newspaper* 27 October

Translation:
The Aobadai Junior High School(WA) in Yokohama City is rare among public junior high schools in Kanagawa Prefecture in that it has dispensed with school uniforms.

3.5.4 Discourse theme

If nouns mentioned for the first time are related to the **theme of a discourse**, they can co-occur with は. This use of は also pertains to the concept of familiarity. The following excerpt is the fifth paragraph of 天声人語 *Tensē-Jingo* 'Heaven's Voice, Men's Words' (18 May 1983) in *Asahi Newspaper* (cited in Hinds, 1987: 99).

Text 3.14

利休**は**客をもてなす日の朝、赤杉の箸材を取り出し、人数に応じて箸を削り、削りたての杉の香りを興したという伝説がある。

Translation:
On the morning of those days on which he was expecting visitors, Rikyu got out some red Japanese cedar wood and whittled just enough pairs of chopsticks for the expected number of visitors. He then presented the guests with the odour of freshly-cut Japanese cedar.

利休 *Rikyū* was a prominent tea ceremony master in Japan (now deceased). 利休 is mentioned for the first time, but the story about 利休 is related to the theme of the article, that is, わりばし *waribashi* 'Japanese wooden disposable chopsticks'. This short paragraph is talking about the chopsticks that Rikyu whittled for his guests.

3.5.5 New episode

In section 3.5.1, we saw that が *ga* refers to new information based on the co-textual information in a text. In sections 3.5.5 to 3.5.7, we will examine the use of が from the perspective of contextualization. This means that が still expresses new information, but 'newness' is defined depending on how the writer contextualizes the text. The writer creates a mental world through which the newness is demonstrated.

Text 3.15 below is the continuation of Text 3.8. What is significant is that おじいさん *ojīsan* is marked by が, as shown in ①, although this is not the first time it is mentioned. Why does the author of this folktale use が here? This can be explained by referring to the concept of a **new episode**. The writer integrates episodes into the text, and each episode consists of an internally coherent sub-story. In this folktale, the new episode begins when the old man returns home and the old couple cut a big peach, while the previous episode describes the story up to the point when the old woman finds the peach and brings it home. The opening of a new episode can be signalled by indentation in the written text; in this regard, episodes are equivalent to paragraphs. In Text 3.15, a new episode is signalled by が, serving to open a new story that follows from the previous episode. The rest of the new episode follows the principles of old and new information. Look at おじいさん and おばあさん *obāsan* in ②, which are again marked by は to indicate their old status in the text. The use of が attached to 男の子 *otoko no ko* in ③ is a clear marker of the new information because this is the first time the information is mentioned in the story. The author manipulates strategies by introducing a new episode into which the primary old/new contrast is integrated.

Text 3.15　桃太郎

①お昼におじいさん**が**帰って来ました。②おじいさんとおばあさんは桃を

切りました。③するとももの中から元気な男の子**が**飛び出しました。

④おじいさんとおばあさんはその子を「桃太郎」と名づけました。⑤おば

あさんはごはんをたくさん作りました。⑥桃太郎はたくさん食べました。

⑦そして桃太郎はどんどん大きくなりました。

Translation:
When the old man came back for lunch, the old man and woman cut the big peach open with a knife. What a surprise! A lovely little boy jumped out of the peach. The old man and the old woman decided to call him 'Momotaro', which means 'peach-boy'. The old woman cooked a lot of food. Momotaro ate a lot, and he grew quickly.

3.5.6　Self-contained fact

From our discussion so far, it can be seen that が *ga* stands in contrast to は *wa* as it does not have any discursive function; that is, it does not serve to connect adjacent sentences. In Text 3.16, however, the first and second sentences use the same word, namely 雨 *ame* 'rain', and at first glance, this seems to support the existence of a discursive tie between the two 雨. We would expect that は should be attached to the second 雨. The use of が is therefore puzzling. How can we explain this? Can we use the notion of a new episode? The answer is no, since the second が introduces a single fact but does not constitute an episode. The puzzle is resolved by suggesting that the information conveyed by ② is **self-contained**. Here, the writer looks independently at the situation in X city where a great amount of precipitation is reported. Although the rain mentioned here refers to the same typhoon mentioned in ①, the reason が is attached to 雨 is that the rainfall in X city is conceived as being independent from its previous mention, and hence is self-contained. It could be argued that X 町 *machi* in ② is marked by は, which might preclude the repetition of は in the same sentence. Although this is an interesting argument, even if は were removed from X 町では *machi dewa*, は would not work out. This validates the existence of the writer's contextualization by which a mental world is constructed in which the rainfall in X city is taken as a self-contained fact.[3]

Text 3.16

①雨は台風１５号の影響で２８日から降り始め、１日夕にいったん子康状態となったが、１日深夜から再び激しくなったという。②X 町では２日午前０時から８時までに９５ミリの雨が降った。

© 2002 *Asahi Newspaper* 3 July

A similar explanation applies to Text 3.17 (slightly modified by the author) taken from a Japanese textbook *Nihongo Chūkyū Dokkai Nyūmon* 'An Introduction to Intermediate Japanese Reading' (1991) by Tomioka and Shima (p. 42 in Chapter 7). In this text, その人 *sono hito* is marked by が despite its reference to 男の人 *otoko no hito*. By using が, the writer distinguishes the fact that he is working in the coffee shop from the fact that he taught the girl, who is the author of this text, the job. The act of teaching is thus considered to be self-contained.

Text 3.17

先週の日曜日に、わたしは友達の家でアルバイトをしました。友達の家は、ケーキ屋さんです。店の中には小さい喫茶店もあります。喫茶店では男の人が一人、働いていて、その人が私に仕事を教えてくれました。

3.5.7 Suspense

Another use of が *ga* to express newness is **suspense**. Consider Text 3.18. One salient characteristic of this function is that が is used several times, and this repeated use evokes a sense of suspense. This serves as a strategy in a story in which the writer intends to evoke excitement in the reader's mind. This use of が would not be found in newspaper articles since they do not need to evoke a sense of suspense – their main role is to provide the reader with current news (see section 3.6 below).

In the extract from a short story, ひとり遊び *Hitori-asobi* 'Single Play', given below, が is used five times to describe a woman whom the main protagonist 隼人 *Hayato* meets in the bar of the hotel where he is staying. 隼人 is married, and he knows that he loves his wife 涼子 *Ryōko*. The use of が triggers an effect such that each statement uttered by the woman is fresh, new and independent, and this effect accordingly introduces a sense of suspense into the passage. Throughout the conversation, 隼人 is overwhelmed by the way the woman talks, behaves and approaches him. This feeling is not evil but pleasant to him. In secret, he is waiting to discover more about this woman, and the reader may be tempted to conclude that they will end up spending the night together. In line 25, the final line of the passage, the woman is marked by は *wa*, and this is where the suspense ends. Note that が is attached to 女の顔 *on-na no kao* 'woman's face' (line 5) and 唇 *kuchibiru* 'lips' (line 7). These two expressions are related to the woman, as they are the parts of her body (see Chapter 6, section 6.1.6 in JL).

Text 3.18

1　「話しかけてもいいですか？」

　　席を移るとすぐに、女**が**言った。隼人を見てはいなかった。自分で運

　　んだグラスを見ながらだった。

　　隼人**は**、何と答えていいのか戸惑った。ただ女を見ていた。[...]

5　いくつぐらいだろう。そう思ったときに、女の顔**が**向いた。

　　「三十二歳、独身、プログラマー」

　　眉の濃い、意思のはっきりした感じの女の、形のいい唇**が**そう言っ

　　て、少し笑ったように思えた。

　　「四十三歳、妻ひとり、息子ひとり。営業マン。名古屋在中」

10　隼人**は**つられたように、そう自己紹介する。女**が**、今度ははっきりし

　　た笑いを浮かべて続けた。

　　「今夜はこのホテルに滞在。そして、フォーローゼスの水割りをみ始

　　めたばかり」[...]

　　「どういう女か、考えているんですか？」

15　女**が**そう訊いた。隼人より先回りしているように思える。

「いや」

隼人は曖昧に言葉を濁した。そして、しばらく時間をおいてから続
ける。

「少しは気のきいたことが言えたらとおもって、考えるんだが
……」[...]

20 正直な気持ちを、彼は言った。女が静かに頷いて、ジントニックの
長いグラスを口に運んだ。

隼人は急にらくになったようにおもった。それで、ひとりになりた
ったのだ、とホテルにいる理由を説明した。

「わかります」

25 女は呟くように言った。そしてグラスの中の氷を鳴らした。

Translation:

1   'May I speak to you?'
The woman(GA) said soon after having changed the seat. She didn't
look at Hayato; she looked at the glass that she had brought to the table
with her. Hayato(WA) was confused, as he didn't know how to reply to
her. He was simply looking at her.
5 He wondered how old she was. At this moment she turned her face(GA)
toward him.
     'Thirty-two. I'm a programmer,' said the woman, with a thick eye-
brow and well-shaped lips(GA). She seemed to have her own clear
opinion. Hayato felt that she also smiled slightly.
     'Forty-three. I have a wife and a son. A businessman. Living in
Nagoya.'
10 Hayato(WA) introduced himself as if he was forced to do so. The
woman(GA) continued – with a clear smile on her face this time.
     'I'm staying in this hotel tonight. I've just started drinking a
whisky.'
     'Are you wondering what kind of woman I am?' asked the
woman(GA).
15 He feels she can foresee what he thinks.
     'No, not really.'
Hayato(WA) intentionally made himself ambiguous. After a break he
continued.

'I'm trying to figure out how I can say something sensible . . .'
20 He(WA) confessed his honest feeling.
The woman(GA) quietly looked at him and drew a long glass of gin tonic toward her mouth.
Hayato(WA) suddenly felt relieved and explained that he was staying in the hotel, as he wanted to be alone.
25   'I understand,' said the woman(WA) with a mutter, and clinked her glass with ice.

3.5.8   Contrast

は is used to express **contrast**. Contrast means that two or more entities are brought into opposition, and this function is independent of new or old information, as described in section 3.5.1, and of discourse strategies, as described in sections 3.5.2 to 3.5.7. The following passage is a short essay about a Sunday pastime.

Text 3.19

①先週の日曜日に、よう子と三郎が街へ買い物に行った。②買い物のあと
で、レストランに立ち寄り昼ごはんを食べることになった。③三郎がレス
トランで食べようと提案した。④しかし、困ったことによう子は和食**は**好
きだが、洋食**は**嫌いだった。⑤二人は結局昼食を取らずに家路についた。

Translation:
Last Sunday, Yoko and Saburo went to town to do some shopping. Afterwards, they decided to drop by a restaurant to have lunch. Saburo suggested eating in a (Western) restaurant. Unfortunately, Yoko likes Japanese food(WA) but does not like Western food(WA). Finally, they decided to go straight home without having lunch.

和食 *washoku* and 洋食 *yōshoku* in ④ are both marked by は, although they are introduced into the discourse for the first time. Since the passage concerns how よう子 *Yōko* and 三郎 *Saburō* spent their time in town last Sunday, neither 和食 nor 洋食 is related to the theme of the passage (section 3.5.4). The reason は is used here is that it serves to express the contrast between two facts: Yoko likes Japanese food but does not like Western food.

Contrast is not always expressed by means of two は, and a single occurrence of は is sufficient to bring about the contrastive meaning in discourse.

102

Text 3.20

①先週の日曜日に、よう子と三郎が街へ買い物に行った。②クリスマスが真近だ。③母へのプレゼント**は**簡単に見つかった。④しかし、父へのプレゼントを見つけるために一苦労した。⑤家に着いたときはもう夜7時を過ぎていた。

Translation:
Last Sunday, Yoko and Saburo went to town to do some shopping. Christmas was approaching. They found a present(WA) for their mother, but had a hard time finding a present for their father. It was past seven o'clock when they arrived home.

In Text 3.20, プレゼント *purezento* 'present' in ① is marked by は *wa*, although this is the first time it is mentioned. From the context of Yoko and Saburo's having to go around town to find a present for their father, we can infer that the use of は implicitly brings two facts into contrast: it was easy to find a present for their mother but not for their father. The adversative conjunction しかし *shikashi* 'but' in ④ is often included when a singly occurring contrastive は appears in a text.

　　　When we deal with ellipsis in section 3.7.2 below, we will show contrast to be an emphatic tool in a narrative. In a sense, contrast and emphasis are two sides of the same coin in that emphasis is at work when two (or more) entities are different. Especially when only one entity is expressed verbally, this entity gains more prominence than the other.

Activity 6

Identify the contrastive は *wa*, which appears in three texts below. Text 3.21 reports the results of a questionnaire surveying people's opinions of America in so-called anti-American countries. Text 3.22 describes everyday life in a village in Papua New Guinea located close to the Indonesian border. Text 3.23 is a report about a baseball athlete who had been in bad shape but who had started to recover from it in a recent game mentioned in the article.

Text 3.21

文化**は**好きだが　中東政策大嫌い

反米１０カ国で米の印象調査

アラブ諸国やフランスなど反米感情の強い１０カ国で、米世論調査が米国のどこが好きで何が嫌いかを尋ねた。ハリウッド映画や米テレビ番組**は**好きだが、イスラエル寄りの中東政策**は**大嫌い、という結果が出た。

© 2002 *Asahi Newspaper* 13 April

Text 3.22

世界で２番目に大きな島、ニューギニア島。熱帯の密林が広がる島の真ん中に、南北約７２０キロにわたる国境が走る。東側がパプアニューギニア、西側**は**インドネシアのイリアンジャヤだ。

© 2002 *Asahi Newspaper* 13 April

Text 3.23

「とにかく自分のスイングをするだけだった。結果が出たのは何より？その通り。」試合後、片岡はぽつり、ぽつりと口を開いた。笑顔**は**見せなかった。

© 2002 *Asahi.com* 19 August

Commentary

In Text 3.21, contrastive は appears in the second sentence of the main text (〜は好きだが、〜は大嫌い). Here, the author compares two results from the survey: people like Hollywood movies and American TV programmes, but they dislike America's Middle East policy, which they feel favours Israel. Contrast is thus utilized to highlight two opposing facts. The headline also contains a contrastive は, but the second は (after 中東政策 *chūtō-sēsaku*) is omitted. Headlines in newspapers are elliptical. This one summarizes the results of the questionnaire (i.e., people like American culture but not American politics).

Text 3.22 contains a single は. The two contrasting entities are Papua New Guinea and Irian Jaya, a state of Indonesia. Since the first entity is marked by が but not by は, we could say that contrastive は is more likely to be used when two entities are enumerated but not opposed. What is at issue in this report may not be the differences between Papua New Guinea and Indonesia, but rather the fact that these two countries closely face each other. If the first noun phrase were marked with は, we could infer that the fact that the two countries occupy the east and west sides of New Guinea Island plays a role in the report, which of course is not the case here.

Text 3.23 also contains a single は. After the game, Kataoka gradually opened his mouth, but he did not show a smile. In Texts 3.21 and 3.22, contrast is also realized lexically (i.e., 'like' versus 'dislike', and 'Papua New Guinea' versus 'Indonesia'), but in this example, two sentences (i.e., his slowness of speech versus no smile) are placed in contrast.

3.6 Sentence-final forms

This section has three subsections. By **sentence-final forms**, we mean the forms that appear sentence-finally and bear a meaning relevant to the sentence. Japanese is abundant in sentence-final forms, but we limit ourselves here to dealing with **past** and **present tense forms** whose functions intertwine with the organization of the discourse.

The first two subsections (3.6.1 and 3.6.2) deal with the strategies used by a journalist when he or she writes a newspaper article. What we generally know about newspapers is that their main purpose is to report current news concisely, embedding basic facts such as 'what happened', 'who did it', 'where it happened' and 'when it happened' into the text. Looking more closely, we come to recognize that journalists use rhetorical strategies by utilizing different tense forms to convey information more effectively and convincingly. That is to say, sentences in newspaper articles are not constructed simply to describe facts but also to convey the journalist's attitudes towards the facts being reported.

How, then, can we interpret the attitudes of a journalist? A key rhetorical strategy might be for the journalist to differentiate facts from commentaries when reporting events. This dichotomy parallels that of foreground and background information. This notion can be traced back to an article entitled 'Aspect and Foregrounding in Discourse' (1979) by the American linguist Paul J. Hopper. The idea was later adopted by Japanese linguists such as Soga (1983) and Makino and Tsutsui (1995) in the study of the switch between -*ta* and -*(r)u* forms of verbs. In general, foreground refers to events that depict the major storyline in a narrative, while background refers to supportive events. It is commonsensical that newspapers report past events, and that facts are cited in the past tense. The notion of background comes into play when the journalist comments

105

on these facts by using the present tense. When the report focuses more on its commentary, the facts can also be cited in the present tense, emphasizing its present validity. These alternations offer mechanisms that allow the journalist to report events more effectively.

The third subsection (3.6.3) deals with a short story. Stories differ from newspaper articles in two significant ways: (i) the writer creates protagonists who participate in events, and (ii) the writer creates a narrator who tells the story. In short stories, too, both present and past tenses are utilized, but present tense does not always play the part of commentary. The use of present tense seems to have an extra function that is absent from newspaper articles, that is, to elaborate on the protagonist's mind.

We stated at the outset of this chapter that texts are created in accordance with principles to maintain coherency (section 3.1). The alternation between fact and commentary is considered one such principle.

In what follows, we examine three representative texts. Each article employs slightly different rhetorical strategies. Text 3.24 deals with national news and figures on the front page. Text 3.25 is a well-known essay column called 天声人語 *tensē-jingo* 'Heaven's Voice, Men's Words', which appears daily at the bottom of the front page. Text 3.26 is an extract from a short story that depicts the protagonist's dramatic visit to her former lover's residence.

3.6.1   Elaboration

Text 3.24 contains a lead followed by the beginning of the main text. The article is concerned with 受精卵診断 *jusēran-shindan* 'a diagnosis of fertilized eggs', which was carried out in a hospital without official permission. Sentence-final forms are marked in boldface. Discuss with other students specific characteristics that strike you as relevant for comprehending the text.

Text 3.24

Lead

体外受精をした受精卵を選別する目的で、子宮に戻す前に検査する受精卵

診断をしたと、神戸市灘区にある大谷産婦人科の大谷徹郎院長 (48)

が４日、①**明らかにした**。０２年から男女の産み分けなどのために３例

②**実施したという**。受精卵診断について、日本産婦人科学会は対象を重い

遺伝性の病気に限り、個別に審査するが、まだ認めた③例は**ない**。大谷院

長は同学会会員だが、学会への④**申請をしていなかった**。

Main Text

大谷院長によると、最初の例は女児を望む⑤３０代女性。０２年末と０３年６月に排卵誘発剤を使って卵子を採り⑥**体外受精をした**。受精卵が八つの細胞に分裂した段階でこのうち二つを吸い出し、性別を決める染色体を調べ、女児になる受精卵を子宮に⑦**戻した**。女性は妊娠に成功し、今月末にも出産する⑧予定という。

© *Asahi Newspaper*, 5 February 2004

Translation:
Dr Ōtani (48), the director of a hospital for obstetrics and gynaecology (大谷産婦人科 *Ōtani Sanfujinka*) in Nada City, Kobe, made it public on the 4th that they carried out a diagnosis in order to single out externally (体外受精 *taigai-jusē*) fertilized eggs (受精卵 *jusēran*). Since 2002, this diagnosis has been carried out three times (3 例 *sanrē*) to identify the gender of a newborn baby (男女産み分け *danjo-umiwake*). The Japanese Society of Obstetrics and Gynaecology has not recognized cases like the above except for a patient who suffered from a severe hereditary disease, and this case is examined separately. Dr Ōtani is a member of this society but did not request permission for the diagnosis.

According to Ōtani, the first case involved a woman in her thirties who wanted a female child. In 2002 and 2003, she underwent external fertilization by taking medicine that induces ovulation (排卵誘発剤 *hairan-yūhatsuzai*) and had her eggs removed. When the fertilized eggs split into eight cells (八つの細胞 *yattsu no saibō*), two were aspirated (吸い出し *suidashi*). The chromosomes (染色体 *senshokutai*) of these eggs, which determine the gender, were examined and the eggs that would result in a girl were returned to the womb (子宮 *shikyū*). This woman successfully became pregnant and is expecting her baby towards the end of this month.

What one might first notice is that the journalist alternates between the past and present tenses of a verb. The past tense is found in ①, ④, ⑥ and ⑦ (marked in boldface), while the present tense is found in ②, ③ and ⑧ (underlined). ⑤ (not marked) does not contain a predicate. The past tense is used to describe an event in the past. What is problematic here is the use of the present tense, since the reports in ② and ③, which contain the present tense, refer to events in the past. This shows that past events are expressed not only by past tense forms but by present tense forms as well. The question is why.

Look at the forms of these predicates more closely. In ②, the journalist uses a quotative form という *toyū* 'to say that' to report the past event; this may produce the effect that what is reported is based not on the journalist's direct observation but on hearsay, while in ③, the present tense 例はない *rē wa nai* underlines that what is reported is presently valid – the implementation of the diagnosis has not yet been officially permitted. These examples show that the journalist uses the present tense to embed rhetorical effects.

Are these rhetorical effects the only strategies at work? The present tense appears to be used instead of the past tense in order to supplement a fact previously mentioned. In other words, ② and ③ elaborate on the statement given in ①; what 大谷院長 *Ōtani-inchō* made public (i.e., the implementation of a diagnosis in his hospital) is elaborated on by the additional information provided by ② (i.e., the frequency of the implementation) and ③ (i.e., no case of implementation without authorization). This function of **elaboration** on previous information is also applicable to ⑧. That is to say, ⑦ describes the event in the past – female eggs were returned to the woman's womb – and ⑧ gives two elaborations: one is that she succeeded in getting impregnated, the other is that she will give birth towards the end of the month. This combination of fact and elaboration is to be regarded as a discursive organization; it makes sense – particularly in the context of newspapers – to combine descriptive and elaborative information. Table 3.3 provides a summary of our discussion.

Table 3.3 *Alternation between past and present tenses in Text 3.24*

No.	Examples	Tense	Functions
①	明らかにした	past	fact
②	実施したという	present	elaboration
③	例はない	present	elaboration
④	申請をしていなかった	past	fact
⑤	３０代女性	∅	∅
⑥	体外受精をした	past	fact
⑦	戻した	past	fact
⑧	予定という	present	elaboration

3.6.2 States and views

Text 3.25 (identical to Text 5.2 in Chapter 5, p. 108, in JL) illustrates another interesting case. Again, the journalist uses a present tense form (underlined) to elaborate on past events (marked in boldface). Verbs in the past tense (marked in boldface) occur four times, as do present tense verbs.

Although it was stated above that the present tense serves as elaboration, elaboration here does not mean the same as it does with regard to the previous text. When we consider the information that ②, ④, ⑤, and ⑧ convey exactly, we recognize that not all of them are reporting facts in the past; instead some of them refer to the journalist's viewpoints or observations.

It appears that two kinds of journalist viewpoints come into question. We call them (i) **perpetuating states** – states that have existed for some time or will continue to exist in the future, and (ii) **perpetuating views** – views commonly accepted by people. The present tense form in Text 3.25 takes the role of expressing the journalist's opinions about the facts, whereas in Text 3.24, the journalist does not go beyond presenting the facts with the present tense.

Text 3.25

今年も２０００人以上が①死亡した。毎年のように繰り返されるイスラム

教の聖地メッカでの②事故である。９０年には１４２６人の死者が③出た。

世界中から２００万人もの巡礼者が集まるだけに混乱が④つきまとう。

メッカ巡礼とあわせて催される犠牲祭はイスラム世界で最も重要な祭りの

⑤一つだ。アフガニスタン・バーミヤンの大仏を破壊したタリバーンも

この期間は爆破作業を⑥中断した。今年は犠牲祭に集まった人々をねら

ったテロが発生、イラクのクルド人自治区で多数の犠牲者が⑦出た。

生活の隅々まで宗教が⑧支配している。

© *Asahi Newspaper* 5 February 2004

Sentence-final forms can be summarized as in Table 3.4 (p. 110). Instead of using the notion of elaboration, the columns are filled by p.state (perpetuating state) or p.view (perpetuating view). A fact is normally followed by the journalist's viewpoint, but the sequence of ⑤ and ⑥ is an exception in which this order is reversed.

Table 3.4 *Alternation between past and present tenses in Text 3.25*

No.	Examples	Tense	Functions
①	死亡した	past	fact
②	事故である	present	p.state
③	出た	past	fact
④	つきまとう	present	p.view
⑤	一つだ	present	p.state
⑥	中断した	past	fact
⑦	出た	past	fact
⑧	支配している	present	p.view

3.6.3   Tied up with the protagonist

While in a newspaper a journalist represents his or her own views at the time of writing, in stories the writer entrusts his or her views with the protagonist. Writers create a narrative world in which plots are devised and presented. Makino (1996: 111–117), examining the occurrence of the present tense in 'Cinderella', remarks that present tense forms concretize the protagonist's strong opinions, and this in turn makes the event more vivid and realistic. Text 3.26 is an extract from 冷たい手 *Tsumetai te* 'Cold Hands'. This short story begins with a narration in which the protagonist 武村比呂子 *Takemura Hiroko* visits the house of her former lover where 秋子 *Akiko*, his wife, warmly welcomes her. Present tense forms occur several times in this passage. Our claim is that the present tense serves to link the event described to the protagonist's mind at the time of narration. Because of this link, the use of present tense is meaningful to the entire plot. Past events are regarded not as things that are completed but that light is cast upon, so they are still relevant to the narration of the story. Surely, this analysis elaborates on the vividness or actualization of an event, since it shows exactly how these concepts work out in a story. It is important to note that, as we already saw in Texts 3.24 and 3.25, alternation between past and present tenses is by itself a literary, or rhetorical, device that brings about dynamism in the narration.

Text 3.26

1　郊外にある築後半年もたっていない、グレーの外壁に四角い

①家だった。白く縁取られた窓枠が品のよいアクセントに②なって

いる。敷地はざっと見たところ五十坪③ぐらいだろう。玄関ドアの前

まできて武村比呂子は黒真珠のネックレスの位置を確かめるように

5 　指先を這わせ、次にそれと揃いになっているイアリングの留め金に

　　も手を④**やってみた**。どちらも昨年の誕生日に夫から贈られた

　　⑤<u>ものだ</u>。淡いピンク色のマニキュアの先が塗りたての

　　状態を保っているを見とどけてから、玄関チャイムを⑥押す。

　　インターホンで訪問者を問いただすこともなく、すぐさまドアは

10 ⑦**開けられた**。ドア・チェーンもすでに⑧**はずされていた**。

　　「いらっしゃい。お電話があってからずっと首を長くして待っていた

　　の。さあ、お入りになって。本当にうれしいわ。十年ぶりですもの」

　　独身の頃よりややふくよかになった秋子だが、思わずこちらの気持

　　ちを明るくさせる、はずむようなしゃべり方は⑨**同じだった**。

15 「いきなり押しかけてきて、ご迷惑じゃなかったのかしら」

　　ベージュのスーツと同色のパンプスをぬぎ、スリッパにはき替えなが

　　ら比呂子は遠慮がちに⑩**たずねた**。午前中に電話をかけ、秋子の都合

　　をきいたものの、同じ日の午後の三時すぎに訪ねてきた

　　⑪**強引さだった**。だが、衝動的な思いつきを、すぐさま行動に移さな

20 かったなら、おそらく一生この家には⑫**こられなかった**だろう。今朝、

　　夫の武村が食事をしながら、夜には仕事がらみの飲み会があるのを

　　思い出し、帰りが遅くなるので夕食はいらない、と言ったとたん、

　　比呂子の気持ちは⑬**固まった**。夫の武村が会社の同僚たちとのつきあ

　　いなどで深夜になるのは珍しくないなずなのに、実際、きょうまで

25 夕食の支度にわずらわされることなくこの家を訪れる機会は何回と

　　あったのに、比呂子は⑭**ためらいつづけてきた**。夫が出勤していっ

111

たあと、比呂子は寝室に置かれている自分専用のライティング・デス

クの引き出しから一通の葉書を⑮だした。消印は三ヶ月前の七月

の上旬、裏側には「新築」「転居」の文字が加わったあいさつ文が

30　⑯印刷されていた。差しだし人は、秋子とその夫である梅田、

ふたりの男の子の名前も⑰そえてある。小学三年、小学一年とわざ

わざつけたしたのは、多分⑱秋子だろう。

© 2002 Tōdō, Shizuko / *Tsumetai Te* (pp. 131–133), Kodansha

The extract begins with a narration about the house into which 秋子's *Akiko*'s family has recently moved. Six predicates have the present tense form (underlined).

Table 3.5 is a suggestive answer to each function of the present tense form. Three forms have an elaborative function. ② elaborates on the house mentioned in the previous narrative, and ⑤ elaborates on the earrings mentioned in the previous narrative. ⑰ elaborates on the postcard that 比呂子 *Hiroko* had received three months before by mentioning that the names of both the parents and their children are written on it. Sentences prior to elaboration all appear in past tense form.

比呂子's inner thoughts are expressed in ③, ⑫ and ⑱. These all occur with an auxiliary だろう *darō*. This auxiliary is used to express the speaker's uncertainty or imprecision about the statement. The lack of assertiveness also softens the statement. When ⑱ 秋子だろう 'It would be Akiko' is used, the speaker expresses her conjecture about 秋子. While だろう in ③ and ⑱ is attached to the present tense form, だろう in ⑫ is attached to the past tense form; 比呂子 is expressing her conjecture about an event that happened in the past.

Another example in which the present tense is used is ⑥ チャイムを押す 'to ring the door chimes'. It clearly refers to 比呂子's action of ringing the doorbell that occurred in the past. The present tense might be used because this moment is seen to evoke 比呂子's emotional tension; it signals the beginning of the highlights of her visit – the topic in the story.

④, ⑦, ⑩, ⑬, ⑭ and ⑮ all contain the past tense. These events describe a dynamic action in the sense that it has a beginning and an end. Consider ⑦. The opening of the door has a beginning (e.g., someone touches the doorknob and moves it inward/outward) and an end (e.g., the door gets opened so that someone can come inside). ①, ⑧, ⑨, ⑪, and ⑯ also contain the past tense, though they describe a non-dynamic past event. Consider ①. What is at issue here is the existence of a new house on the day when 比呂子 visits 秋子. Likewise, in ⑧, the issue is that the door chain was already unlocked when she arrived at the house. It concerns not the dynamic action of unlocking the door chain but rather its unlocked state. Why are these events expressed by the past tense? It may be because the opening of the door or the unlocked state of the door chain is not considered relevant to 比呂子's mind at the time of narration. These facts in the past are treated separately from her present psychological state. When we compare ⑯ and ⑰, it is striking they do not use the same tense, although both are concerned with the same postcard, that is, what is written on it (a greeting sentence in ⑯ and the names of the family in ⑰). ⑯ might use past tense because it describes a fact about the postcard that 比呂子 received, whereas the use of present tense in ⑰, which we classified as elaboration above, may also establish a link between 秋子's family and 比呂子's emotions evoked by her decision to visit her former lover's house. The contrast between past and present creates a dynamism in the narration that makes her emotions vivid. It is possible to use past tense in ⑰, but it may not express 比呂子's rising emotions as successfully.

Table 3.5 *Alternation between past and present tenses in Text 3.26*

No.	Example	Tense	Function
①	家だった	past	description of the past
②	なっている	present	elaboration
③	ぐらいだろう	present + Aux	比呂子's inner thought
④	やってみた	past	description of the past
⑤	贈られたものだ	present	elaboration
⑥	玄関チャイムを押す	present	比呂子's inner thought
⑦～⑪	See text	past	description of the past
⑫	来られなかっただろう	past + Aux	比呂子's inner thought
⑬～⑯	See text	past	description of the past
⑰	そえてある	present	elaboration / 比呂子's inner thought
⑱	秋子だろう	present + Aux	比呂子's inner thought

3.7 Ellipsis

3.7.1 What is ellipsis?

When a customer C asks a shop assistant S in a department store about the price of a watch (4a), the answer C receives from S may be (4b).

(4) a Customer: そこの時計はいくらですか。
        Soko no tokē wa ikura desuka
        How much is the watch?
     b Shop assistant: ２０００円です。
        Nisen-en desu.
        2000 yen.

When C points to the watch in the shop, the referent of the watch is activated in C's and S's mental representations. What is noteworthy in S's utterance is that he gives only the price of the watch, the minimal information necessary. His answer is minimal because he minimizes the effort of conveying a message (see Makino and Tsutsui 1986: 23). If the information already exists in the user's consciousness, there is no need to repeat it. When we omit or do not express a linguistic form overtly which is underlyingly present, we are speaking **elliptically** (see Halliday and Hasan 1976: 144, cited in Hinds 1986: 106). A general consensus shared by scholars in Japanese linguistics is that Japanese is abundant with ellipsis (Hinds 1986; Iwasaki 2002; Makino and Tsutsui 1986, among others), mainly because Japanese tends to leave pragmatically retrievable information unspecified (Iwasaki 2002: 9). The short dialogue (4) is a case in point. It appears that what language users basically do in discourse, written or spoken, is to try to present new information and suppress already activated information. In (4) the new information is the price of the watch – the information C is eager to obtain. Since the watch is known to C and S, only its price needs to be made explicit. New information (e.g., the price of the watch) stands in contrast to old information (e.g., the watch C is pointing to). Old information tends to be omitted whereas new information cannot be, precisely because it serves as the main resource for the structuring of a communication (Dooley and Levinsohn 2001: 65).

An understanding of ellipsis is tied up with what the discourse is talking about or, more precisely, the concept of **discourse topic**. Discourse topic is a 'theme' around which the writer's mind revolves while constructing a text. In Chafe's words (1994: 120), discourse topics are identified as ideas of events, states and references that participate in the discourse. Although these ideas are not easy to represent as definitive pictures, they influence the way our thinking is organized in discourse. The assumption is that ellipsis occurs when the writer's active and coherent thought, that is, the discourse topic, is tied with a specific unit of the discourse. In Western literature this unit is called 'episode' (Van Dijk 1982), whereas in Japanese literature, it is dubbed 段落 *danraku* 'paragraph' (Maynard 1998: 81–84). The idea is that discourse consists of psychological segments that represent coherency (see section 3.1 for the term 'coherence'). The entire discourse is, so to speak, the sum of these units, each of which contains a topic to be talked about. Let us call this unit **discourse unit** for the sake of

114

simplicity in this book. One interesting observation made about Japanese discourse is that an initial sentence of this unit has an entity marked by a topic marker は *wa*. An overt mention of this entity in subsequent sentences is avoided on the grounds that it is already activated in the reader's mind. This section examines extracts from 'Calling You', which neatly represents the occurrence of ellipsis and its relation to the discourse unit.

Text 3.27

1	**わたしは**おそらくこの高校で唯一の、携帯電話を持っていない女子高
	校生だ。その上、カラオケにも行かないし、プリクラを撮ったことも
	ない。今時こんな人間は珍しいと、自分でも思う。校則では禁止され
	ているけれど、携帯電話なんてだれでも持っている。正直なところ、
5	教室でクラスメートがちらつかせるたびに、平静でいられなくなる。
	教室に着信のメロディーが流れるたびに、取り残された気分になる。
	みんながあの小さな通信機に話しかけているのも見ると、
	あらためて自分には友人がいないのだと気付く。

© 2003 Otsu, Ichi /*Calling You* (p. 6), Kadokawa

Translation:
I(WA) should be the only student in this high school who does not have a mobile telephone. Besides, I do not go to *karaoke*. Neither do I take a photograph of myself. I consider that a human like me is rare in this world. Everyone has a mobile telephone, although it is prohibited by school regulations. To be honest, I lose my calmness whenever my classmates show off their mobile telephones. Whenever the receiving tones ring, I feel isolated. When I see my classmates talk to the communication machine, I re-recognize that I do not have friends.

Text 3.27 is the beginning of the story. The first-person narrator わたし *watashi* 'I' is a female high school student and the central figure in this story. She describes her relationship to the mobile telephone. This relationship can be considered a discourse topic. わたし appears only once in the first sentence. Although the subsequent sentences continue to speak of her in terms of the mobile telephone, わたし does not reappear but remains suppressed. This suppression is motivated by the writer taking it for granted that the reader knows the passage is talking about the protagonist わたし. That is to say, even without an overt reference to わたし, the reader is able to recognize the relationship between わたし and new information about her. For instance, the reader knows that it is わたし who does not go to *karaoke*. Likewise, it is わたし who loses calmness each time her classmates show off their mobile telephones. The link between わたし and the event described in each sentence is established through the discourse topic. The passage organized by this link constitutes a discourse unit that represents coherent ideas about the female student. Table 3.6 summarizes the distribution of old and new information. New information is given in a propositional form.

Table 3.6

Line	Old	New
1	わたしは	携帯電話を持っていない
2	(∅ わたしは)	カラオケに行かない
2	(∅ わたしは)	プリクラを撮らない
3	(∅ わたしは)	こんな人間は珍しいと思う
5	(∅ わたしは)	平静でいられない
6	(∅ わたしは)	取り残された気分になる
8	(∅ わたしは)	友人がいないと気づく

When a new discourse topic is introduced in a different paragraph, the passage starts with わたしは again, as shown in Text 3.28.

Text 3.28

1	**わたしは**話をするのが下手で、だれかに話しかけられると、つい身構えてしまう。心の中を見透かされまいと、よそよそしい返事をしてしまう。相手の話にどうリアクションを返せばいいのかわからず、曖昧に笑って失望させてしまう。そして、それらの失敗を繰り返すのが怖
5	くて、だれかと話をすることから遠ざかってしまう。

© 2003 Otsu, Ichi / *Calling You* (p. 6), Kadokawa

This passage continues to describe わたし, who has trouble making friends with her classmates, in person. It is evident that this new discourse topic is connected to the previous discourse topic in Text 3.27 in the sense that her timidity in socializing, as described here, is the cause of her not having a mobile telephone. It is noteworthy that this passage is organized similarly to the previous one. First of all, the first sentence has わたし marked by は; second, the first-person narrator is suppressed in the subsequent sentences; and third, the unit focuses on describing わたし.

But it is important to keep in mind that the omission of the topic in this story is not as regular as we have just observed. First of all, it is often quite hard to determine exactly where one discourse unit begins and another ends. As we will see in section 3.7.2, わたし recurs, though it could be omitted. For example, between Texts 3.27 and 3.28, which we have categorized as two different discourse units, are seven intervening sentences. These sentences express two instances of わたし overtly, as shown in Texts 3.29 and 3.30. This implies that it might be too simplistic to conclude that a text is composed of 'discourse units' that explain why ellipsis occurs.

Activity 7

Table 3.7 summarizes the distribution of topic and focus in Text 3.28. There are four sentences in total. Complete the table by filling in the new information in the column. Information must be in a propositional form.

Table 3.7

Line	Old	New
1–2	わたしは	身構える
2		よそよそしい返事をする
3–4		
4–5		

3.7.2 When わたし becomes overt?

This section presents four cases in which ellipsis does not take place, that is, わたし *watashi* 'I' becomes overt. This will give you an idea of when the writer needs to make the information overt despite its already being activated in the reader's mind. These examples are extracted from the first four pages of 'Calling You' (pp. 6–9).

3.7.2.1 わたし *is contrasted with another entity*

Text 3.29 is an immediate follow-up to Text 3.27. Here わたし is made overt, possibly because it expresses contrast. わたし is contrasted with her classmates. While her classmates are close to each other thanks to the mobile telephone, わたし is isolated from this network. Without the overt presence of わたし, the contrast cannot be realized here.

Text 3.29

教室のみんなは携帯電話を通じて網の目のようにつながっているが、そこに**わたしは**含まれていない。みんなが手をつないで楽しそうに笑っているのに、自分だけが輪の外で小石でもけっている気分だ。

© 2003 Otsu, Ichi /*Calling You* (p. 6), Kadokawa

3.7.2.2 わたし *receives emphasis*

When わたし *watashi* is given special emphasis, it reappears in the text. Text 3.30 is the passage that immediately follows Text 3.29. Here わたし appears again. This time it functions as the receiver of a phone call. The sentence containing わたし explains why she does not have a mobile telephone. The previous sentence is a **cleft construction** (X は Y だ) in which the predicate is clefted to the front, whereby the fact that she does not have a mobile telephone is foregrounded. The cleft sentence already explains that わたし has no one to talk to. In other words, the sentence with わたし is a repetition of the same fact. Repetition reactivates the significance of her isolation. Although contrast is not explicit here, emphasis is placed on わたし because of an implicit contrast that exists between わたし (who does not receive phone calls) and her classmates (who receive phone calls). If わたしに were deleted, the emphatic meaning attached would disappear. The sentence would sound awkward as well.

Text 3.30

本当はみんなのように携帯電話を持ちたい。しかし話をしてくれる人がいない。持たないようにしているのはそのためだ。**わたしに**電話をかけてくれる人など、どこにもいないから。ついでに言えば、いっしょにカラオケへ行ってくれる人も、いっしょにプリクラを撮ってくれる人もいない。

© 2003 Otsu, Ichi / *Calling You* (p. 6), Kadokawa

Another emphatic expression is found in Text 3.31, in which わたし *watashi* is embedded in a cleft construction. This construction foregrounds the fact that it is わたし and no one else in the classroom who always leaves school the earliest. The reason is that she has no commitments after school; she does not belong to a club, neither does she have someone to go out with. Here again, the passage stresses her isolation. Similar to Text 3.30, the emphatic use of わたし implies a contrast between her and her classmates. Although no explicit mention of her classmates is made in this passage, their role as a contrasted counterpart is easily inferable. It is impossible to delete わたし here.

Text 3.31

一日の授業が終わると、クラスの中で一番早く学校から立ち去るのは、いつも**わたし**だった。

© 2003 Otsu, Ichi / *Calling You* (p. 9), Kadokawa

3.7.2.3 わたし *is the target of an action*

When わたし *watashi* functions as the target of a denoted action, it becomes overt in the text, as illustrated in Texts 3.32 and 3.33. わたし is presented as having an awkward existence (Text 3.32) because she cannot make friends with anyone. Everyone therefore treats her cautiously in much the same way as they would an abscess. In the classroom, わたし is entirely alone; she feels comfortable only in the library (Text 3.33). Because the library is the only place that accepts her, わたし is made overt so as to stress that there is an exception. The omission of わたしを in both texts would result in a sense of oddness in the sentences in which it occurs. Here again, as in the other two cases above, the overt expression of わたし is motivated by her unique existence at school that distinguishes her from her classmates. The actions mentioned here, 'treatment of her' and 'acceptance of her', are targeted only at わたし. No one else in the classroom receives these actions.

Text 3.32

春にこの高校へ入学してからというもの、だれとも親しくなることができないでいた。結局、教室の中で特異な存在となってしまい、だれもが腫れ物を触るように**わたしを**取り扱った。

© 2003 Otsu, Ichi / *Calling You* (p. 7), Kadokawa

Text 3.33

昼休みになると、よく図書館を訪れた。教室には居場所がなかったし、学校内で**わたしを**受け入れてくれる場所はそこだけだった。

© 2003 Otsu, Ichi / *Calling You* (p. 8), Kadokawa

3.7.2.4 わたし *serves as an experiencer*

When a topic serves as an implicit subject who experiences a denoted event, as shown in Texts 3.34 and 3.35, it becomes overt in the text. Contrary to the other examples above, わたし *watashi* is marked with は in these cases. In Text 3.34, the phrase is embedded in a noun modification, and it is impossible to delete it. Though this impossibility may not be due to the noun modification *per se*, わたし serves as an experiencer who feels thankful to the heater located at the window because it emits warm air. In contrast, it is possible to remove the phrase in Text 3.35. If it is removed, the sentence loses the accentuation placed on わたし. The presence of accentuation is to be attributed to the repetition of the expression 想像する 'to imagine' (see Activity 1 in Chapter 2, pp. 47–49). The repeti-

119

tion implies that the imagination is an integral part of わたし's isolated existence. It is therefore meaningful to highlight わたし, since she is the experiencer of this act and knows the value of this imagination.

Text 3.34

> 館内は静かで、空調の設備が整っている。窓際にあるヒーターから、暖か
> い空気が出ていた。すぐ風邪をひく**わたしにとっては**ありがたい。

© 2003 Otsu, Ichi / *Calling You* (p. 8), Kadokawa

Text 3.35

> いつしか自分だけの携帯電話を想像するのが楽しくなる。**わたしには**この、
> 想像をするという行為が重要だった。

© 2003 Otsu, Ichi / *Calling You* (p. 9), Kadokawa

Exercise

Choose your favourite text and examine whether it exhibits cases of ellipsis. Try to explain when ellipsis is used in your text and what functions it serves.

Notes

1   See Text 3.26, which narrates the beginning stage of 比呂子's visit to 秋子's new residence.
2   A higher degree of continuity with the て-form was originally proposed by Ono (1991), who studied a procedural discourse (i.e., a recipe). Instead of highlighting the 'subordinate' relationship between S1 and S2, his study adopts the statistic method to examine the continuity between S1 and S2 in terms of changes in participant, time, place and use of the comma. That is, continuity between S1 and S2 is not conceptualized qualitatively, as indicated in this book, but measured quantitatively.
3   When sentences express naturally occurring phenomena, they are called 現象文 *genshōbun* 'phenomenal sentence' in Japanese linguistics (see Nagano 1986: 134–135). These sentences typically take が *ga* to mark the subject. An example sentence with が in Text 3.16 could be considered 現象文 as it verbalizes merely what has happened in X city.

4 Language and culture

Culture can be understood as the attitudes, behaviours or habits shared by the members of a society. The shared knowledge allows us to know how to communicate with other members of a society and how to interpret their behaviour. Culture can represent what the entire society shares, or it can portray more restricted aspects of society. For instance, what is shared by each ethnic group of a multicultural society (e.g., Singapore and Malaysia) can be considered culture. Culture can also represent trends or shared properties of groups of people according to age, education, profession or the degree of formality in a society. Sometimes these are called 'micro-cultures' (Neuliep 2003: 22) or 'subcultures' (Gudykunst 2004: 43) as opposed to the larger dominant culture. The title of this chapter, 'Language and culture', suggests that language is related to certain aspects of people's attitudes in a society. In one sense, language comes into existence through culture and evolves along with it; consequently, the use of language reflects the ways people behave in a given society.

This chapter will not be an exhaustive description of the relationship between language and culture in Japanese society; instead, it will focus on five selected domains: gender (4.1), in-groups and out-groups (4.2), politeness (4.3), honorifics (4.4), and young people (4.5). These domains characterize the reality of much of contemporary Japanese society and demonstrate their importance as reflected in the Japanese language.

4.1 Gender

The distinction between being a woman and being a man in Japanese society plays a significant role in use of the language. Grammatical forms that reflect this difference include pronouns in the first and second person (e.g., 私 *watashi* 'I', あなた *anata* 'You') (4.1.1), lexical items (e.g., 親父 *oyaji* 'father', お袋 *ofukuro* 'mother') or prefixed words (e.g., お買い物 *okaimono* 'shopping', お野菜 *oyasai* 'vegetable') (4.1.2), and sentence/word-final particles (e.g., わ, ぞ) (4.1.3).

4.1.1 Personal pronouns

The use of **personal pronouns** is distinguished not only by differences in gender but also by the degree of formality in a given speech situation.

Table 4.1 *Personal pronouns in the first and second person*

Formality	First person, 'I'		Second person, 'you'	
	men	**women**	**men**	**women**
formal	私 *watakushi* 私 *watashi*	私 私	あなた *anata*	あなた
informal	僕 *boku* 俺 *ore*	私 あたし *atashi* あたい *atai*	あなた 君 *kimi* あんた *anta* おまえ *omae*	あなた あんた
offensive	俺		おまえ きさま *kisama* てめえ *temē*	あんた

Table 4.1 is based on statements in major previous studies (Shibatani 1990: 371; Tsujimura 1996: 373; Iwasaki 2002: 293, among others) showing that gender differences arise when the speaker and addressee are situated in a more informal setting. The forms of the first and second person pronouns in a formal setting are identical regardless of gender: 私 *watakushi/watashi* for the first person and あなた *anata* for the second person. However, three further forms of the second person (君 *kimi*, あんた *anta* and おまえ *omae*) are used in men's informal speech, while only one further form (あんた) is used in women's informal speech.

In specific situations in which two parties strongly disagree or are quarrelling, offensive forms are employed. But while men's speech has four offensive forms (俺 *ore* 'I', おまえ 'you', きさま *kisama* 'you', てめえ *temē* 'you'), women's speech has only one (あんた), which has the same form as the informal one. This lack of impolite expressions in women's speech may be explained by the fact that women were generally considered more genteel than men in traditional Japanese society. In this respect, Backhouse's words (1993: 99) are appropriate: 'Women typically operate nearer the genteel end of the cline, whereas men's usage ranges more widely and, particularly in informal speech, may take in robust, even "vulgar" items normally avoided by women.' Holmes (2001: 156) points out that 'across all social groups women generally use more standard forms than men', one reason being that women are 'more status-conscious than men' (ibid.: 157).

Especially in informal speech situations, the distinction between men's and women's speech is disappearing in present-day Japan. The growing popularity of the use of 俺 and 僕 by young women was remarked upon as early as the 1970s (Jugaku 1979). One reason appears to be that use of the male register has enabled young women to cast off a sense of powerlessness or subservience that was attached to the position of women in traditional Japanese society (Akiba-Reynolds 1998: 300). Text 4.1, an extract from 出直しといで！ *Denaoshitoide* 'Do it again', gives you a hint as to how おまえ is used by a female student, 茜 *Akane*, who responds rudely to a male classmate's words. The male student also uses おまえ towards her, but this merely signals their casual relationship. She could use あんた according to Table 4.1, but the interaction in this *manga*-drawing implies that she uses the *omae*-code to overcome gender disadvantages, or, to put it differently, to become equal to her male interlocutor linguistically and, hence, socially.

Text 4.1  おまえもね！

© 2003 Isshiki, Makoto / *Denaoshitoide!* (p. 140), Kodansha

Personal pronouns in the second person are normally used as address forms in conversation – forms used when the speaker addresses his or her interlocutor. It is worth mentioning that the use of these forms often depends on the interpersonal relationship between the speaker and addressee. That is to say, gender difference *per se* is not a crucial factor in using personal pronouns in all speech situations. For instance, Table 4.1 states that おまえ and あんた are used by men in informal speech. However, their actual use is influenced by the ways in which the participants

123

interact with each other. When a man talks to his wife or his girlfriend in everyday conversation, おまえ would be used more frequently, while あんた would be used by a man with a female friend (e.g., a classmate), both having a good friendship but not necessarily an intimate relationship.

Consider あんた *anta* 'you', the form used by women in both informal and offensive situations. The dialogue in Text 4.2, extracted from the drama ふぞろいの林檎たち *Fuzoroi no Ringo-tachi* 'Uneven Apples', contains あんた employed by the elder sister 愛子 *Aiko* with her younger brother 良雄 *Yoshio*. Because they are not having a row or disagreement, あんた pertains to an informal register. What is intriguing is that the understanding of the use of あんた goes beyond the scope of gender or informality, taking the interpersonal relationship between the participants into consideration. Despite the informal speech setting, 良雄 does not use あんた with his sister (he could do so according to Table 4.1) but instead addresses her as 姉さん *nēsan* 'elder sister', the reason being that he is younger than she. This instance shows that age difference rather than gender or formality difference influences the way the second person is addressed.[1] In addition, 愛子 addresses 良雄 by his given name (line 1) rather than using the personal pronoun あんた as she draws his attention to her query (see the original text).[2] This further indicates that the choice of the second person as an address form depends on the conversational management.

Text 4.2 あんた

愛子「良雄」

良雄「なに？」

愛子「なにしてんの？**あんた**（と小声）」

良雄「なにしてるって、コーヒーを、**姉さん**が、いま」

愛子「（二階に聞こえないように）そんなこといってんじゃないの」

良雄「どんなこといってんのさ」

愛子「日曜日に、あんなの、連れてきて（と二階を見る）」

良雄「聞こえるだろ」

愛子「どうしてひとの奥さんばっかり連れて来るの」

良雄「だから、彼女はやっと妊娠したんだよ」

愛子「**あんた**が相手じゃないんでしょう？」

良雄「あ、当たり前じゃない」

124

愛子「なんで**あんた**が世話をやくの？」

良雄「だから、亭主がいなくなっちゃったんだって」

愛子「バカな男と結婚するから」

© 1991 Yamada, Taichi / *Fuzoroi no Ringo-tachi* (p. 214), Magazine House

Historically speaking, personal pronouns used to belong to different speech registers. おまえ was originally written as 御前 *omae* and, as the *kanji* indicate, it was used for people whose status was higher than the speaker's. Towards the end of the Edo Period (1600–1868), 御前 started to be used for people of an equal or lower status to the speaker's; this change made it possible for couples or lovers to use 御前 as a signal of intimacy (Tsujimura et al. 1991: 147). Similarly, きさま was originally written 貴様 *kisama* in *kanji* and was an honorific expression, but around the middle of the Meiji Period (1868–1912) it became an expression of insult (ibid.: 194). Between the Kamakura (1185–1333) and Edo Periods, 俺 started to be used independent of formality and gender, and finally ceased to be used by women towards the end of the Edo Period (ibid.: 177).

In addition to personal pronouns, common nouns are also used to refer to the first and second persons, in which gender differentiation does not play a role. 家 *uchi* or 内 *uchi* 'home, house' refers to the speaker's family members. お宅 *otaku* 'your home, house' refers to the addressee's family members. Demonstratives such as こちら (informally こっち) and そちら (informally そっち) (see also Table 2.1 in Chapter 2) can also be used to refer to the first and second persons, respectively. An example for こっち is illustrated in line 64 of Text 4.12; the speaker 良雄 *Yoshio* uses it to describe himself in terms of his rank in the company where he works. An example for そっち is found in line 15 in Text 4.4; 綾子 *Ayako* uses it to refer to 良雄, her friend, with whom she converses. An example for うち *uchi* is seen in Text 2.14, Chapter 2, as repeated as Text 4.3 here (shortened). In this context, うち in lines 3 and 8 refers to 綾子 and her husband. 綾子's utterance in line 3 can be translated into English as 'Ultimately, we are the happiest, aren't we?'.

Text 4.3　うち

1　綾子「お父ちゃん」

　実「なんだよ？」

　綾子「（部屋の方から微笑して現れ）結局、**うち**が一番幸せね」

　実「幸せ？」

5　綾子「岩田さんとこもあまりうまく行ってないみたいだし、陽子さん

　　　も仲手川さんも独身だし、晴江さんは自殺さわぎだし」

　　実「人生ってもんは、そんなもんよ」

　　綾子「うまく行ってるの、**うち**だけじゃない」

4.1.2　Lexical and prefixed words

Certain **lexical** and **prefixed** items differentiate men's and women's speech. Kinship terms such as 親父 *oyaji* 'father' and お袋 *ofukuro* 'mother' appearing in informal settings are used exclusively by men. When we end a letter, Japanese expressions corresponding to 'sincerely' or 'with best wishes' are differentiated by gender; かしこ *kashiko* is used exclusively by women, and 敬具 *kēgu* by men. 草々 *sōsō* is used by both genders.

In contrast, the politeness prefix お, which was used exclusively by women in traditional Japanese society, tends now to be used by both genders. For example, お冷 *ohiya* 'cold water', お金 *okane* 'money', お勘定 *okanjō* 'bill', お酒 *osake* 'alcohol', お弁当 *obentō* 'lunch box', お正月 *oshōgatsu* 'New Year', お昼 *ohiru* 'midday, afternoon, lunch' , お茶 *ocha* 'tea' , おでん *oden* 'Japanese hotchpotch', お浸し *ohitashi* 'boiled vegetables with dressing (e.g., soy sauce)' and お開き *ohiraki* 'adjournment' all contain the prefix and are rarely used without it (see more examples in Tsujimura et al. 1991). By contrast, women appear to still use household terms more frequently when attached by お, for example, お買い物 *okaimono* 'shopping', お野菜 *oyasai* 'vegetable', お肉 *oniku* 'meat', お塩 *oshio* 'salt', お砂糖 *osatō* 'sugar'. Men may not use these words with the prefix. Not all household terms can be attached with お: ×おまな板 *omanaita* 'cooking plate', ×おコロッケ 'croquette', ×お牛乳 *ogyūnyū* 'milk', ×おわさび *owasabi* 'grated Japanese horseradish' and ×おほうれん草 *ohōrensō* 'spinach'. The meanings of at least two words, おにぎり *onigiri* 'Japanese rice balls' and おしぼり *oshibori* 'wet towels served before a meal', change if the prefix is removed. にぎり means a piece of hand-rolled *sushi,* and しぼり can mean either a tie-dyed fabric or the aperture of a camera. Both men and women can use each of these words.[3]

The prefix お can also be used to express **irony**. As seen in Text 4.1, お is prefixed to 勉強 *benkyō* 'study' to indicate that the speaker means the opposite of what he says (see Chandler 2002: 134–135; Hebron 2004: 151; and Matthews 1997: 187 for the notion of 'irony'). That is to say, the use of the politeness prefix implies the opposite of the meaning of the word to which it is attached. Some scholars (Gibbs 1994: 13; Hebron 2004: 151, to name just a few) treat irony as one figurative language (see also Chapter 2, section 2.5). The male student knows that 茜 *Akane* belongs to a group of problematic students and that she is unlikely to change her attitude towards learning. This assumption may have led him to speak ironically and use the politeness prefix to imply the opposite of what he says. More precisely, he is proposing that she had better study hard, but he regrets that she is not doing so at present and may not do so in the future. His irony or sarcasm derives from his awareness of this incongruity.

4.1.3 Particles

The use of particles is another measurement that distinguishes men's and women's speech. Recall that you have learned case particles in Chapter 7, section 7.5 in JL. These particles indicate syntactic and semantic relations between the elements in a sentence. The purpose of this section is to demonstrate how **interactional particles** – particles used to fulfil the speaker and addressee's communicative intent – function in discourse. The concept 'interactional' emphasizes that the use of particles is germane to the ways in which speech participants (i.e., speaker and addressee) act towards one another. When we speak Japanese, gender differentiation is one important criterion when choosing an appropriate particle. Accordingly, the speaker's choice of an appropriate particle makes the conversation more communicative and successful.

Let us first examine the functions of each particle based on con-structed examples. ね *ne* and よ *yo* are two frequently occurring particles (see Table 4.2 below). Although they are employed by both genders (as illustrated in examples (1), (2), (3), (4), (5), (6), (8), (11), (12), (14), (17) below), gender is also differentiated (as illustrated in (7), (9), (10), (13), (15), (16), (18), (19), (20) and (21)). Gender differentiation often depends on the element that precedes the particle. To illustrate, the particle かしら *kashira* is inserted before ね (9) in women's speech, whereas the interroga-tive particle か *ka* is inserted into men's speech (10), both conveying the same state of affairs. In formal speech – the speech characterized by the maintenance of social hierarchy between speaker and addressee – these particles often do not differentiate gender (i.e., they are used by both men and women). For example, (4) and (5) both refer to the speech between teacher and student regardless of their gender differentiation; the former is uttered by a student who uses です as a signal of politeness to his teacher (see section 4.3 below), while the latter is spoken by a teacher who does not use it, signalling his higher social status. It is possible to rephrase (5) as 早いわね *hayaiwane* to emphasize that the speaker is a woman.

Generally speaking, the use of よ allows the speaker to be assertive, thereby articulating his or her (strong) position, whereas the use of ね

127

establishes a congenial atmosphere between speaker and addressee. Examples (9), (10) and (11) do not permit よ on the ground that か *ka* and かしら *kashira*, which express uncertainty/indetermination, do not go with the assertiveness encoded in よ. Similar to ね, gender differentiation tends to be made by the element that precedes よ. (14), (16) and (20) are more appropriate for men's speech than their alternatives (13), (15) and (19), which are more appropriate for women. (14) could be used by a woman, and it sounds more assertive than (13). Compare the elements that come before the particle: (14), (16) and (20) contain 反対だ *hantaida* 'be opposed to', うまい *umai* 'tasty' and 来い *koi* 'come!', whereas (13), (15) and (19) contain 反対, 美味しいわ *oishiiwa*, and 来て *kite*. When よ is followed by ね, as in (21), the speaker's assertiveness is softened, which in turn increases the speaker's friendliness. It would be odd to say 来いよね because a strong order form 来い is assertive by itself (see Chapter 1, section 1.3), and it therefore does not go with ね.

Other particles (i.e., の *no*, わ *wa*, かしら *kashira*, ぜ *ze*, ぞ *zo*, さ *sa* and な *na*) are more gender-sensitive in their own right. (24) and (25) are usually used by women to give an explanation; の is a shortened form of のだ *noda* (see Chapter 1, section 1.1.1). もの *mono* in (25) is more often used by children, boys or girls, as well as by young women. It has a contracted form もん *mon*. (26) is an interrogative sentence used by both men and women in a colloquial setting. Particles such as かしら *kashira*, さ *sa* and な *na* can be used by both men and women in certain speech settings. When someone is surprised or wonders (32) (33), criticizes harshly (42), utters a strong opinion (45), speaks to him/herself (48) (49) or is puzzled (50), gender distinction is not normally made. It is possible to say 重いわ *omoiwa* (as opposed to (48)) or 変だわ *hendawa* (as opposed to (49)) to emphasize that the speaker is a woman.

The marking of particles by INFORM in Table 4.2 indicates they are used only in informal speech, as opposed to ね and よ, which are used in both informal and formal speech. We have observed in Table 4.1 that first and second person pronouns exhibit gender distinction when the speech situation is informal. The same rule appears to be at work with interactional particles. For example, (1), (4), (6), (12) and (17) contain the formal forms です and ます. Formal forms are not always to be equated with forms used in formal situations, but more formal (that is, polite) forms are preferred when the speech is formal because people tend to be more polite. We can conclude that the more informal the speech situation is, the more obvious gender distinction becomes.

Table 4.2 *Meanings of interactional particles*

Particle	Meaning	Example	Male	Female
ね *ne*	Confirmation, agreement	(1), (2), (3), (4)	ね, だ**ね**	ね, だ**ね**
	Admiration, wonder, surprise	(5)	ね	ね
	Speaker's opinion/mild statement	(6), (7), (8)	ね, だ**ね**	ね
	Softening a question	(9), (10)	か**ね**	かしら**ね**
	Softening speaker's opinion/answer	(11)	かしら**ね**	かしら**ね**
よ *yo*	Strong intention of the speaker	(12)	よ	よ
	Emotion of the speaker	(13), (14)	よ, だ**よ**	よ
	Judgement of the speaker	(15), (16)	よ	よ, わ**よ**
	Appealing to the addressee in order, request and agreement	(17), (18)	よ	よ
	Appealing to the addressee in invitation	(19), (20), (21)	よ	よ, よ**ね**
の *no* INFORM	Explanatory statement	(22)	Ø	の, な**の**
	Persuasion	(23)	の	の
	Explanation	(24), (25)	Ø	の, も**の**
	Posing a question	(26)	の	の
わ *wa* INFORM	Statement	(27)	Ø	わ
	Opinion	(28)	Ø	わ
	Admiration, surprise	(29)	Ø	わ
かしら *kashira* INFORM	Posing a question	(30)	Ø	かしら
	Self-questioning	(31)	Ø	かしら
	Astonishment, doubt	(32), (33)	かしら	かしら
ぜ *ze* INFORM	Seeking agreement	(34)	ぜ	Ø
	Appealing to addressee with opinion	(35)	ぜ	Ø
	determination	(36)	ぜ	Ø
ぞ *zo* INFORM	Strong self-statement	(37)	ぞ	Ø
	Strong self-oriented opinion	(38)	ぞ	Ø
	Strong self-oriented determination	(39)	ぞ	Ø
さ *sa* INFORM	Strong statement	(40)	さ	Ø
	Casual agreement/disagreement	(41)	さ	Ø
	Strong objection	(42)	さ	さ
な *na* INFORM	Intensifying speaker's emotion	(43), (44)	な	Ø
	Strong opinion	(45)	な	な
	Seeking agreement	(46)	な	Ø
	Request	(47)	よ**な**	Ø
	Statement	(48), (49)	な	な
	Posing a question	(50)	か**な**	か**な**

(1) 佐藤さんです**ね**。{M/F}
Satō-san desu ne
You're Mr/Ms Satō, aren't you?

(2) 佐藤さん**ね**。{M/F}

(3) 佐藤さんだ**ね**。{M/F}
Satō-san da ne

(4) 先生、テストは木曜日です**ね**。{M/F}
Sensē tesuto wa mokuyōbi desu ne
Teacher, is the test on Thursday?

(5) 高尾君はとても覚えが早い**ね**。{M/F}
Takao-kun wa totemo oboe ga hayai ne
Takao, you're quick in learning.

(6) 明日は雨です**ね**。{M/F}
Asu wa ame desu ne
It will rain tomorrow.

(7) 明日は雨**ね**。{F}

(8) 明日は雨だ**ね**。{M/F}

(9) 埼玉県は関東地方だったかしら**ね**。{F}
Saitama-ken wa kantō-chihō datta kashira ne
I wonder if Saitama Prefecture is in the Kantō District.

(10) 埼玉県は関東地方だったか**ね**。{M}

(11) A: 松田さん、もう授業終わりましたか。
Matsuda-san mō jugyō owarimashita ka
Mr./Ms. Matsuda, did the class finish?
B: どうかしら**ね**。{M/F}
Dō kashira ne
I don't know.

(12) 私は明日のお別れ会に必ず出席します**よ**。{M/F}
Watashi wa ashita no owakare-kai ni kanarazu shusseki shimasu yo
I am going to attend a farewell party tomorrow.

(13) 私はその意見に反対**よ**。{F}
Watashi wa sono iken ni hantai yo
I do not agree with the opinion.

(14) 私はその意見に反対だ**よ**。{M/F}

(15) あの日本料理店は美味しいわ**よ**。{F}
Ano nihon-ryōriten wa oishīwa yo
The foods in that Japanese restaurant are tasty.

(16) あの日本料理店はうまい**よ**。{M}

(17) 人のアイディアを盗んではいけません**よ**。{M/F}
Hito no aidia o nusun dewa ikemasen yo
Don't steal someone's ideas.

(18) そろそろ寝ましょう**よ**。{F}
Sorosoro nemashō yo
Let's go to bed soon.

(19) 明日のパーティに必ず来て**よ**。{F}
Ashita no pātī ni kanarazu kite yo
Do come to the party tomorrow.

(20) 明日のパーティに必ず来いよ。{M}

(21) 明日のパーティに必ず来てよね。{F}

(22) A: これ、あなたのペン？
　　　Kore anata no pen?
　　　Is this pen yours?

　　 B: いいえ、違う**の**。弟のペンな**の**。{F}
　　　Īe chigau no Otōto no pen nano
　　　No, it's not mine, but my brother's.

(23) あなたは、勉強だけしてればいいの。{M/F}
　　Anata wa benkyō dake shitereba ī no
　　Do study only.

(24) A: 遅かったね。
　　　Osokatta ne
　　　You're late.

　　 B: バスが来なかった**の**。{F}
　　　Basu ga konakatta no
　　　The bus didn't come on time.

(25) A: 甘いものばかり食べてはいけません。
　　　Amai mono bakari tabete wa ikemasen
　　　Don't eat sweets only.

　　 B: おいしいんだも**の**。{F}
　　　Oishīnda mono
　　　They are tasty.

(26) あした行く**の**？{M/F}
　　Ashita iku no?
　　Are you going out tomorrow?

(27) この箱、重い**わ**。(see (48)) {F}
　　Kono hako, omoi wa
　　This box is heavy.

(28) 明日は雨だ**わ**。{F}
　　It's going to rain tomorrow.

(29) びっくりした**わ**。中田さんが結婚したなんて。{F}
　　Bikkuri shita wa. Nakata-san ga kekkon shita nante
　　I'm surprised because Mr/Ms Nakata got married.

(30) A: だれが部屋に入ったの**かしら**。{F}
　　　Dare ga heya ni haitta no kashira
　　　Who entered the room?

　　 B: さあ (see (50))
　　　Sā
　　　I don't know.

(31) お財布どこに置いたの**かしら**。{F}
　　Osaifu doko ni oita no kashira
　　I wonder where I put aside my wallet.

(32) あいつ正気**かしら**。{M}
　　Aitsu shōki kashira
　　Is he serious?

131

(33) あの人正気**かしら**。{F}
Ano hito shōki kashira
Is that man serious?

(34) さあ、行こう**ぜ**。{M}
Sā ikōze
Let's go.

(35) この焼き鳥、おいしい**ぜ**。{M}
Kono yakitori oishī ze
This yakitori is tasty.

(36) 明日から、酒はやめる**ぜ**。{M}
Ashita kara sake wa yameru ze
I'm determined to stop sake from tomorrow on.

(37) あれ、変だ**ぞ**。(see (49)) {M}
Are hen da zo
Look, it's strange.

(38) さあ、行く**ぞ**。{M}
Sā, iku zo
Okay, let's go.

(39) 明日から、酒はやめる**ぞ**。{M}

(40) それは、当たり前**さ**。{M}
Sore wa atarimae sa
That's natural.

(41) A: 結婚する気がないんじゃないの。
   Kekkon suru ki ga nainjanai no
   You may not want to get married.
   B: そんなことない**さ**。{M}
   That's not true.

(42) こんな夜遅くまで何していたの**さ**。{M/F}
Kon-na yoru osoku made nani shite itano sa
What have you been doing so late at night?

(43) チューリップの花が本当にきれいだ**な**。{M}
Chūrippu no hana ga hontō ni kireida na
Flowers of tulips are very pretty.

(44) 大ちゃん、大きくなった**な**。{M}
Dai-chan ōkiku natta na
Dai, you've grown.

(45) 私は・俺はそう思わない**な**。{M/F}
Watashi / Ore wa sō omowanai na
I don't think so.

(46) この手紙出してくれる（だろう）**な**。{M}
Kono tegami dashite kureru (darō) na
Can you send this letter?

(47) 明日早く来いよ**な**。(M)
Ashita hayaku koi yona
Come early tomorrow.

(48) この箱重い**な**。(see (27)) {M/F}
This box is heavy.

(49)　あれ、変だ**な**。 (see (37)) {M/F}
　　Look, it's strange.
(50)　A: だれが部屋にはいったのか**な**。{M/F}
　　　　Dare ga heya ni haittano kana
　　　　Who entered the room?
　　　B: さあ。 (see (30))
　　　　I don't know.

It is important to remark that particles such as ね *ne* and さ *sa* are not only used sentence-finally but can be placed word-finally as well. In Japanese grammar, the former is classified as 終助詞 *shū-joshi*, while the latter is classified as 間投助詞 *kantō-joshi*.

女: いい天気**ね**。
　　*Ī tenki**ne***
　　It is a fine day, isn't it. (sentence-final)
女: 今日**ね**、私学校休むわ。
　　*Kyō**ne**, watashi gakkō yasumu wa*
　　Listen, I will be absent from school today? (word-final)

The functions of these two variants are not the same. When ね is used sentence-finally, the speaker requests either an agreement or a confirmation (see (1) to (4) above); when it is used word-finally, it draws the hearer's attention to the speaker. By using さ sentence-finally, the male speaker responds to his addressee by showing casual agreement (see (41) above), while when it is used word-finally, it functions as an attentive marker, like ね, as shown below. Note that a word-final さ can also be used by women to serve the same function.

女: 二人分高いんじゃない。
　　Futari-bun takainjanai
　　Isn't it expensive to pay for the two?
男: いい**さ**。
　　*Ī**sa***
　　It's okay. (sentence-final)

男: 今日**さ**、俺学校休むよ。
　　*Kyō**sa**, ore gakkō yasumu yo*
　　Listen, I will be absent from school today. (word-final)
女: 今日**さ**、私学校休むわ。
　　*Kyō**sa**, watashi gakkō yasumu wa*
　　Listen, I will be absent from school today.

Activity 1

Let us explore the drama ふぞろいの林檎たち *Fuzoroi no Ringo-tachi* 'Uneven Apples'. The conversations between two protagonists, 良雄

Yoshio and 綾子 *Ayako*, take place in Yoshio's room, as shown in Texts 4.4 and 4.5. They have spent one night together by mistake (4.4), and the following morning they feel guilty (4.5). Find sentence-final particles and list them according to men's and women's registers.

Text 4.4

1	良雄「(灯りをつけ、上がったところで、濡れたコートも脱がずに立っている)」
	綾子「(入って来て)こういう時は、実家へ帰ればいいんだけど、結婚する時、親が反対したのを押し切ったから、今頃、ひどい人だな
5	ていえないし、行くとこなくて―」
	良雄「上がれよ」
	綾子「いいの？迷惑でしょう？」
	良雄「いいさ」
	綾子「ありがとう。濡れちゃって。ちょっとお茶だけ貰えると―」
10	良雄「ドア、閉めて」
	綾子「うん(とドアを閉める)」
	良雄「(それを見ている)」
	綾子「ひどい顔なの」
	良雄「―」
15	綾子「(気がついて)どうかした？そっちも、なんかあった？」
	良雄「ああ―」
	綾子「なに？」
	良雄「まいったよ」
	綾子「どうした？」
20	良雄「まいったよ (と急に綾子の方へ行き綾子を抱きしめる)」
	綾子「(ドアに背をつけて)どうした？」
	良雄「みんな、行っちまった」
	綾子「みんなって？」

良雄「部下を、俺なりに大事にしてるつもりだった。外国人にも、

25 やさしくしてるつもりだった」

綾子「うん」

良雄「みんな、甘い男だとおもってたんだ。腹ン中で笑っていたんだ」

綾子「—」

良雄「みんな、行っちまった」

30 綾子「—」

良雄「 (急に綾子の唇を求める)」

綾子「ダメ (と横を向く)」

良雄「 (自制し)ああ—」

綾子「人妻だもの」

35 良雄「ああ (とゆっくりはなれる)」

綾子「でも— (とその良雄を見て)でもいい。人妻だっていい

(と抱きついて行く)」

二人、唇を求め合ってしまう。

© 1991 Yamada, Taichi / *Fuzoroi no Ringo-tachi* (pp. 147–148), Magazine House

Text 4.5

炬燵の前に、正座してうつむいている綾子。良雄、その前でコーヒーを

注いでいる。

1 良雄「はい (とコーヒーを前へすべらせる)」

綾子「 (うなずく)」

良雄「フフ、どんどん元気なくなっちゃうんだなあ。」

綾子「フフ」

5 良雄「無理にでも、パンぐらい食べて」

綾子「 (うなずく)」

良雄「元気出そうよ」

綾子「 (うなずく)」

良雄「いいね？昨夜は二人とも、どうかしてたんだ。忘れよう。」

10 綾子「 (うなずく)」

良雄「その方がいいんだろ？」

綾子「 (うなずく)」

良雄「なんかずるいようだけど—」

綾子「ううん。一晩ぐらいのことで、私も今までの人生、こわす

15 気ないし」

良雄「—ああ」

綾子「新宿のビジネスホテルで泊まったってことにするから」

良雄「うん—」

綾子「絶対に、かくしてね」

20 良雄「ああ」

綾子「結局、私—あの人を愛していると思う」

良雄「—うん」

綾子「でも、少し、勝手だから、このくらいのこと、したっていい

のよ」

25 良雄「 (苦笑)」

綾子「いい思い出にするわ」

良雄「—ああ」

綾子「一生、かくすけど—」

良雄「ああ」

Commentary

The way the protagonists 良雄 *Yoshio* and 綾子 *Ayako* converse is characterized by the use of final particles. By observing these forms, the reader may identify the gender the speaker belongs to. Table 4.3 summarizes the distribution of particles used by 良雄 and 綾子. Each form is accompanied by its function, indicated by [ ].

Table 4.3 *Actual usage of interactional particles in Texts 4.4 and 4.5*

Particle	良雄 *Yoshio*	T4	T5	綾子 *Ayako*	T4	T5
ね	①いいね [confirmation]		9	⑦かくしてね [seeking for agreement]		19
よ	②上がれよ [invitation]	6		⑧このくらいのこと、 したっていいのよ		23–24
	③元気出そうよ [speaker's intention]		7	[forceful judgment]		
	④まいったよ [expressing emotion]	18/20				
の				⑨いいの？ [question]	7	
				⑩ひどい顔なの [statement]	13	
				⑧このくらいのこと、 したっていいのよ [persuasion]		23–24
もの				⑪人妻だもの [explanation]	34	
わ				⑫いい思い出にするわ [opinion]		26
さ	⑤いいさ [casual disagreement]	8				
なあ	⑥元気なくなっちゃうんだなあ [intensifying emotion]	3				

Particles ね and よ are used by both genders, though よ is used most frequently. Note that the expressions in which these particles appear are not interchangeable. The part preceding the particle needs to be modified. For instance, ①いいね and ②上がれよ may become いいわね and 上がってよ if they are used by 綾子 *Ayako*, while ⑦ぜったいにかくしてね may become ぜったいにかくせよ or ぜったいにかくせよな if 良雄 *Yoshio* uses them. As mentioned above, the preceding word gives rise to gender distinction. In other words, preceding elements such as ② 上がれ 'Come in' and ⑦ かくして 'Hide it' differentiate the gender: the former is a strong order form used most frequently by men (see Chapter 1, section 1.3.1), while the latter is a request form that lacks forcefulness (see Chapter 1, section 1.3.4).

By contrast, ⑤, ⑥, ⑩, ⑪ and ⑫ distinguish gender by use of the particle, and the preceding part has a neutral form, that is, ⑤ いい 'okay' (dictionary form of the adjective), ⑥ and ⑪ だ (copula), ⑩ 顔 'face' (noun), and ⑫ する 'do' (dictionary form of the verb). な is always added to a noun such as 顔 when の is used (see example (22) above). Prolonging the vowel /a/ in な /na/ gives rise to なあ. The prolongation occurs when the speaker embeds his emotions into the utterance. Since 良雄 and 綾子 regret that they spent the night together, 良雄 intensifies his emotion particularly when he observes 綾子 not eating and drinking, showing her low spirits.

⑨いいの？ is uttered by 綾子 here, but this expression can be used by a man, as demonstrated in Text 4.6. いいの？ *īno* 'Is it okay?' is certainly a question (see also (26) above) but, more importantly, it serves to check whether what the speaker has said is true. In Text 4.4, 綾子 double-checks whether she can really enter his room (line 7). In Text 4.6, another scene in the drama, 良雄 uses the same expression in response to 陽子 *Yōko*, his female friend, who is offering him to come to her house.

Text 4.6

陽子「うちへ来ない？この下、白衣なの。着替えるの面倒くさくて」

良雄「**いいの？**」

陽子「いいわよ、久し振りじゃない」

© 1991 Yamada, Taichi / *Fuzoroi no Ringo-tachi* (p. 15), Magazine House

Apart from particles, it is worth mentioning a couple of expressions that mark men's speech. For example, 良雄 uses the male register as in 行っちまった *itchimatta* 'They are gone' (line 22 in Text 4.4), which can be paraphrased as 行っちゃった *itchatta* in women's speech. Its equivalent in formal speech is 行ってしまいました *itteshimaimashita* (see also Chapter 1, section 1.2.4). The use of the first person pronoun 俺 'I' (line 24 in Text 4.4) also points to men's speech. よう in 忘れよう *wasureyō* (line 9, Text 4.5) counts as men's speech; its equivalent in women's speech is 忘れましょう *wasuremashō*. The expression ああ *Ā* 'yes' (lines 15, 19, 26 and 28 in Text 4.5) uttered by 良雄 is a signal of consent pertaining to men's speech. As we examined in section 1.2.1 in Chapter 1, だろ *daro* (line 11, Text 4.5) in men's speech makes a confirmation. Its equivalent in women's speech is でしょ *desho* (its non-contracted form is でしょう *deshō*), as seen in line 7 in Text 4.4.[4]

4.2　In-groups and out-groups

4.2.1　Family

Japanese language pays special attention to the distinction between members of social groups called **in-groups** and **out-groups**. People who are inside an in-group are referred to as 'うち' *uchi* 'inside', while people who are outside an in-group, that is, in an out-group, are referred to as そと *soto* 'outside' or よそ *yoso* 'another place'. うち (内 or 家 in *kanji*) is an equivalent of 'home', 'house', or 'family', as used in expressions such as 内の中で犬を飼う *uchi no naka de inu o kau* 'to keep a dog in the house', and 内中で祝う *uchijū de iwau* 'to celebrate within the whole family'. In contrast, そと (外 in *kanji*) or よそ (他所 in *kanji*) refers to what does not pertain to home, house, or family. Strictly speaking, the boundary between in- and out-groups is not clear-cut but instead depends on a given speech situation or on the relationships between those people participating in the speech. As a rule of thumb, families are in-groups, while groups outside a family are generally considered out-groups.

When people take part in a conversation, the distinction between **reference** and **address terms** is indispensable. Reference terms are used when speakers talk about a person who does not participate in the conversation, while address terms are used when speakers address their interlocutors directly in a conversation. The choice of a reference or address term is made by considering which group, in or out, the speaker and hearer belong to. This system can be set down in five basic relationships: (i) OUT to IN about P (see (51a)), (ii) IN to IN about P (see (51b)), (iii) IN to OUT about P (see (51c)), (iv) OUT to IN (see (51d)), and (v) IN to IN (see (51e)). As in (i) to (iii), P indicates a person who is referred to in a conversation (the use of a reference form). When P is absent, as in (iv) and (v), participants speak to each other (the use of address form). As shown in Tables 4.4 and 4.5 (p. 141), these relationships are realized by using kinship terms (terms indicating the kinship relations) or individual names. Some forms are suffixed by a politeness marker さん or 様, while others have no such suffix.

Let us illustrate five scenarios in which you (as a son in the family) interact with persons from in- and out-groups. When an out-group person (e.g., a salesperson) visits your house and asks you the whereabouts of your father (P), he can either use お父さん *otōsan* or お父様 *otōsama* (more polite than the former) to refer to your father, as shown in (51a). Your answer would be something like (51c) in which you use 父 *chichi* to refer to your father. Now your father has returned home (e.g., after work) and you talk to your father. As shown in (51e), you use a polite form to address him. After returning from a park, your father goes out again. Your sister asks you where your father is, as in (51b). Here, she uses お父さん

otōsan as a reference form, since he is not present in the conversation. When the salesperson visits your home in the evening, your father is at home and he is shown a new product. The salesperson may address your father by saying お父さん *otōsan* to hear his opinion, as in (51d).[5]

(51) a. **お父さん・お父様**はご在宅ですか。 OUT → IN (REFERENCE)
      Otōsan / Otōsama wa gozaitaku desuka
      Is your father at home?

    b. **お父さん**どこに行ったの。 IN → IN (REFERENCE)
      Otōsan doko ni ittano
      Where is Dad?

    c. **父**は会社です。 IN → OUT (REFERENCE)
      Chichi wa kaisha desu
      My father is at work (literally, in the company).

    d. **お父さん**はこの製品をどうお思いですか。
      OUT → IN (ADDRESS)
      Otōsan wa kono sēhin o dō ōmoi desu ka
      How do you find this product?

    e. **お父さん**、一緒に公園に行こうよ。 IN → IN (ADDRESS)
      Otōsan issho ni kōen ni ikō yo
      Dad, let's go to the park together.

While IN → IN and OUT → IN can be used for both reference and address forms, most IN → OUT forms are employed as a reference only, except 兄貴 *aniki* 'elder brother' and 姉貴 *aneki* 'elder sister', which can be used to address the speaker's elder brother or sister in casual speech, as illustrated in (52). Consider Table 4.4.

(52) **兄貴・姉貴**一緒に街へ行こうよ。
      Aniki / Aneki issho ni machi e ikō yo
      'My elder brother/my elder sister, shall we go to town?'

Tables 4.4 and 4.5 summarize kinship terms.[6] Forms in boldface are used for both reference and address, while forms not in boldface are used for reference (exceptions are illustrated in (52)). Forms marked by * are used only as address forms.

(53) and (54) below illustrate further examples. In (53a), the wife introduces her husband to an out-group member (e.g., her neighbour, friend or colleague). (53b) and (53c) refer to situations in which the wife asks her husband to run an errand by using two address forms: the second person pronoun あなた *anata* (see section 4.1) and his name suffixed by さん. (53d) exemplifies an out-group member asking the wife whether her husband is at home. This person uses a reference form prefixed by ご *go*. When an out-group person speaks directly to her husband, he uses the same form ご主人 as an address form (53e). (54) illustrates the relationship between a mother and her daughter. If the mother talks to her daughter,

Table 4.4 *Kinship reference & address forms I*

In → Out	In → In	Out → In	Meaning
父・親父	お父さん	お父さん・お父様	father
母・お袋	お母さん	お母さん・お母様	mother
兄・**兄貴**	お兄さん	お兄さん	elder brother
姉・**姉貴**	お姉さん	お姉さん	elder sister
祖父	おじいさん	おじい様・おじいさん	grandfather
祖母	おばあさん	おばあ様・おばあさん	grandmother
おじ	おじさん	おじさん	uncle
おば	おばさん	おばさん	aunt

Table 4.5 *Kinship reference & address forms II*

In → Out	In → In	Out → In	Meaning
弟	own name	弟さん	younger brother
妹	own name	妹さん	younger sister
息子	own name	ご子息様・息子様・息子さん・own name	son
娘	own name	お嬢様・娘さん・お嬢さん・own name	daughter
甥	own name		nephew
姪	own name		niece
主人・夫・旦那・亭主・ハズ	*あなた・お父さん・own name	ご主人様・ご主人・own name	husband
家内・妻・ワイフ	*おまえ・お母さん・own name	奥さん・奥様・own name	wife

the daughter is addressed by her own name, as in (54a). The suffix (ちゃん *chan*) is a diminutive form, verbalizing the speaker's intimacy with the addressee. If the mother introduces her daughter to an out-group member, she says (54b). When an out-group person refers to the daughter, he uses お嬢様 *ojōsama* or お嬢さん *ojōsan* (54c). When an out-group member addresses the daughter, お嬢さん might be preferred to お嬢様 (54d). If

141

the out-group person knows her name, it might be more common to use her own name in the context of (54c) and (54d). The character 嬢 refers to a girl or a woman. お *o* is a politeness prefix in much the same way as ご *go*.

(53) a. 私の主人です。　IN → OUT (REFERENCE)
　　　Watashi no shujin desu
　　　This is my husband.

　　 b. **あなた**、スーパーに行って焼き魚買ってきて。
　　　Anata sūpā ni itte yakizakana katte kite
　　　IN → IN (ADDRESS)
　　　Darling, can you go to the supermarket and buy fried fish?

　　 c. **たかしさん**、スーパーに行って焼き魚買ってきて。
　　　Takashi-san sūpā ni itte yakizakana katte kite
　　　IN → IN (ADDRESS)
　　　Takashi, can you go to the supermarket and buy fried fish?

　　 d. **ご主人**はご在宅ですか。　OUT → IN (REFERENCE)
　　　Goshujin wa gozaitaku desu ka.
　　　Is your husband at home?

　　 e. **ご主人**はこの製品をどうお思いですか。　OUT → IN (ADDRESS)
　　　Goshujin wa kono seihin o dō ōmoi desu ka
　　　What do you think about this product?

(54) a. **美香ちゃん**、スーパーに行って焼き魚買ってきて。
　　　Mika-chan sūpā ni itte yakizakana katte kite
　　　IN → IN (ADDRESS)
　　　Mika, can you go to the supermarket and buy fried fish?

　　 b. 私の**娘**です。　IN → OUT (REFERENCE)
　　　Watashi no musume desu
　　　This is my daughter.

　　 c. **お嬢様・お嬢さん**はもう何歳になりましたか。
　　　Ojōsama / san wa mō nansai ni narimashita ka
　　　OUT → IN (REFERENCE)
　　　How old is your daughter?

　　 d. **お嬢さん**、学校は楽しいですか。　OUT → IN (ADDRESS)
　　　Ojōsan gakkō wa tanoshii desu ka
　　　Are you enjoying school?

Texts: How address/reference forms (IN→IN) are used

The following excerpts taken from 日本の歴史 *Nihon no Rekishi* 'Japanese History' (1982) edited by Kasahara give you an idea of how address and reference forms are used in different in-group situations. These scenes take place shortly after the end of World War II (i.e., after 1945) and describe traditional family relationships. The unprefixed forms 父さん *tōsan* 'father' and 母さん *kāsan* 'mother' are used (Text 4.7); the former is a reference form and the latter is a self-reference form. The grandfather calls his grandson by his name (i.e., 進 *Susumu*) without adding a suffix (Text

4.8). あなた *anata* and おまえ *omae* are used by the couple. おまえ is used when the husband draws his wife's attention (Text 4.9); he is asking her opinion about a picture in a newspaper that shows the destroyed houses in the war. When their dramatic reunion comes about, the husband calls his wife by her name (Text 4.10). It would be odd for him to call her おまえ in this context. His wife calls him あなた. It is hardly possible for her to use his name here. When she draws his attention, she still uses あなた to her husband (Text 4.11). In contemporary Japanese society, modern wives may not use あなた as frequently as they did at that time.

Text 4.7

© 1982 Shueisha / *Nihon no Rekishi* (p. 80) Vol. 18

Text 4.8

© 1982 Shueisha / *Nihon no Rekishi* (p. 80) Vol. 18

Text 4.9

© 1982 Shueisha / *Nihon no Rekishi* (p. 26) Vol. 18

Text 4.10

© 1982 Shueisha / *Nihon no Rekishi* (p. 64) Vol. 18

Text 4.11

© 1982 Shueisha / *Nihon no Rekishi* (p. 80) Vol. 18

4.2.2 Company

The concept of in-groups and out-groups can be applied to communities such as a company, as shown by (55). (55a) is uttered when someone outside the company asks whether the president is in. (55b) can be uttered by a secretary of the president in response to the query in (55a), while (55c) can be uttered by a colleague of Mr Hayashi, an employee, in a context in which someone from outside wants to talk to or meet him. 社長 *shachō* is an honorific title used for the president in a company. This title can be used without being accompanied by さん *san*, as in (55b), because the president and his secretary are regarded as members of the in-group, just like a son and his father are in the in-group, as shown in (51c) above. Similarly, (55c) refers to a situation in which a colleague of Mr Hayashi answers the telephone and says that Mr Hayashi is on leave today. A reference to Mr Hayashi without using さん by his colleague indicates that they are in-group members. This relationship resembles the scenario in which a younger brother refers to his elder sister as 姉 *ane* when someone from an out-group asks about her.

(55) a. **社長様・社長さん**はいらっしゃいますか。 OUT → IN (REFERENCE)
       Shachō-sama/Shachō-san wa irasshaimasu ka
       Is the president in?

   b. **社長**はただいま外出中です。 IN → OUT (REFERENCE)
       Shachō wa tadaima gaishutsu-chū desu
       The president is out.

   c. **林**は本日は休みです。 IN → OUT (REFERENCE)
       Hayashi wa honjitsu wa yasumi desu
       Mr Hayashi is on leave today.

So far, company context seems to parallel family context. Where address forms are concerned, however, we encounter some differences. Recall that when family members address each other, polite forms are used (e.g., お父さん *otōsan* 'father', お兄さん *onīsan* 'elder brother'). Consider (56). The president is addressed by his subordinate without the addition of a politeness suffix (社長 *shachō*) (56a), while Mr Hayashi, an employee of the company, is addressed by his colleague with a suffix (林さん *hayashi-san*) (56b). If they are considered to be in-group members, as we have seen in (55), it is logical to expect that they should have the same address form. But the differing ways of addressing the president and Mr Hayashi imply that categorizing members within a company is not the same as within a family. Address terms at the workplace largely depend on the status or rank of the people who work there.

(56) a. **社長**、おはようございます。 (subordinate → President)
       Shachō ohayōgozaimasu (ADDRESS)
       (Mr) President, good morning.

145

b. **林さん**、おはようございます。
(colleagues in the same rank)
Hayashi-san ohayōgozaimasu (ADDRESS)
Mr Hayashi, good morning.

Another difference between family and company is in the use of self-reference forms. Recall from Text 4.7 that the mother calls herself 母さん *kāsan* when she is with her children. But in the workplace, the president can hardly call himself as 社長さん. Likewise, the sectional chief cannot refer to himself as 課長さん *kachō-san*. This is because 社長 and 課長 indicate their status within the company. Kinship terms are by no means titles; they merely indicate the relationships between members of a family. Table 4.6 summarizes examples (55) and (56).

Table 4.6 *Reference & address forms in a company*

In → Out	In → In	Out → In	Meaning
社長	社長	社長さん・社長様	President
林	林さん・林君	林さん・林様	Mr/Ms Hayashi

Activity 2

The following conversation is taken from ふぞろいの林檎たち *Fuzoroi no Ringo-tachi* 'Uneven Apples'. It takes place in 陽子's *Yōko*'s room, where old friends gather for the first time in many years. Look carefully at the words marked in boldface, and state whether the forms used are address forms or reference forms. When the forms are address forms, explain the social relationship they represent. Note that 綾子 *Ayako* and 実 *Minoru* are a married couple.

Text 4.12

1　陽子「そんなに変った？」
　　実「変んない」
　　良雄「変んない」
　　綾子「変らない」
5　陽子「変らないわけないでしょ。まったく（とコップ酒をのむ）」
　　フフ、とみんなも苦笑してのむ。
　　実「しかし、あれだよな、昔の仲間っていうのはいいよなあ。一年ぶ

りとか三年ぶりとかで逢ったってさ、すぐ気持ち解け合うし、気心し

れてるし」

10 健一「俺の気心知れてるか？①**お前**」

実「そうやって偉そうなこというとこ、ちっとも変ってねえじゃね

えか」

良雄「ほんと」

陽子「仕事が好きで自信たっぷりで」

15 健一「え？ (と苦笑)」

陽子「いま考えてることは、早く帰らねえと明日が大変だ」

健一「よしてよ」

陽子「昔の連中としんみりしてる暇はねえ」

実「いえてる」

20 陽子「明日の午後の段取りを確認したかなあ (と健一の口真似風にい

う)」

健一「いいよ、もう (と苦笑)」

実「②**お前**の気心ぐらい知れてんだから」

陽子「そう」

25 良雄「まあ、俺たちの年齢は仕事もわかって来て、一番忙しい時期で

はあるけど」

実「③**お前**はそれほどギンギンじゃないだろ」

良雄「そうでもないさ」

実「まだ④**お前**班長やってのか？」

30 綾子「⑤**お父ちゃん** (たしなめる)」

健一「⑥**お父ちゃん** (からかう)

実「外へ出たら、⑦**お父ちゃん**ていうなっていってるだろ」

陽子「いいじゃないの」

実「離れて歩けっていったって、すぐ子供しょって並んでくるから

35 体裁悪くて」

健一「成長しねえな、⑧**お前**も (と叩く)」

実「⑨**お前**はしてんのかよ？」

陽子「してるつもりねぇ (皮肉)」

健一「きびしいな (と苦笑)」

40　良雄「いや、この頃はさ、運送業はもう人集めよ、人が集まらなくて、年から年中もう、その対策でさ」

実「仕事はあるんだよな」

良雄「そうよ。仕事は、とってくればいくらでもあるけど、人がいなくて」

45　実「同じよ、こっちも。管理職になったらもう、若いやつがやめて行くんでよ」

陽子「やだ、管理職？」

実「⑩**課長**よ」

健一「そうかよ」

50　良雄「すげえじゃない」

綾子「ううん、やめないように、みんな⑪**課長**にしたのよ」

実「冗談いうなよ」

健一「みんな⑫**課長**ってことはないだろうけど」

綾子「そうなの。特に⑬**この人**貫禄がないから、名刺にせめて

55　⑭**課長**とかつけてやろうって」

実「⑮**亭主**のね、出世をね、そういうさめた目で見て、どうするんだよ？おめでとうって、単純に喜ぶってとこが、本当に⑯**こいつ**ないんだよ」

陽子「⑰**課長**なんてすごい」

60　綾子「全部あわせて十一人の会社だもの」

実「あ (コップをとり) 酔って来たんだよ、⑱**お前**。だからのむなっていったろう」

良雄「 (そのコップをとり) とり上げることはないだろ (と綾子へ

渡しながら) こっちはやっと⑲ **係長** だけど」

65 陽子「そうなの (祝福の声)」

良雄「早くはないけど――」

© 1991 Yamada, Taichi / *Fuzoroi no Ringo-tachi* (pp. 20–21), Magazine House

Commentary

Table 4.7 summarizes the uses of address and reference forms in Text 4.12. All company terms are used as reference forms in this text.

Table 4.7 Address versus reference forms in actual usage

No.	Example	Address	Reference
①	お前	◯	
②	お前	◯	
③	お前	◯	
④	お前	◯	
⑤	お父ちゃん	◯	
⑥	お父ちゃん	◯	
⑦	お父ちゃん		◯
⑧	お前	◯	
⑨	お前	◯	
⑩	課長		◯
⑪	課長		◯
⑫	課長		◯
⑬	この人		◯
⑭	課長		◯
⑮	亭主		◯
⑯	こいつ		◯
⑰	課長		◯
⑱	お前	◯	
⑲	係長		◯

お前 *omae* 'you' is used seven times (① ② ③ ④ ⑧ ⑨ ⑱), each time as an address form. In all cases (except ⑱) the form is used when a man speaks to his close friend, either man or woman. Since the situation is a conversation between friends who know each other well, it is quite natural to use お前. お前 in ⑱ is used by 実 *Minoru* to call 綾子 *Ayako*, who is his wife.

149

お父ちゃん *otōchan* 'father' appears three times. ⑤ is used by 綾子 to address her husband 実. In Japanese kinship terms (see Table 4.4), the father is called 'father' as he is viewed from his children's kinship relationship (i.e., he is their father), and this address form is used by all members of the family. This means that family members are categorized by the status of the youngest member. Thus, a mother can address her daughter お姉ちゃん *onēchan* (literally 'elder sister') if a family member is younger than her daughter (i.e., she has a younger sister or younger brother). As shown in 実's utterance in ⑦, some parents may prefer not to represent their fatherhood or motherhood in public. The use of お父ちゃん enables 健一 *Kenichi* to make fun of 実 by addressing him as お父ちゃん ⑥. お父ちゃん in ⑦ is a repetition of the way 綾子 addressed her husband; it therefore does not function as an address form. The use of ちゃん signals the informal or casual relationship of the participants in the conversation.

この人 *kono hito* (literally 'this person') in ⑬ is a reference form for her husband 実. 綾子, his wife, is humbling him before their friends, as she thinks that he lacks dignity. This form is used only when the speaker refers to his or her in-group members (e.g., married couples or close friends) who share an equal social status. Children, for example, cannot use this form to refer to their parents. こいつ ⑲ refers to 綾子. This form is normally used by a man to his wife or girlfriend.[7]

By using 亭主 *tēshu* (literally 'husband') in ⑮, 実 refers to himself as 綾子's husband. This form is self-reference. Other alternative forms such as 旦那 *dan-na* and 主人 *shujin* given in Table 4.5 are not suitable here.

課長 *kachō* occurs five times (⑩, ⑪, ⑫, ⑭ and ⑰). This word is not an address form but a reference form in all instances; people are talking about 実's title in the company where he works. ⑩ differs slightly in that 実, who had been promoted to section chief, responds to 陽子's *Yōko*'s surprising reaction (line 59) by giving more details about his status in the company. ⑩ is self-reference.

係長 *kakarichō* ⑲ is used to refer to 良雄's status in his workplace. Similar to ⑩, 良雄 uses his title to describe himself. This form, too, is self-reference.

4.3 Politeness

ます-forms (e.g., 行きます *ikimasu* 'to go' or 食べます *tabemasu* 'to eat') or です-forms (e.g., かわいいです *kawaīdesu* 'to be pretty' or しずかです *shizukadesu* 'to be quiet') are treated as **polite forms**. For instance, it is natural for a teacher to use a polite form when he or she talks to his or her students in the classroom, as shown in (56), because it is appropriate for the teacher, who officially ranks higher than the students, to maintain a formal relationship with them by using a polite form. In other words, the difference that exists between the social positions of teacher and students pertains to a formal speech situation, and as such the teacher demonstrates politeness or good manners through the social distance created by polite forms. In (56), a classroom teacher notifies his pupils that the homework has to be submitted by next week by using a polite request form (see Chapter 1, section 1.3.5 above).

(56)　先生: では、みなさん来週までに作文を提出して**ください**。
　　　Sensē: *Dewa, mina-san raishū made ni sakubun o tēshutsu shite kudasai*
　　　Teacher: Now, everyone, please submit the essay by next week.

Formal situations are realized not only when people of different social status interact with each other (e.g., teacher versus students) but also when people who have the same social status interact. When students meet for the first time, the following conversation might be heard.

(57)　学生 1：今日学校へ**行きます**か。
　　　Gakusē 1: *Kyō gakkō e ikimasu ka*
　　　　　　Are you going to school today?
　　　学生 2：いいえ、**行きません**。
　　　Gakusē 2: *Īe ikimasen*
　　　　　　No, I am not.

In (57), two students are not familiar with each other. (56) and (57) exemplify the use of polite forms in Japanese when the speech situation is formal; the speaker and addressee attempt to maintain social distance. In informal speech where speaker and addressee are familiar to each other and do not need to maintain social distance, informal forms (i.e., dictionary forms) are used, as in (58).

(58)　学生 1：今日学校へ**行く**？
　　　Gakusē 1: *Kyō gakkō e iku?*
　　　　　　Are you going to school today?
　　　学生 2：ううん、**行かない**。
　　　Gakusē 2: *Ūn ikanai*
　　　　　　No, I am not.

Polite forms are also used when two people do not communicate properly, which creates distance. 土屋君 *Tsuchiya-kun* and 茜 *Akane* are from the same high school and know each other well. When 土屋君 makes it public that he likes 茜, 茜 uses the polite forms どなた *donata* (versus its informal form だれ *dare* 'who') and でした *deshita* (versus だった *datta*) not because she does not know him, but because she does not really understand what he has said.

Text 4.13 どなたでしたっけ？

© 2003 Isshiki, Makoto / *Denaoshitoide!* (p. 22), Kodansha

Note that people can be polite only when they have a speech partner with whom to communicate. A polite form can switch to a non-polite form in the same environment when the speaker stops drawing attention to his addressee. In other words, 'murmurs' or 'exclamations' are not subject to formality on the grounds that these are self-contained expressions. Imagine a scene in which a shop assistant is demonstrating how to prepare かっぱ巻き *kappa-maki* 'sushi roll with cucumbers' in a supermarket. She might first say something like (59a), (59b) and (59c) in sequence.

(59) a. ごはんの上にきゅうりを**のせます**。
        Gohan no ue ni kyūri o nosemasu
        Place pieces of the cucumbers on the rice.
      b. のりでごはんを**巻きます**。
        Nori de gohan o makimasu
        Roll the rice with seaweeds.
      c. 包丁で小さく**切ります**。
        Hōchō de chīsaku kirimasu
        Cut the sushi rolls into small pieces with a knife.

She may then say (60) as soon as she notices that the knife does not cut the sushi rolls. This form is not marked by です (e.g., おかしいです), although her speech takes place in the same environment of (59), where she has customers in front of her. This plain form in (60) is directed to the shop assistant herself, not to the customers.

(60) **おかしい**な。
        Okashī na
        Strange!?

If (60) is replaced by 痛い *itai* 'Ouch!' as the result of an error made by the shop assistant, its polite form (e.g., 痛いです *itaidesu*) is not used either, because exclamations are also self-contained expressions (see also Makino and Tsutsui 1995: 39).

4.4 Honorifics

Honorifics, or 敬語 *kēgo*, refer to the way a speaker expresses respect or honour to people who are of a higher social rank. The Japanese language has two forms of honorifics: **respect** and **humble honorifics**. Using honorifics is another means of expressing politeness in that the speaker shows his well-manneredness in accordance with his personal relationship with the other.[8] Unlike polite forms, however, honorifics are not used to establish a formal relationship. In actual speech, honorific forms are often accompanied by ます to emphasize formality. As shown in (61a), いらっしゃいます (いらっしゃる is its dictionary form) consists of an honorific form (for 来る 'come' or 行く 'go') and a polite form ます. In a situation in which two close colleagues are conversing, it is possible, as in (61b), to use an honorific form without ます. The speaker is well-mannered but does not need to be formal. (61b) is an interrogative accompanied by a rising intonation.

(61) a. 佐藤さん、明日のパーティに**いらっしゃい**ますか。
        Satō-san ashita no pāti ni irasshaimasuka
        Mr Sato, are you coming tomorrow?
      b. 佐藤さん、明日のパーティに**いらっしゃる**？
        Satō-san ashita no pāti ni irassaru
        Mr Sato, are you coming tomorrow?

4.4.1 Respect honorifics

Respect honorifics, or 尊敬語 *sonkē-go*, are used to express the speaker's respect for another person. The person who deserves respect appears in the subject position. Respect honorifics are realized by using three different forms: (i) a special respect form, (ii) the passive form, or (iii) the お-verb-になる form.[9] Table 4.8 displays 25 verbs (see also Hinata 2000: 46–47). You may notice that not all verbs have three forms. (62) to (65) are representative examples.

In (62) and (63), the speaker shows respect to 中田先生 and 田島課長.

(62) 中田先生が食事を**召し上がっ**ております。
      Nakata-sensē ga shokuji o meshiagatte orimasu
      Teacher Nakata is eating a meal.
(63) 田島課長がお部屋で**お待ちになっ**ております。
      Tajima-kachō ga oheya de omachi ni natte orimasu
      The chief executive, Mr Tajima, is waiting in the room.

Although some verbs have three forms, their meanings are not always identical. For example, respect verbs are preferred to お-verb forms when describing a fact (62) or making a request (64). When a verb does not have

153

Table 4.8 *Representative examples of respect honorifics*

	Verbs	Meaning	Respect forms	Passive forms	お-Verb-になる
1	食べる	eat	上がる・召し上がる	食べられる	お食べになる
2	飲む	drink	上がる・召し上がる	飲まれる	お飲みになる
3	行く	go	いらっしゃる	行かれる	お行きになる
4	来る	come	いらっしゃる・見える	来られる	お越しになる・おいでになる・お見えになる
5	いる	stay	いらっしゃる	おられる	—
6	言う	say	おっしゃる	言われる	—
7	くれる	give	くださる	—	—
8	する	do	なさる	される	—
9	着る	wear	召す	着られる	お召しになる
10	聞く	ask	お耳に入る	聞かれる	お聞きになる
11	書く	write	—	書かれる	お書きになる
12	読む	read	—	読まれる	お読みになる
13	待つ	wait	ご存知です	待たれる	お待ちになる
14	知る	know	—	—	—
15	もらう	receive	—	—	—
16	あげる	give	—	—	—
17	やる	give	—	やられる	おやりになる
18	見る	see, watch	—	見られる	ご覧になる
19	借りる	borrow	—	借りられる	お借りになる
20	会う	see, meet	—	会われる	お会いになる
21	貸す	lend	—	貸される	お貸しになる
22	受け取る・訪問する	receive	—	受け取られる	お受け取りになる
23	訪ねる・訪問する	visit	—	訪ねられる・訪問される	お訪ねになる
24	わかる・引き受ける	understand, accept	—	—	おわかりになる・お引き受けになる
25	気に入る	be fond of	お気に召す	気に入られる	お気に入りになる

a respect form but instead has passive and お-verb-する forms, the latter appears to be more prevalent (65).

(64) お菓子を召し上がってください。
    (△お食べになってください)
    Okashi o meshi-agatte kudasai
    Please have some sweets.

(65) 本を**お読みになって**ください。(×読まれてください)
    Hon o oyomi ni natte kudasai
    Please read the book.

4.4.2 Humble honorifics

Humble honorifics, or 謙譲語 *kenjō-go*, are used by the speaker to humble himself in order to honour the status of his speech partner who deserves respect. Humble honorifics are realized by using two different forms: (i) a special humble form, and (ii) the お-verb-する form. Table 4.9 displays the same 25 verbs as in Table 4.8.[10]

In (66), the speaker expresses his respect to his addressee by using the humble form of 受け取る *uketoru* 'to receive'. The humble honorific can be expressed in two ways: one is to use a lexical form 拝受する (拝受いたす employs two humble forms) (66a), and the other is to use a morphologically complex form お受け取りする (お受け取りいたす employs two humble forms) (66b).

(66) a. お手紙を**拝受しました・拝受いたし**ました。
      Otegami o haiju shimashita / haiju itashimashita
      It is my honour to receive your letter.
    b. お手紙を**お受け取りしました・お受け取りいたし**ました。
      Otegami o ouketori shimashita / ouketori itashimashita
      It is my honour to receive your letter.

You may already know that Japanese people customarily say いただきます *itadakimasu* before a meal (67). This form was originally a humble form of 食べる *taberu* or 飲む *nomu*, to which the polite form ます *masu* was attached. The speaker humbles himself to thank the person who has prepared the meal. In present-day Japan, language users may not be conscious of the presence of humbleness in this expression, since its function as a marker of starting a meal has been entirely conventionalized in society.

(67) **いただき**ます。
    Itadakimasu
    Enjoy your meal.
    (literally: 'It is my honour to have a meal.')

Note that humble and お-verb forms are not always interchangeable.

Table 4.9 *Representative examples of humble honorifics*

	Verbs	Meaning	Humble forms	お-Verb-する
1	食べる	eat	いただく・頂戴する	—
2	飲む	drink	いただく・頂戴する	—
3	行く	go	参る・うかがう・上がる	おうかがいする
4	来る	come	—	—
5	いる	stay	おる	—
6	言う	say	もうす・申し上げる	—
7	くれる	give	—	—
8	する	do	いたす	—
9	着る	wear	—	—
10	聞く	ask	うかがう・承る・拝聴する	お聞きする
11	書く	write	—	お書きする
12	読む	read	拝読する	お読みする
13	待つ	wait	—	お待ちする
14	知る	know	存じる・存じ上げる	—
15	もらう	receive	いただく・頂戴する・たまわる	—
16	あげる	give	さしあげる・進呈する	おあげする
17	やる	give	さしあげる・進呈する	—
18	見る	see, watch	拝見する	—
19	借りる	borrow	拝借する	お借りする
20	会う	see, meet	お目にかかる	—
21	貸す	lend	—	お貸しする
22	受け取る	receive	拝受する・いただく	お受け取りする
23	訪ねる・訪問する	visit	伺う・上がる・参上する	お訪ねする・ご訪問する
24	わかる・引き受ける	understand, accept	承知する・かしこまる	—
25	気に入る	be fond of	—	—

When the speaker is going to read a book written by Professor X, he uses the お-verb form (68). When he has already read the book, the humble verb will be used (69). This contrast is not applicable to all verbs in Table 4.9.

> (68) これからX先生のお書きになられた本を**お読みいたし**ます。
> *Korekara X-sensē no okaki ni narareta hon o oyomi itashimasu*
> I am going to read the book written by Professor X.
> (69) 先日、先生がお書きになられた本を**拝読いたし**ました。
> *Senjitsu sensē ga okaki ni narareta hon o haidoku itashimashita*
> I read the book you have written with honour the other day.

As shown in [68] and [69], お読みする and 拝読する are humble honorifics for 読む *yomu* 'to read'. Since する also has its humble form いたす *itasu*, the whole expression duplicates a sense of humbleness, which strengthens the expression of respect.

Activity 3

Having studied the two types of honorifics, let us explore how they are used in actual situations. Examining three extracts from 日本の歴史 *Nihon no rekishi* 'Japanese History' (1982) edited by Kasahara, identify the honorific forms and explain who uses honorifics to whom. Texts 4.14 and 4.15 describe formal meetings, while Text 4.16 illustrates an informal meeting. Read from top to bottom and from left to right.

Commentary

Two points need to be mentioned. First, the occurrence of honorifics is independent of the formality of the speech situation. This claim is supported by the co-existence of honorifics with formal and informal uses of the language. The background of Texts 4.14 and 4.15 is a formal meeting where government officials are having a discussion: です *desu* and ます *masu* forms are frequently used by the participants. In contrast, Text 4.16 is an informal meeting where people with the same social status are having a casual discussion: the particle ぞ *zo*, which expresses the male speaker's strong opinion, and the plain form だ *da* are the markers of informality here.

    Second, the honorifics used in these texts are all humble honorifics. Speakers humble themselves to show respect to the person they are talking to (Texts 4.14/15) or are going to talk to (Text 4.16). In a meeting, formal or informal, in which two or more people discuss a certain topic, humble forms appear to be preferred to respect forms. The question is why. We learned in section 4.4.1 that the use of respect honorifics is grammatically restricted in that the person who receives respect has to be in the subject

Text 4.14 総理どういたしましょうか 'The Prime Minister, what shall we do?'

© 1982 Shueisha / *Nihon no Rekishi* (p. 80) Vol. 18

Text 4.15 わたしがお答えします 'I will answer that'

© 1982 Shueisha / *Nihon no Rekishi* (p. 80) Vol. 18

position. This means that respect is directed to the agent who wilfuly performs an action. In Text 4.15, the performer of an action wilfuly answers the question (お答えします *Okotae shimasu* 'I will answer that'). However, the referent of the subject is the first person, and it would be odd for the first person to respect himself. If the subject is in the second or third

Text 4.16 うかがおう 'Let's ask for the Emperor's opinion'

© 1982 Shueisha / *Nihon no Rekishi* (p. 80) Vol. 18

person, it is possible for the speaker to use respect honorifics such as 部長がお答えになられますか *Buchō ga okotae ni nararemasuka* 'Head, will you answer the question?' or 部長がお答えになられます *Buchō ga okotae ni nararemasu* 'The Head of the division will answer the question'. Similarly, in Text 4.14, the person who raises a question (どういたしましょうか *Dō itashimashōka* 'What shall we do') cannot respect himself, and thus he uses the humble honorific, showing his respect to the President (総理 *sōri*), the person he is talking to. In Text 4.16, the use of the humble honorific うかがう *ukagau* 'to ask' is natural because it is the *samurai* who is going to talk to the Emperor (ミカド *Mikado*) to ask for his opinion. Since the Emperor's action is not at issue here, it is adequate for the *samurai* to use a humble honorific to show respect to the Emperor, who has a higher status. Note that ご意見 *goiken* 'opinion' is a polite form of 意見.

These texts convey the interesting fact that, although further investigation is needed, three randomly selected texts make more frequent use of humble honorifics than of respect honorifics.

4.5 Young people

Young people in modern Japanese society form an important cultural domain. **Young people's language** is called 若者ことば *wakamono-kotoba* or 若者用語 *wakamono-yōgo* in Japanese. This language was brought to our attention during the 1980s – the time that inaugurated a shift to today's global economy (see Cameron 2000: 341) – and it still enjoys popularity owing to its productive power to invent new words and expressions that characterize aspects of contemporary Japanese society, or, to put it more precisely, what young people think about or feel in response to the society in which they live. Young people's language has the following socio-cultural characteristics:

(70) a. It is used in groups.
      b. It is used in informal settings.
      c. It is spoken language.
      d. It does not distinguish between men's and women's speech.
      e. It does not create social hierarchy.

Young people's language differs from the other variations demonstrated from 4.1 to 4.4 in that it actually belongs to a subculture. This is why you normally do not learn young people's language in the classroom, whereas the other variations, which belong to the larger culture, are part of the Japanese language syllabus. It is worth mentioning that young people's language is not merely the language used exclusively by young people. While most of its expressions are short-lived in society, some survive and continue to be used by other generations (Kamei 2003: 7).[11]

Another characteristic of young people's language is that it is linguistic, that is, its coinage is not random but follows the system of the Japanese language. Note that four features, as shown in (71), pertain to the concepts we have studied in previous chapters (including chapters in JL):

(71) a. It arises from morphological processes (clipping (4.5.1), affixation (4.5.2), and reduplication (4.5.3)).
      b. It arises from changes in original meaning (4.5.4).
      c. It arises from being less direct (4.5.5).
      d. It arises from changes in grammar (4.5.6).

The following sections provide examples for each category in (71) to show how young people's language is created. Examples are taken mainly from 現代用語の基礎知識 *Gendai-yōgo no Kiso-chishiki* 'An Encyclopedia of Contemporary Words' (2003: 1133–1137).

4.5.1 Clipping

Clipping refers to the shortening of long words. This is also termed 'truncation' by some authors (Kaiser et al. 2001: 575). Original words are reduced usually to three or four morae. As shown in the examples below, a word can be clipped in one of three ways: (i) the first two morae and the final two morae of the new word are taken from the original word (①, ②, ③), (ii) the first two/three morae and the final mora of the new word are taken from the original word (④, ⑤, ⑥), and (iii) the first or final part of the original word is deleted (⑦, ⑧).

(72)
    ①ドタキャン dotakyan ← **dotan**ba de **kyan**seru
        'to cancel something at the last moment'
    ②カゲレン kageren ← **kage** de **ren**syū
        'to practice secretly'
    ③よしぎゅう yoshigyū ← **yoshi**noya no **gyū**don
        'beef bowl at Yoshinoya'
    ④きもい kimoi ← **kimo**chi-waru-**i** 'to feel unwell'
    ⑤なつい natsui ← **natsu**kasii 'to feel yearning for'
    ⑥めんどい mendoi ← **mendo**kusai 'tiresome'
    ⑦セブン sebun ← **sebun**-irebun 'Seven Eleven' (= convenience
        store)
    ⑧リーマン rīman ← sara**rīman** 'salaried man'

4.5.2 Affixation

Affixation attaches a prefix or suffix to a base (see Chapter 5, section 5.6 in JL). There are four types of affixes. The first type produces a nominal expression with a special meaning. 系 *kē* normally refers to 'family line' (e.g., 日系米人 *nikkē-bējin* 'Japanese-American'), but when attached to a word like ジャニーズ *Janīzu*, a singing group consisting of young men, the whole word ジャニーズ系 refers to a type of young men who resemble, in their manners or outlook, the members of the group. いやし系 *iyashikē* refers to a person or an object that soothes one's mental pains. いやし is derived from the verb 癒す *iyasu* 'to soothe, heal'.

    リアン is related to *rian* in English, as in *vegetarian*. Although *rian* in English by itself is not an affix, *rian* occupies the final three morae in Japanese. Young people use it to refer to people who behave a certain way. ジベタリアン *jibetarian* thus indicates people who gather (often sit on the ground) in front of a convenience store (e.g., セブンイレブン *sebun-irebun* 'Seven Eleven'). ジベタ comes from 地べた *jibeta* 'ground'.

    Similarly, スト *suto* comes from *st*, the final part of *economist* or *stylist*, referring to people with a similar behaviour. ビニスト thus refers to people who often go to the convenience store.

    The second type of suffix is る *ru*, which produces a verb. In examples ④ to ⑧, part of the original word (consisting of two morae) is combined with the suffix. じもる *jimoru* is derived from 地元 *jimoto* 'local', referring to people who enjoy themselves in their own place (where they were born and brought up).

    The third type of suffix is い *i*, which produces an adjective. Like other examples with る *ru*, this suffix is attached to a part of the original word. グロい *guroi* 'unpleasant' is a combination of the first two morae of the original word グロテスク 'grotesque' and the suffix い.

The fourth type of suffix is an aspectual marker てる *teru*, which is attached to part of the original word to express the progressive aspect (see Chapter 7, section 7.4 in JL for the notion of 'aspect'). Instead of saying グロバる with the suffix る (see above), グロバッてる emphasizes the continuity of the situation. This expression refers to people who frequently speak about 'globalization'.

(73)

Nominalizing suffix:
①ジャニーズ系 *Janīzukē*
②いやし系 *iyasikē*
③ジベタリアン *jibetarian*
④ビニスト *binisuto*

Verbalizing suffix:
④じもる *jimoru* ← **jimo**to + る
⑤ビニる *biniru* ← **conveni**ence store + る
⑥カフェる *kaferu* ← **cafe**teria + る
⑦プクる *pukuru* ← **ippuku** + る
⑧吉る *yoshiru* ← **Yoshi**noya + る

Adjectivizing suffix:
⑨グロい *guroi* ← **gro**tesque + い

Aspectual suffix:
⑩グロバッてる *gurobatteru* ← **globa**lization + てる

4.5.3 Reduplication

Young people also coin new words by **reduplication** (repetition of the same word). ① and ② have almost the same meaning: someone cannot afford doing anything else because he is fully occupied. いっぱいいっぱい is a reduplication of いっぱい 'full'. あっぷあっぷ is a phenomime and is used not only by young people but also by people in general in Japan. It describes someone floundering in water and almost drowning. のりのり ③ comes from 乗り気 *noriki* 'enthusiasm, interest', implying that someone is very enthusiastic about doing something or is in a good condition to do something. のり is derived from clipping, and the clipped word is reduplicated. ラブラブ ④ comes from the English word *love* and is reduplicated, referring to couples who are in love.

(74)

①いっぱいいっぱい *ippai-ippai* 'fully occupied'
②あっぷあっぷ *appu-appu* 'fully occupied'
③のりのり *nori-nori* 'be in a good condition'
④ラブラブ *rabu-rabu* 'to be in love'

4.5.4 Meaning extension

Words can be assigned a new meaning based on their original meaning. おいしい *oishī* ① originally means 'delicious', but it is **extended** to mean 'advantageous' or 'lucky' by young people. For example, おいしいアルバイト *oishī arubaito* means a part-time job that pays you more money than your workload might justify. This meaning reminds us of an extended meaning of the synonym うまい 'delicious' in modern Japanese that has a positive meaning as 'good, skilled' (e.g., うまい考え *umai kangae* 'good idea', スキーがうまい *sukī ga umai* 'to be good at skiing').

アツい *atsui* ② originally refers to something hot due to high temperature (see also Chapter 6, section 6.2 in JL), but its meaning extends to mean what is currently in fashion. Young people say あの曲アツいな *Ano kyoku atsui na* to mean that 'That song is popular'.

イタい *itai* ③ is originally an adjective meaning 'painful'. For instance, we say お腹がいたい *Onaka ga itai* 'I have a stomachache.' This physical pain can be extended to the mental sphere, as in 離婚の話はいたい *Rikon no hanashi wa itai* 'It is painful to talk about divorce.' In young people's speech, イタい can refer to someone whose presence does not match the given atmosphere because he is not suited to attend the place or event. They would thus say あの人イタいね *ano hito itai ne* to mean that the person is at an inappropriate place.

(75)
> ①おいしい *oishī*
> ②アツい *atsui*
> ③イタい *itai*

4.5.5 Indirectness

Some words reduce the directness of an expression when they are reformulated. As shown in (76) below, directness is reduced by inserting characters (① and ④) or phrases (② and ③). This new use of words is not normally found in standard Japanese grammar. A conventional expression is provided in parentheses for each expression.

From ① to ③, the speaker tries to avoid expressing things directly since this would have a negative connotation. Consider ①. In Japanese society, it is not considered favourable that a woman should not be good at doing household chores. In standard Japanese grammar, 人 *hito* 'person' is used to describe a second or third person (あなた・彼は冷たい人だ *anata/kare wa tsumetai hito da* 'You are/He is a cold **person**.'). By using 人 to the first person (i.e., the speaker), which is unusual in standard Japanese, the person's lack of skill is backgrounded. At the same time, she succeeds in distancing herself from the statement.

Likewise, X じゃないですか 'isn't it X?' contains a contracted form じゃ derived from では, while ない is a negative adjective referring to the absence of something. This expression is normally used when the speaker describes a third person (e.g., his acquaintance) and seeks agreement or consent from the addressee (あの人は吾妻さんでは・じゃないですか *Ano hito wa Azuma-san dewa/ja naidesuka* 'Isn't that person Mr Azuma?'). This is a strategy for conducting a conversation smoothly instead of speaking bluntly. When the speaker uses it to describe himself, he softens the statement about himself.

入ってる *haitteru* is a shortened form of 入っている *haitte iru*, indicating that something is inside a place. ビールが冷蔵庫に入ってる *Bīru ga reizōko ni haitteru* tells us that there is beer in the refrigerator. おやじ入ってる *Oyaji haitteru* does not mean that おやじ 'an old or middle-aged man' (not 'father' [see Table 4.4 in section 4.2.1]) is located inside something; instead it is used when someone looks or behaves like an old man. This reminds us of a metaphoric extension in that おやじ does not refer literally to an old man, but instead represents people who have the traits that characterize an old man (see Chapter 2, section 2.5.1 for the notion of 'metaphor'). ロリ *rori* is a clipped word from ロリータ *Rorīta*, which refers to the Lolita complex. ロリ入ってる *rori haitteru* refers to girls who look like Lolita; that is, they have a young face and teenager's clothes that may attract middle-aged men affected by the Lolita complex. Note that the verbal expression 入ってる can be treated as an example of simile (see Chapter 2, section 2.5.2) to the extent that it expresses similarity between two entities. ジャニーズ系 can also be treated as an example of indirectness.

(76)

①~人

私って家事できない**人**だから *Watashitte kaji dekinai **hito** dakara*

(私は家事ができないから) 'As I can't do household chores.'

②~じゃないですか

私ってコーヒー好き**じゃないですか**

*Watashitte kōhī suki**janaidesuka***

(私はコーヒーが好きじゃないです) 'I don't like coffee.'

③~入ってる

おやじ**入ってる** *Oyaji **haitteru***

(おやじのようだ) 'X looks like an old man.'

ロリ**入ってる** *Rori **haitteru***

(ロリータのようだ) 'X looks like a Lolita.'

④~系 (see (73) ①)

ジャニーズ**系** *Janīzuke*

(ジャニーズのような) 'X looks like a member of ジャニーズ.'

4.5.6 New grammar

Young people also use grammatical elements of standard Japanese in different ways. The conventional usage of the grammatical expression is provided in parentheses, while the new usage is highlighted in boldface. The four expressions mentioned here are related to the typical activities of waitresses or waiters in service sectors such as restaurants or coffee shops in Japan, such as taking an order or receiving money from customers for their meal. In ① to ④, particles (から, で, に) are used in a peculiar way. ④ also contains the past tense; this usage is not found in standard Japanese.

①　**から**お預かりします。(Øお預かりいたします)
1000 円**から**お預かりします。
*Sen-en **kara** oazukari shimasu*
I have received ¥1000.

②　**で**いいです。(がいいです)
コーヒー**で**いいです。
*Kōhī **de** īdesu*
I would like to have a cup of coffee.

③　**に**なります。(でございます)
から揚げ**に**なります。
*Karāge **ni** narimasu*
Here is a fried chicken.

④　**から**で**よかった**でしょうか。(Øでよろしいでしょうか)
五千円**から**で**よかった**でしょうか。
*Gosen-en **karade yokatta** deshō ka*
All right, I have received ¥5000 from you.

Activity 4

Manga often exhibit the language of young people. Two drawings below describe everyday life in a high school. In Text 4.17, 茜 *Akane* and 山田素直 *Yamada Sunao* are to go to the schoolmaster's office because of their low grades. In Text 4.18, 茜's classmate 仁子 *Jinko* is talking to 茜 in a casual manner. Can you identify examples of young people's language? If you find some, explain which linguistic processes are at work.

Commentary

There are two instances of young people's language in these texts: バックレる *bakkureru* and マジ *maji*. Both words are created by deleting a part of the original word, that is, they are examples of clipping (see 4.5.1). バックレる, derived from しらばくれる *shirabakureru*, demonstrates a sound alteration in which /k/ is geminated (see Chapter 2, section 2.1, p. 16 in JL). The original word しらばくれる means that someone pretends not

Text 4.17

© 2003 Isshiki, Makoto / *Denaoshitoide!* (p. 138), Kodansha

Text 4.18

© 2003 Isshiki, Makoto / *Denaoshitoide!* (p. 140), Kodansha

to know something, while バックレる implies that someone intentionally escapes from his or her duty. The new meaning is related to the original in the sense that one ignores something. As shown in Text 4.17, バックレる is applied to a school context in which 茜 *Akane* and 素直 *Sunao* fail to perform their duty as students (i.e., they do not attend classes).

マジ comes from まじめ *majime*, which has three meanings: (i) 'serious', (ii) 'earnest' and (iii) 'honest'. Here マジ is related to the first and second meanings. マジに恋をする, as seen in Text 4.18, means that X loves Y seriously/earnestly. This word can also be used emphatically. For example, マジに疲れた 'really tired' does not refer to one's seriousness, but instead emphasizes that someone is tired. This intensifying function is absent from Text 4.18.

These two instances show that newly coined words do not normally maintain their original meaning in a straightforward manner. One reason for this change appears to be that words are created as society changes. Meanings encoded in words are susceptible to societal changes, or, to put it differently, words are perhaps coined to a certain extent to represent these changes. Hence, newly coined words do not always remain around for long since the new culture in a society is often short-lived.

Trask (1996: 12–13) states that the causes of language change are many and various, one of which is the language user's awareness of fashion. This awareness is most noticeable among teenagers, who are particularly prone to using trendy words and disliking words that are old hat. Fashion is certainly an important element in language change, but it is by no means the only one. What else, then, can trigger changes in language? Consider that, when language is spoken, it is easier for a speaker to embed his emotions. For example, the gemination of /k/ in バックれる might also signal the speaker's emphatic emotions, as we also mentioned with respect to にっぽん *nippon* and にほん *nihon* (see Text 2.7, Chapter 2, p. 39 in JL). Thus, emotions can be a crucial element leading to language change. Gender differences may also contribute to language change.

An important final point is that new words cannot arise without the grammar of Japanese. Neither バックれる nor マジ can be accepted if they do not fit with the moraic structure of Japanese. It goes without saying that culture influences the patterns of language use, though it is certainly not the only resource that influences language.

Notes

1   If 良雄 *Yoshio* gets furious about 愛子 *Aiko*, he may use あんた *anta* 'you' to her. The use of あんた here means that not only gender or formality but also the interaction between the participants plays a role in choosing the appropriate language form.
2   In the original text, 良雄 *yoshio* was conversing with 耕一 *kōichi* and 幸子 *sachiko* in a living room. 愛子 *aiko* comes to the place and joins the conversation. At this moment, she addresses Yoshio by his given name.
3   Words with お are often called 美化語 *bikago* 'language of beautification'. These words are typically used to signal the speaker's refined and elegant manner of language use (see Tsujimura et al. 1971: 400–403).
4   As a recent study (e.g., Okamoto and Shibamoto Smith 2004) has revealed, there is no direct correspondence between being a woman (biologically) and use of women's language. It is apparent that women's speech or men's speech as employed in Japanese discourse

is composed of socio-cultural, ideological or contextual factors in addition to linguistic. See also note 1.

5   The salesperson can also address your father by his family name. In a normal situation, his family name should be given priority, but お父さん can be preferred when he functions as the father in a conversation.

6   Two expressions, お嬢様 *ojōsama* and お嬢さん *ojōsan*, have a special connotation apart from their use as an address term. They both refer to women, particularly young women, who are brought up in wealthy families and who behave in a manner that shows they are spoiled and inexperienced with the outside world. The first variant is more frequently used for this meaning.

7   こいつ is derived from 此奴 *koyatsu*, meaning 'this person'. It can be used negatively when the speaker expresses hatred or contempt, or positively when the speaker expresses intimacy. It has the related forms そいつ *soitsu* and あいつ *aitsu* (see Table 2.1 in Chapter 2).

8   Honorifics constitute the major part of what is generally called 待遇表現 *taigū-hyōgen* 'expression of levels of socialization'. This use of language pays special attention to the social status of the interlocutors and their interpersonal relationships.

9   The reason the passive form is used for honorifics might be due to the fact that the passive form in Japanese has the meaning of spontaneity or 自発 *jihatsu* (see Chapter 7, section 7.3.1 in JL). Ōno (1966: 74–77) claims that Japanese people show respect to 'something that is autonomous and hence occurs independently'. In ancient Japan, nature was venerated and at a later period God or Emperor received great respect (see also Kikuchi 1994: 120–122).

10 Not all verbs accept the お-verb-する form. For example, お食べする *otabesuru* or お飲みする *onomisuru* sounds odd and お行きする *oyukisuru* or お言いする *oīsuru* are unacceptable (see also Ishiguro 2005: 109).

11 One striking example might be the use of から *kara* (see section 4.5.6.) when a shop assistant receives money for payment from the customer. During her visit to Japan in March 2007, the author noticed that から as a signal of reception was frequently used in various shops and restaurants.

5 Radio talk

In the previous chapters, we have been dealing with written language. This chapter investigates spoken language. Recall that in Chapter 7 of JL (see Activity 4), we discussed how spoken language differs from written language using drama scripts. The language we examine here is also categorized as 'spoken' but it differs significantly from the spoken language we examined previously in that this chapter deals with **naturally occurring conversation**. This refers to speakers' creating conversations in real time. Conversations in drama scripts do not occur naturally but are created by a dramatist; the speakers in a drama are the creatures of the writer. One important characteristic of naturally occurring conversations is that they are, more often than not, accompanied by verbal or non-verbal elements that are otherwise semantically empty in isolation (e.g., backchannels, hedges, laughs). These elements become meaningful when the speakers employ them as devices to communicate with each other. Seen this way, spoken interaction does not merely present information[1] but also demonstrates **social relations** between speaker and listener. By 'social' we mean the varying degrees of interpersonal relationships between people who constitute a society. For example, if someone asks his or her interlocutor a question, a social relationship that may arise is the speaker's expectation of the listener's response. Drama scripts need not be concerned with this aspect of social relationships precisely because they do not presuppose authentic participants.

In this chapter, we focus on **radio talk**, one genre of conversation. Radio talk refers to 'talk on the radio', or to adopt Hutchby's words (1991: 135), 'all forms of talk encounterable on radio, from DJ talk through interview to phone-in talk'. According to Halliday (1985: 46), a paradigm form of spoken language is natural spontaneous conversation. Radio talk is not always spontaneous as broadcasters sometimes design it, but talk represents, by definition, a use of spoken language (see Hutchby 2006: 3), as it is delivered on the spot, and hence, is a genuine instance of natural conversation.

The term **talk** is often used interchangeably with the term **conversation**. *The Cambridge Advanced Learner's Dictionary* (2005: 272) defines conversation as follows:

A talk between two or more people in which thoughts, feelings and ideas are expressed, questions are asked and answered, or news and information are exchanged.

Oxford Dictionary of English provides a similar definition (2005: 378):

A talk, especially an informal one, between two or more people, in which news and ideas are exchanged.

According to these definitions, conversation is a general term for spoken interaction carried out by people who have common interest. In this chapter, the terms are also used interchangeably, but talk is considered one subset of conversation and used especially when interaction has a 'single focus' (to adopt a now classic remark by Bales et al. (1951, cited in Schegloff 1972 [1968]: 376). For example, we refer to 'in-studio talk', 'talk show', 'mundane talk', 'phatic talk', 'hedged talk' and so on (see also Bloomer et al. 2005: 40; Goffman 1981: 14).

The chapter draws on what we call **in-studio talk** broadcast by the International Channel in Singapore. This radio channel is responsible for a two-hour Japanese programme broadcast on Monday to Friday from 7a.m. to 9a.m. The author collected the data used in this Chapter by tape-recording the talks and then carefully transcribing them. In-studio talks refer to radio talks conducted in a studio (hence, the name) and broadcast live. In a talk programme entitled 'Welcome to the Studio' (ウェルカム ツゥ スツゥディオ in Japanese[2]), a male broadcaster speaks with a guest in a casual manner for about 15 minutes. His major role is to interrogate the guest about his or her profession and personal interests. Topics include the guest's past experiences, career, achievements, hobbies and likes/dislikes. The age of the participants is not made public.[3]

This chapter will give you an overview of Japanese spoken interaction, based on the data at hand. We draw on two recordings, which we call Talk I (3 April, 2006) and Talk II (17 April, 2006), respectively. Sections 5.1 to 5.4 focus on Talk I only. While introducing basic notions essential to understanding talk in interactions in general, the discussion revolves around the following three questions: (i) how talk begins and ends (5.1 and 5.2), (ii) how participants sustain the talk (5.3), and (iii) what strategies participants use while talking (5.4). Section 5.5 includes two activities that are based on extracts from Talk II. Section 5.6 presents the whole text of Talk I, which adopts the standard transcript notations (e.g., see Atkinson and Heritage 1984: ix–xvi; Bloomer et al. 2005: 43–48; Sack et al. 1974: 731–733).

5.1 Opening a talk

At the beginning of an in-studio talk, the host (H) initiates the talk with the stereotypical expression, 'ウェルカム ツゥ

スツゥディオの時間がやってまいりました 'Welcome to the programme "Welcome to the Studio", (literally: 'The time for "Welcome to the Studio" has arrived'). The general procedure in such a programme is that H first introduces a guest (G) by identifying his or her name and profession followed by more specific topics in the course of a talk. In Text 5.1, the beginning of the programme, H welcomes a female guest to the studio who will soon start working for the radio programme to which she is now invited as a guest.

A talk comes into existence when two people begin with a verbal exchange. The basic rule for a talk is that one person speaks at a time; it rarely happens that two people speak at the same time. While one person talks, the other listens as there is an interest in an ongoing verbal interaction. Units of talk are called **turns**. A turn refers to the part during which one speaker talks before the next speaker takes a turn. Turns are exchanged between speakers; no single speaker dominates the talk from the beginning to the end. This cooperative joint work is called **turn-taking**; speakers take turns in conversation to hold the floor. Consider Text 5.1. H's turn occupies the first three lines, and in line 3, H greets G by saying おはようございます *ohayōgozaimasu* 'Good morning'. G's first turn in line 4 begins at the point at which H has finished his turn. G attends to H by greeting him back.[4]

Text 5.1

1 H:	ウェルカム ツゥ スツゥディオの時間がやってまいりました	
2	今朝は桜木桃子さんにスタジオに来ていただいております	
3	→ おはようございます	
4 G:	→ おはようございます::	
5 H:	リスナーの方 桜木桃子さんといわれても (.) よう分かんない	
6	と思うんですが ちょっともうちょっと (1.0) しゃべっていただけ	
7	ますか	
8 G:	→ そうですね だれだおまえはですよね	
9	ええとあのう 実は (1.0) え 4月から毎週月曜日のモーニングナビゲー	
10	ションの担当をさせていただくことになりました	
11	えっと 声の仕事は (1.0) ええ:: 五年前からやっているんです	
12	けれども =	

© 2006 3 April FM96.3

Translation:
1 H: Welcome to the programme 'Welcome to Studio'.
2   This morning we have Ms Momoko Sakuraki as our guest in the studio.
3   Good morning.
4 G: Good morning.
5 H: Our listeners may perhaps not recognize who Momoko Sakuraki
6   is
7   Would you mind introducing yourself briefly?
8 G: Sure. I agree they may ask who I am.
9   Well, I will be in charge of 'Morning Navigation' every
10   morning from April.
11–12 Well, I have been engaged in 'voice work' for five years.

H's utterance (line 3) and G's responding turn (line 4) construct a paired utterance, or more technically, an **adjacency pair**, consisting of the first pair part (the first speaker's utterance) and the second pair part (the second speaker's utterance). In lines 6 and 7, H asks G to introduce herself, and G does so accordingly in lines 9–12, informing the listener of her responsibility for a programme called 'Morning Navigation'. As shown here, adjacency pairs are not always immediately linked; G inserts an utterance (line 8) into the pair, expressing her compliance with the self-introduction and adding a brief comment on it. This type of utterance that intervenes is called **insertion** (referring to one utterance) or **insertion sequence** (referring to more than one utterance) (Pridham 2001: 28). Since the topic of such an insertion is related to that of the main sequence in which it occurs, the question asked is normally answered after the insertion. Observe that G answers H's main question from line 9 after her insertion in line 8.

Table 5.1 (p. 173) is a list of possible adjacency pairs based on Bloomer et al. (2005: 58). Some partly shortened examples are taken from Talk II.

5.2   Closing a talk

Towards the end of a talk, the host (H) returns to the profession of the guest (G), praising, in one way or another, the contributions she has made and will make in the future. In Text 5.2 (p. 174), H politely articulates his best wishes to G three times (lines 427, 432, 434). The replies from G are very general; the way she responds is customary and polite (lines 428 and 433). The use of polite expressions may help the participants 'settle the affairs' (Stenström 1994: 11) smoothly. We can say that H and G are

Table 5.1 List of possible adjacency pairs

	First pair part	Second pair part
1	Greeting おはようございます *ohayōgozaimasu* 'Good morning'	Greeting おはようございます *ohayōgozaimasu* 'Good morning'
2	Question 奥さんは仕事お持ちですか *okusan wa shigoto omochi desuka* 'Does your wife have a job?'	Answer いいえ *īe* 'No'
3	Apology 申し訳ございません *mōshiwake gozaimasen* 'I apologize'	Acceptance 気になさらないでください *kini nasaranaide kudasai* 'Don't mention it'
4	Compliment すばらしい作品ですね *subarashī sakuhin desu ne* 'That's a wonderful masterpiece'	Thanks ありがとうございます *arigatō gozaimasu* 'Thank you'
5	Opinion めずらしいお名前ですね *mezurashī onamae desu ne* 'Your name is unique, isn't it?'	Agreement そのとおりです *sono tōri desu* 'That's right'
6	Accusation あなたが悪い *anata ga warui* 'It is you who is wrong'	Denial いいえ、私のせいじゃない *īe watashi no sē janai* 'No, it's not my fault'
7	Offer お手伝いしましょうか *otetsudai shimashō ka* 'Shall I give you a hand?'	Acceptance ありがとうございます *arigatō gozaimasu* 'Thank you'
8	Request 曲をご紹介してください *kyoku o goshōkai shite kudasai* 'Can you introduce the song?'	Acceptance はい *hai* 'Yes, certainly'
9	Thanks 今朝はお忙しいところありがとうございました *kesa wa oisogashī tokoro arigatō gozaimashita* 'Thank you for coming despite your busy schedule'	Thanks ありがとうございました *arigatō gozaimashita* 'Thank you very much'

both engaged in so-called **phatic communion**, to adopt Malinowski's notion (1972 [1923]). Topics handled in this part of the talk are peripheral to the core part of the talk, but the purpose of this communion seems to create a pleasant atmosphere in which to close the talk in a friendly and successful manner. These non-transactional and ceremonial exchanges are

173

extremely salient at the end of a radio talk, particularly when the host has invited a guest onto the programme.

Text 5.2

423 H:	え 桜木桃子を<u>サポート</u>していただけるかと思います	
424 G:	よろしくお願いいたします	
425 H:	じゃまずはえ: 振れ触れ桜木桃子	
426 G:	はい	
427 H: →	来週からがんばってください	
428 G: →	ありがとうございます　ど [うぞよろしく	
429 H:	[今朝はお忙しいというかあ (laugh)	
430	ええ　大変な時でございますけれども	
431 G:	はい (laugh)	
432 H: →	来週楽しみにしてます　今朝はありがとうございました	
433 G: →	どうもありがとうございました　よろしくお願いいたします	
434 H: →	これからがんばってください	
435 G:	はい	

© 2006 3 April FM96.3

Translation:
423 H: They will be supporting Momoko Sakuraki.
424 G: I hope they will. (literally: 'Please send my regards to them')
425 H: First of all, hurray, hurray, Momoko Sakuraki!
426 G: Yes. (meaning 'Thank you')
427 H: I wish you all the best from next week on.
428 G: Thank you for your encouragement.
429–30 H: You may now have a busy or hard time.
431 G: Yes (laugh)
432 H: Look forward to the next week. Thank you for coming this morning.
433 G: Thank you for inviting me. I send my regards to my future listeners.
434 H: I wish you success. (literally: Please make further efforts)
435 G: Thank you. (literally: Yes, I will).

5.3 Maintaining a talk

A talk continues to be maintained after its opening and before its reaching a closing point. In a radio talk, an **exchange** between the host (H) and the guest (G) plays an important role in sustaining a talk. A normal procedure in an in-studio talk is that H initiates an exchange by making a statement, asking a question or putting forward a request, and these acts are responded to, answered and accepted by G. It is rare for G to initiate a talk. Stenström (1994: 88) provides the following diagram that neatly illustrates the basic relationships between the initiator and the respondent. Each row in the left white column corresponds horizontally to a row in the right white column. For example, when H makes a statement, it is expected to be replied to by G. Likewise, when a question is asked or a request is made, it is expected to be answered by G.

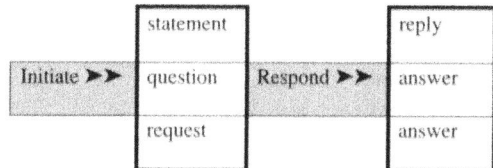

Diagram 5.1 *Basic schema for exchange*

5.3.1 Statement and reply

The most frequently used strategy by H in Talk I is to make a statement. Table 5.2 gives an overview of the tokens of statement–reply. H makes a statement 22 times in total, and G replies to it in three different ways, by acknowledging, commenting on or disagreeing with what H has said.[5]

Table 5.2 *Tokens of statement–reply*

| Initiation | Response | | | Total |
| | Reply | | | |
	Acknowledge	Comment	Disagree	
Statement	17	3	2	22

Acknowledgement indicates that G accepts what H has said as valid information. Text 5.3 takes place at the beginning of a talk when H introduces G's profession, pointing out that G is currently in charge of an on-board programme for Singapore Airlines. H's utterance is interrupted by G's exclamation (line 18). G's acknowledgement appears in line 21 where G accepts H's statement formulated in lines 17 and 19.

Text 5.3

17 H:	(***) ね シンガポールエアラインズの	
18 G:	あららららら	
19 H:	[機内で::え::番組をお持ちということなんですね	
20 G:	[(laugh)	
21 G: →	はい	

© 2006 3 April FM96.3

Translation:
17 H: Singapore Airlines.
18 G: Oh, my! (expressing surprise)
19 H: On board, er, you're in charge of a programme, aren't you?
20 G: (laugh)
21 G: Yes.

Comment indicates that the respondent not only accepts the initiator's utterance, but also comments on it by saying that what was just said is 'good', 'bad' or 'pitiful', etc. Text 5.4 shows that G (lines 186 and 188) admires H's assumption that many listeners may request the song (that G has just requested), implying that they may also like G's voice as a moderator.

Text 5.4

184 H:	これじゃやるとするとリスナーの方から::どんどんどん (laugh)
185	リクエストをかかってくるかもしれないですね
186 G:→	ねえ:
187 H:	ねえ
188 G:→	ねえ:そうなったらいいですね::=

© 2006 3 April FM96.3

Translation:
184–5 H: If we do this, then many listeners may constantly request this song.
186 G: I hope so.
187 H: I hope so, too.
188 G: Yes, I wish they would do that. (literally: it would be good if it becomes so)

Disagreement indicates that the respondent does not accept what the initiator has said. In Text 5.5, H suspects (or perhaps teases her by saying) that G should receive training in how to drink alcohol because aeroplane crews might have many unemptied wine bottles when their routine flight is over. In line 158, G objects to his assumption. As Table 5.2 shows, disagreement occurs only twice in the entire programme (see G's utterance in lines 151 and 153 in Text 5.25 below).

Text 5.5

157 H: 　ね そ こで鍛えられたのかなと思いました
158 G: → そんな<u>不良みたい</u>なことしませんよ (laugh)

© 2006 3 April FM96.3

Translation:
157 H: I thought you may have been trained there.
158 G: I will not do such a misdeed. (laugh)

5.3.2 Question and answer

Questions are asked to seek new information and the majority of questions are directed from the host (H). Questions are formed by attaching an interrogative marker か *ka* at the end of a sentence. As shown in Table 5.3, the way G presents her answer is characterized in two ways: direct and indirect. A **direct answer** indicates that G answers immediately after H's question (that is, G's turn begins at the point at which H's turn ends), while an **indirect answer** indicates that G's answer is somewhat circumlocutory; that is, it is articulated later in her utterance. Examples of a direct answer are given in Texts 5.6 to 5.10, while Text 5.11 is an example of an indirect answer. Table 5.4 shows how direct and indirect questions are subcategorized into three functions.

Table 5.3 *Tokens of question–answer*

Initiation	Response		Total
	Answer		
	Direct	Indirect	
Question	17	3	20

Table 5.4 *Types of answers*

	Answer		Total
	Direct	Indirect	
Proper	13	1	14
Supplementary	4	0	4
Implicit	0	2	2

Proper means that the answer is exactly what is asked for. Text 5.6 illustrates a case in point. H receives a short and exact answer from G.

Text 5.6

22 H:	あれも二時間 (1.0) 一時間番組ですか
23 G: →	二時間[です

© 2006 3 April FM96.3

Translation:
22 H: Is that a two-hour or one-hour programme?
23 G: A two-hour programme.

Proper answers tend to occur more frequently when questions are formed with a WH-word (WH refers to the first two letters of interrogative words such as 'what' or 'why' in English). Text 5.7 contains どういう *dōyū* 'what kind of'. Text 5.8 contains 何が *naniga* 'what', while Text 5.9 contains 何で *nande* 'why'. WH-words in Japanese do not always begin with 何 (reads as 'nani' or 'nan').

Text 5.7

35 H:	前はどういうお仕事をされていたんですか
36 G: →	前はですね 実は あのう 空飛ぶお姉さんでございました

© 2006 3 April FM96.3

Translation:
35 H: What kind of job did you have previously?
36 G: Previously, in fact, er, I was a flying woman (meaning 'stewardess').

Text 5.8

174 H:	桜木桃子さんのリクエスト曲 (.) 何がよろしいですか
175 G: →	山下達郎さんの君の声に恋してる

© 2006 3 April FM96.3

Translation:
174 H: What song would you like to request, Ms Sakuraki?
175 G: 'I'm in love with your voice' by Tatsurō Yamashita.

Text 5.9

176 H:	これはまた何で
177 G: →	これは(1.0) まあこれからまあリスナーの方にこういう風に (.)
178	思っていただけたらなという (laugh)(*h)
179 H:	なるほど
180 G:	はい 希望が[こもっています

© 2006 3 April FM96.3

Translation:
176 H: Why is that? (meaning 'why did you choose this song')
177–8 G: That's, well, because I would like my future listeners to consider me this way.
179 H: Oh, I see.
180 G: Yes, that articulates my hope.

A **supplementary** answer provides more information than what was asked for in the question. Text 5.10 illustrates that H asks a polarity question (asking for 'Yes' or 'No'). G refers to the fact that what she actually did was to fail to change her shoes. From this exchange, it is clear that G does not answer H's question with 'Yes' or 'No' but modifies it in a way that adds supplementary information. In Chapter 2, section 2.4, we dealt with conventional implicature. The way G responds to H can be considered conventional in the sense that we conventionally know that this exchange has a primary force to provide the accurate information about 'what' exactly she has forgotten rather than saying 'Yes' or 'No'.

Text 5.10

243 H:	＝靴忘れてるんですか
244 G: →	履き替えるのを忘れちゃったんです

© 2006 3 April FM96.3

Translation:
243 H: Did you forget your shoes?
244 G: I forgot to change my shoes.

An **implicit** answer indicates that the answer given by the respondent does not touch on the core of the question, but only implies something related to it. The more indirect the answer is, the more implicit it appears to become. Text 5.11 shows that G does not answer H's question directly; she reconfirms the question (line 194) and, after H's positive reply (line 195), only implies (line 196) that she has made mistakes by saying that it will become the next day if she explains the whole story (meaning that she has made so many mistakes that the story will need a day to be told). This exchange can also be understood metonymically in that what G says in line 196 only expresses part of what G means by her utterance. Because of the given conversational context, we are able to draw the right inference about the unstated utterance (see Chapter 2, section 2.5.4 for a description of the notion 'metonymy').[6]

Text 5.11

193 H:	何か失敗談ちょんぼは
194 G:	ちょんぼですか
195 H:	ええ
196 G: →	は ええ もう明日になってしまいます:: (laugh)

© 2006 3 April FM96.3

Translation:
193 H: Have you made some mistakes?
194 G: Mistakes?
195 H: Yes.
196 G: Yes, certainly. Have we got until tomorrow? (laugh).

A slightly different type of question is when the speaker asks for the information about which s/he has only some imprecise knowledge. This is found in Text 5.12 where H's question contains an ambiguous word いろんな *iron-na* 'various'. G perceives the lack of the core information in H's utterance (line 62) and provides the right word in her turn (line 63). Because G's answer is exactly what he needed, H's repetition, attached by an interactional particle ね, marks his agreement/confirmation (see Chapter 4, section 4.1.3 for a description of the notion 'interactional particle').

Text 5.12

62 H:　　いろんな::放送するんじゃないんですか
63 G: → 機内アナン [ス
64 H:　　　　　　[機内アナンス [ね

© 2006 3 April FM96.3

Translation:
62 H: You make such and such announcements, don't you?
63 G: Board announcement.
64 H: Yes, board announcement.

Questions are not always formed by adding the particle か. As shown in Text 5.13, repeating the other party's utterance (信じられないこと *shinjirarenaikoto* 'what one cannot believe') and adding というますと *toīmasuto* (the polite form of the quotative というます *toīmasu* plus particle と *to*) to it makes a question (see ⑧ in Text 3. 24, Chapter 3, where you can find the neutral form of the quotative という *toyū*). By taking the form of 'reporting', this expression functions as a question, and this way of asking a question sounds more polite. Because G is a guest (and H will be her boss from the following week), it sounds like G is attending to H diplomatically.

Text 5.13

365 H: ええ信じられないこと
366 G: → 信じられないことというますと
367 H: つい最近は (2.0) くまの (1.0) たん汁を飲むんですよ

© 2006 3 April FM96.3

Translation:
365 H: What one cannot believe
366 G: What is it that one cannot believe?
367 H: These days, we eat bear liver soup.

5.3.3 Request and answer

H makes a request using てください *tekudasai*-form (see Chapter 1, section 1.3.5 for a description of the notion 'request') three times. Three other expressions (いただけますか *itadakemasuka* (lines 6-7); いただきたいと思います *itadakitai to omoimasu* (line 101); V-願いたいんですが *negaitaindesuga* (lines 402-3)) are included as a request. As indicated in Table 5.5, G's responses are all compliances. Evading or rejecting a request occurs neither in Talk I nor in Talk II. This may be precisely due to the nature of radio talk, which aims to create a pleasant, and not argumentative, atmosphere for both participants and listeners. G demonstrates her compliance by saying はい *hai* 'OK' (Text 5.14), そうですねえ *sōdesunē* 'Let me think' (Text 5.15).

Table 5.5 *Tokens of requests–answers*

	Responses			
	Answer			Total
Initiation	Comply	Evade	Reject	
Request	6	0	0	6

Text 5.14

191 H: それじゃ曲を (.) ご紹介してください
192 G: → はい　山下達郎で君の声に恋してる

© 2006 3 April FM96.3

Translation:
191 H: OK, can you introduce the song?
192 G: Yes, sure. 'I'm in love with your voice' by Tatsurō Yamashita.

Text 5.15

402–3 H:	<u>ぜひお聞かせ願いたいんですが</u>
404 G:→	<u>そうですねえ</u> (1.0) あのう 今日 (.) はかなり (1.0) くだけました
405	けれども (.) わりと A 括弧 C なんです 実は
406 H:	うん
407 G:	<u>ですから</u> (.) あんまり オブラードにくるまずに
408 H:	はい
409 G:	素の (.) 桜木桃子が出せたらいいなと思っております
410 H:	ん
411 G:	一方通行でなくてね

© 2006 3 April FM96.3

Translation:
402–3 H: I'm eager to hear.
404–5 G: Let me think, well, I was quite informal today but I'm often an 'A equals C' type. (meaning formal/inflexible)
406 H: Yes.
407 G: Therefore, without wrapping myself in a wafer.
408 H: Yes.
409 G: I wish to disclose the way Momoko Sakuraki exactly is.
410 H: Yes.
411 G: Not like a one-way street.

5.4 Conversational strategies

This section deals with strategies people use when they talk. These strategies occur in any part of a talk. Generally speaking, strategies refer to plans that help people achieve success. In a conversational context, participants employ strategies to make the talk more purposeful. In other words, they do not exchange the utterances mechanically but frequently embed 'small words', lexical or non-lexical, in an utterance. Let us call the act of embedding these words **conversational strategies** through which we get the message across effectively. Note that the users of these strategies may not always be conscious of them, however. We say 'Ouch!' when a stranger steps on our foot in a crowded commuter train. We may also say 'What a stench!' when we suddenly smell something unpleasant while walking along a street. These reactions are automatic – not resulting from the speaker's planned scenario; they occur in response to the 'context of the situation' (see also Chapter 1, section 1.3), or to put it simply, the circumstances of a situation under which something is said.[7] The fact that we say 'Ouch!' is not dependent on what we thought about doing or intended to do but it is our natural, spontaneous reaction to the unexpected incident. Despite its spontaneity, saying 'Ouch!' as a means of expressing pain permits the affected person to 'socialize with' the other party. Embedding 'small words' (e.g., backchannels (5.4.1), hedges (5.4.2), hesitations (5.4.3)) or employing 'tools' (e.g., interruptions (5.4.4), repetitions (5.4.5), laughs (5.4.6)) in spoken utterance resembles, so to speak, the act of exclamation in the sense that all these strategies fulfil certain social functions in the context of a situation. In what follows, we take a closer look at six strategies prominent in Talk I.

5.4.1 Backchannels

Backchannels are termed あいづち *aizuchi* in Japanese.[8] This notion was first introduced by Yngve (1970) who refers to words in English such as *yes* or *uh-huh* as backchannels articulated by a listener. These little words serve as short messages that the listener sends to the speaker. Since conversation is a social interaction, as Yngne also argues (ibid.: 568), merely taking a turn cannot be a sufficient social activity unless the listener pays attention to the speaker and sends a message, if appropriate, as a signal of attentiveness. By doing this, the listener gives 'speaker support' to the speaker (Pridham 2001: 18). These supporting words do not carry their own meaning but become meaningful when used as backchannels. Consider Text 5.16 in which the guest (G) describes an event. While she talks, the host (H) frequently sends backchannels. Clearly differentiating all the backchannels used here is by no means an easy task, but let me give you some hints: a group of words such as う *u* (line 213), うん *un* (line 215), え *e* (line 221) seem to function as an attentive marker, typically showing the listener's interest in the episode told, while another group of words such as そうです *sōdesu* (line 223) and ええ *ē* (line 226) function not only as attentive markers but also signal the listener's agreement with what the speaker has explained.[9] Representative words used for backchannels in Talk I are listed in Tables 5.6 and 5.7, giving a bird's eye view of what kind of backchannels are at work in Japanese radio talks. Table 5.6 compiles non-lexical words (they do not have their own meaning), while Table 5.7 compiles lexical words (they have their own meaning). Refer to Text 5.25, the whole text of Talk I, for examples mentioned in these tables.

Backchannels occur at the boundary of a meaningful unit, be it a word, phrase or sentence. In Text 5.16, G tells a story about her making mistakes in a chronological order between lines 208 and 238 (H interferes with G's story-telling from lines 220 to 227). Backchannels are inserted at the point at which G has reported an event or a self-contained happening. For example, the connective て is attached to four verbs in lines 232 to 236 and backchannels appear three times (lines 233, 235 and 237). The next text, Text 5.17, exemplifies a case in which the occurrence of backchannels does not depend on the occurrence of events but they occur at the point of meaningful constituents of a sentence.

Text 5.16

199 G:		ええとですね　仕事::ええと学生上がりで一番初め::にもう
200		あのう:: (1.0) え航空会社の
201 H:		あ::
202 G:		え
203 H:		そそそれで社会経験なく学生からそく入られた
204 G:		そうです
205 H:		うん
206 G:		なったんですが
207 H:	→	はい
208 G:		もうはじめの何回かのフライトでですね
209 H:	→	ん
210 G:		えーと制服を着て (.) タクシーに乗って (.)
211 H:	→	はい
212 G:		家からでるんですけれども
213 H:	→	う
214 G:		あのう::その頃家の中で (.) あのうシンガポールですからね
215 H:	→	うん
216 G:		ビーチサンダルを履いてたんですね
217 H:	→	ああまあ[ね
218 G:		[家の中でリ[ビング家の中でです 外ではなくて
219 H:		[はいはいはいはい

185

220 H:　まあ素肌　素足というと

221 G: → え

222 H:　大理石で寒いし

223 G: → そうです

224 H:　といってといってなんやいうてやっぱ: そういう

225　　　サンダルっぽいとか

226 G: → ええ

227 H:　スリッパ系 [シンガポール履きますよね

228 G:　　　　　　　[スリッパ

229 G:　スリッパ代わりですよね　スリッパ代わりに家では (1.0)

230　　　あのうビーチサンダルを履いてたんですけども

231 H: → え

232 G:　あのう (***) を着て

233 H: → うん

234 G:　バックを持ってお化粧ばっちりして

235 H: → うん

236 G:　タクシーに乗って

237 H: → うん

238 G:　空港に着いたらですねビーチサンダル履いてたんですねえ

239 H:　(laugh)

240 G:　(laugh)

241 H:　ああ

242 G:　もう<u>真っ青</u>になりました =

Translation:
199–200 G: Well, job, er, in an airplane flight just after my graduation.
201 H:　　　Oh
202 G　　　Yes
203 H:　　　You began the job immediately after your graduation without professional experience.

204 G:	Yes, I did.
205 H:	Yes.
206 G:	So, I became a stewardess.
207 H:	Yes.
208 G:	Already in my beginning flights.
209 H:	Um.
210 G:	Well, I put on my uniform and took a taxi.
211 H:	Yes.
212 G:	I left home.
213 H:	Um.
214 G:	Well, at that time at home, well, in Singapore.
215 H:	Um.
216 G:	I was wearing beach sandals.
217 H:	Yeah, I see, I see.
218 G:	At home, yes, at home, not outside.
219 H:	Yes, yes.
220 H:	Ok, bear skin, bear foot.
221 G:	Yes.
222 H:	It's cold because of marble stones.
223 G:	That's right.
224–5 H:	That's why we wear sandals.
226 G:	Yes.
227 H:	We wear a pair of slippers or something like that in Singapore.
228 G:	Slippers.
229–30 G:	Instead of slippers, I was wearing beach sandals instead of slippers at home.
231 H:	Yes.
232 G:	Er, I put on (***)
233 H:	Um.
234 G:	Held a bag and had perfect make-up.
235 H:	Um.
236 G:	Took a taxi.
237 H:	Um.
238 G:	Arrived at the airport and I had beach sandals.
239 H:	(laugh)
240 G:	(laugh)
241 H:	Oh.
242 G:	I turned completely pale.

Text 5.17

97 H:	それじゃ::これからの番組も
98 G: →	ええ
99 H:	そういう形でみんなねリスナーの方が癒される (.)
100 G: →	はい
101 H:	番組を作っていただきたいと思います

© 2006 3 April FM96.3

Translation:
97 H: Well, then, programmes from now on.
98 G: Yes.
99 H: In that way, all listeners will feel relieved.
100 G: Yes.
101 H: I wish you will create such a programme.

Table 5.6 *Non-lexical words used for backchannelling*

	Japanese	Line	Transcription	Meaning
①	あらららら	18	ararararara	surprise, unexpectedness
②	はい	21	hai	positive response
③	あっ	43	aʔ	surprise
④	う::ん	48	ūn	admittance
⑤	え	70	e	positive response
⑥	うん	76	un	attentiveness
⑦	ほ::	79	hoo	admiration
⑧	はいはい	90	haihai	positive response
⑨	はあはあ	92	hāhā	attentiveness
⑩	う	256	u	acknowledgement
⑪	おお	280	ō	surprise
⑫	まあ	371	mā	surprise

Table 5.7 Lexical words for backchannelling

	Japanese	Line	Transcription	Meaning
①	そうですね	8	sōdesune	agreement
②	そうですね	13	sōdesune	acknowledgement
③	そうですか	134	sōdesuka	acknowledgement
④	はいはいはいはいはい	140	haihaihaihaihai	emphatic acknowledgement
⑤	なるほどね	146	naruhodone	agreement
⑥	なるほど	179	naruhodo	agreement, admiration
⑦	まあね	217	māne	acknowledgement
⑧	そうです	223	sōdesu	agreement

5.4.2 Hedges

A **hedge** is a linguistic device by which the speaker avoids being straight to the point, being blunt or sounding authoritative to his or her interlocutor. English has different devices to soften or weaken the force with which something is said; the use of a modal verb (***could** you make a cup of tea* instead of the use of an imperative), a tag question (*make a cup of tea **would you***) or lexical items such as *perhaps, conceivably, sort of, I think, admittedly, by any chance* are considered hedges (Holmes 1995: 74–5; Pridham 2001: 92). Because of their softening/weakening functions, hedges are regarded as the means to express **politeness** – an expression of concern for others or a non-intrusive behaviour (Holmes 1995: 4–5).[10] Text 5.18 is a small collection of lexical items that serve as hedges in Talk I. All the expressions soften the speaker's utterance. Hedges are indicated in boldface and are not always translatable into English. An attentive reader may have noticed that そうですね *sōdesune* can be used as a backchannel as well as a hedge. そうですね as shown in Table 5.7 is considered a signal of attentiveness sent from the listener, while そうですね (line 74) in Text 5.18 serves to prepare for G's polite answer. Some thirty years ago, Lakoff (1975) claimed in her retrospective study that hedges are considered salient features of women's language because they express imprecision or incertitude. A large body of studies have since modified Lakoff's hypothesis one way or another (see Cameron 2000 as an example). It goes without saying that, as shown in Text 5.18, hedges are indeed employed not only by G but also by H, indicating that their occurrence is not dependent on gender but is liable to be influenced by the context of the situation. It is self-evident that, in the context of a radio talk, H is the host serving as a facilitator of a talk, while G is the guest making an effort to be a 'correct' respondent. Hedges might be used in accordance with the degree of interpersonal relationship between the host and the guest, where gender may no longer play the most important role.

189

Text 5.18

5 H: リスナーの方、桜木桃子さんと (.) いわれても (.) よう分かんない
6　　と思うんです**が**
31 H: というお名前をいただいたときに
32　　あの声で**ですね**私何回かあの:: 出張のつらさを**ですね** (1.0)
33　　癒されたことがあると思うんです**けれども**
71 H: ああいうのって**やっぱ**何か何となくその (1.0) しゃべる**というか**
74 G: (***)　そうですね (.) **やはり** (.) 自分のその時の声の調子っていう
75　　のもあります**けど**
105 H: まさしく今日でございます**けど** この後え::ソロデビューの前の
106　　プレ (.) デビュー**みたいな**形になっております　え:::

© 2006 3 April FM96.3

Translation:

5–6 H:　Our listeners may not realize who Ms Momoko Sakuraki is, but

31–3 H:　I think many of us have experienced that the tiredness of our business trip is reduced by the voice of the person with that name.

71 H:　That kind of thing is, kind of, something like a chatting.

74–5 G:　Let me think, I must say, it also depends on the condition of my own voice, but.

105–6 H:　It is exactly today, but after this, er, today is kind of a pre-debut prior to the solo-debut, er

5.4.3　Hesitations

Hesitations are sounds or a stretch of sounds that the speaker uses when starting to speak or when making a brief pause in the middle of speaking. This happens when the speaker does not find the right or adequate expressions/ideas immediately. Hesitations are produced by two means: (i) when the speaker inserts extra sounds or signals (e.g., まあ *mā*/その *sono*) into his/her speech (see Table 5.8) or (ii) when the speaker prolongs (or geminates [see Chapter 2, section 2.2.3 in JL]) the final vowel of a word (e.g., あと::: *atō*) (see Table 5.9). It is important to note that words such as ②あのう *anō*, ③ええ *ē* lexically integrate a prolonged vowel (that is, prolongation by itself is not a signal of hesitation but the occurrence of that word in speech). By contrast, words such as ⑨あと:::, ⑪ください の:: do not lexically contain a prolonged vowel word-finally (that is, prolongation is seen as a sign of hesitation).[11] Koide (1983) calls this phenomenon いいよどみ *īyodomi* in Japanese, meaning that speech does not advance because of phonetically-caused slowness. Hesitations and hedges resemble each other in their functions, but the former do not normally help the speaker perform indirectly or less authoritatively but may merely indicate the disfluency of an utterance. Note, however, if you haven't done so already, that there are cases where it is hard to make a clear demarcation between hedge and hesitation; in other words, it may happen that the speaker avoids being direct by being disfluent in speaking.[12]

Table 5.8

	Japanese	Line	Transcription
①	ええと	9	ēto
②	あのう	9	anō
③	ええ::	11	ē
④	こう	85	kō
⑤	まあ	171	mā

Table 5.9

	Japanese	Line	Transcription
⑥	出発::	26	shuppatsu::
⑦	あと:::	52	ato:::
⑧	いろんな:::	62	iron-na:::
⑨	座ってください の::	68	kudasaino::
⑩	あの::::	66	ano::::

5.4.4 Interruptions

When the listener interrupts the speaker's turn and makes his/her own turn, this act is referred to as **interruption**. When interruption happens, the previous speaker does not normally finish his/her turn completely, and there is a brief **overlap** between both speakers (lines 137 and 138 in Text 5.19). In Talk I, interruptions are initiated more frequently by the host (H), though, overall, its occurrence itself is not frequent. Similar to back-channels, they occur at the end of a meaningful unit. In the case of Text 5.19, H's interruption might be caused by the fact that the guest's (G) utterance (lines 136 and 137) is sufficient for H to ask a question related to the topic of discussion. The difference between backchannels and interruptions is that with the former, H plays a supportive role, facilitating the continuation of G's talk, whereas with the latter, H exerts power, which can change, modify or advance the direction of a talk.

Text 5.19

134 H:	そうですか (laugh) たとえばそのワイン系とかいろんな::ジャンル
135	問わず
136 G:	ジャンル問わず (.) あのう::量はそんなに飲めないんですけども基
137	本的に苦くなければ大丈夫です [にが
138 H: →	[ビールは駄目ということですか

© 2006 3 April FM96.3

Translation:
134–5 H: Oh, do you. Let's say, you like wine or any drink regardless of genre.
136–7 G: Regardless of genre, well, I can't drink too much, but anything will do if it is not bitter. Bitter.
138 H: You mean you can't drink beer.

5.4.5 Repetitions

When participants talk, they occasionally repeat the previous utterance or part of it. We call this phenomenon **repetition**. Table 5.10 demonstrates four instances. Note that repetition does not occur for its own sake but typically when particular information is focused on in an exchange. With regard to the first two cases, the speakers put a certain emphasis on the information referred to or talked about. With regard to the last two, the speakers agree on the information mentioned. In ①, G may not want to disclose the name of the company she is working for. In ③ and ④, H acknowledges the word he did not come up with previously.

Table 5.10

	Line		Previously said	Repeated	Line	
①	15	H	実はある某	某	16	G
②	282	H	一切	一切	283	G
③	63	G	機内アナンス	機内アナウンスね	64	H
④	331	G	アイマスクですか	アイマスク	332	H

5.4.6 Laughs

Laughs form an integral part of radio talk. The guest (G) in Talk I laughs frequently, though what she laughs about is not always funny. Towards the end of Text 5.16 (see above), both the host (H) and G laugh because the mistake G made was humorous (imagine a scene in which a stewardess, formally dressed and perfectly embellished with make-up, finds herself in a pair of beach sandals at an international airport). The act of laughing may nurture an exchange between speaker and addressee. In a sense, it plays a **metapragmatic** role; that is, it conveys a message beyond the use of language. When G laughs, her laugh is a reaction to her own utterance. As Sack (1992: 570–572 [Spring 1972]) points out, laughing is something people do together in talk, bonding them through emotions that they share. Laughing is thus seen as a communicative quality that serves to enhance the flow of talk. Note, however, that people laugh neither in the same way nor to the same extent. People laugh loudly about something funny, while people also laugh gently about something that is not funny. In Talk I, most of G's laughs belong to the second type and she laughs more often than H. It is striking that it typically occurs after an exchange in which G has provided new information to which H responds. Consider lines 44, 67, 96 and 129 in Text 5.25 (section 5.6). The laughs in these lines serve as a follow-up turn to the preceding adjacency pair, playing an evaluative (or metapragmatic) role. G might be using laughs to assure H that her previous utterance is true. We could say that G's use of laughs in these four cases may articulate her femininity. The role of laughs in Text 5.3, given here as Text 5.20, might be slightly different; G laughs (line 20) after her surprise (line 18) and it overlaps with H's second turn (line 19) in which he reveals she is currently in charge of an on-board programme for Singapore Airlines. The laugh here may show her hesitant acceptance of H's statement (line 17).

Text 5.20

17 H:	(***) ねシンガポールエアラインズの
18 G:	あらららら
19 H:	[機内で::え::番組をお持ちということなんですね
20 G: →	[(laugh)
21 G:	はい

© 2006 3 April FM96.3

In Text 5.21, G laughs after H has confirmed the new information (line 55) G has given (line 54). This type of laugh can be interpreted as showing G's humbleness, as the laugh precedes G's restatement (lines 56–57) where she mildly modifies the extent of her previous utterance by stating that she only visited the same places. The modification of her utterance may reduce the effect of her sounding proud or posh.

Text 5.21

52 H:	あと :::ほとんどないんじゃないんですか南米ぐらいじゃないで
53	すか
54 G:	南米中近東ですかね
55 H:	中近東
56 G: →	(laugh) いやでも (.) あのそんなに行ってないんです 外資系の会
57	社ばかりでしたので 日本人は同じような所しか飛ばないんです

© 2006 3 April FM96.3

Translation:
52–3 H: The other countries are not many but perhaps South America?
54 G: South America and the Middle East, I think.
55 H: The Middle East.
56–7 G: (laugh) No, but, well, I haven't been to many countries. I have worked for foreign companies and Japanese normally fly to similar places only.

In Text 5.22, G laughs (line 129) after she has responded to H (line 127) and H acknowledges G's answer (line 128). The second laugh (line 131) serves as G's reconfirmation. The third laugh occurs in the middle of G's utterance (line 133). In all three cases, laughing is an indicator of the respondent's positive reaction to the topic of the talk.

Text 5.22

124 H:	あのう::桜木桃子さんの趣味は
125 G:	趣味 (1.0) ええと (.) 実はですね
126 H:	はい
127 G:	食べるのが好きなんで料理も好きなんです
128 H:	ほ::

129 G: → (laugh)

130 H: 食べるのも好き料理もすき

131 G: → はい (laugh)

132 H: お酒の方はどうですか

133 G: → はい もう (laugh) 大好きでございます

© 2006 3 April FM96.3

Translation:
124 G: Umm, What is your hobby, Ms Sakuraki?
125 G: Hobby, er, in fact.
126 H: Yes.
127 G: I like eating and I like cooking.
128 H: Oh.
129 G: (laugh)
130 H: Like eating and like cooking.
131 G: Yes.
132 H: How about drinking?
133 G: Yes, I like (laugh) it very much.

5.5   Talk II

Activity 1

Text 5.23 is the beginning of an in-studio radio talk tape-recorded on 17 April 2006. In this talk, the host (H) introduces a male guest whose name is Mr Kanemori and who works for Tanpopo System Ltd. Pick out adjacency pairs and make a list explaining the relationship between initiator and respondent. Look at the list you have produced and consider what types of initiation and response are carried out. Also, make a list of backchannels, hedges or hesitations used in this talk and explain their functions (Note: there is no translation of this text).

Text 5.23

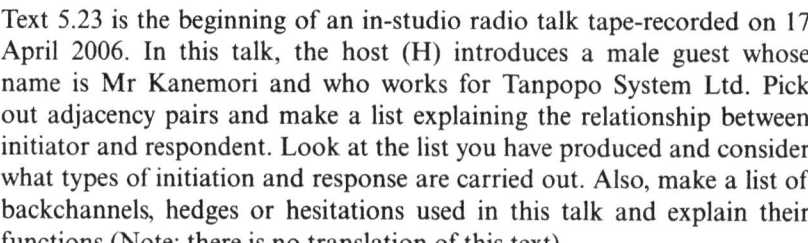

1 H: ウェルカム ツゥ スツゥデオ の時間がやってまいりました

2 H: けさはたんぽぽシステムサービスプライベートリミテッド社のジ

3　　ェネラルマネージャーでいらっしゃいます金森佳久さんにスタ

4　　ジオに来ていただいております

5 H: おはようございます

6 G: あっ おはようございます

7 H: めずらしいお名前ですね 金森[さん]　お金の森と書い[て]

8 G:　　　　　　　　　　　　　[そう::]　　　　　　　　　[ですね]

9 G: もとはあのう::ま私実際あのう九州の佐賀の出身なんですけども

10 H: はい

11 G: お 実際はそのう名古屋の方(.)に多い(.)名前[だというふうに聞いて

12 H:　　　　　　　　　　　　　　　　　　　　　　[はあ:

13 G: いますね

14 H: そうですか

15 G: ええ

16 H: あのう小学校やとかでいじめられませんでしたか

17 G: いや まあね よくある金森ですからね (laugh) よくありますよ (laugh)

18 H: 関西ですとね 何か

19 G: え::: あります そうそう ええ

20 H: あのうたんぽぽシステムサービスというこれ名刺をいただくとあの

21　　 たんぽぽ銀行の (.) ロゴですよね

22 G: そうですよね

23 H: え

24 G: え あのう家はたんぽぽ旧たんぽぽ銀行の情報子会社 (.) として え

25　　 ま あシンガポールにあのう設立された会社なんですけれども

26 H: はあ:　シンガポールはどういうことやっとられるんですか

27 G: 今ではですね銀行さんのお::システムメインテナンス

28 H: はい

29 G: それからあとは まあ 日系企業さんのですね

30 H: ええ

31 G: まあ システム主にい::メインテナンス作ったりとか

32 H: はあ

33 G: そういうことやってるところです

```
34 H: しかし銀行さんていうますと ATM から始まってほんとにもうセキ
35    ュリティーが完璧じゃないとね
36 G: そうですね　ですから一番気を遣うのはまあお金勘定はともかく
37    なんですけれどもね セキュリティーを非常に気を遣っていま
38    すよねえ
39 H: そうですか　そういうノーハウをほんとにもう長年蓄積されてい
40    ると
41 G: そうですね　まあ我々はその分について高い面識を持ってやって
42    ますので非常に自信を持ってやってるとこですね
```

© 2006 17 April FM96.3

Commentary

There are seven adjacency pairs, which are marked by '/' (e.g., 5/6 means
that the first pair part is on line 5 and the second is on line 6). '&' is used
when one pair part extends over more than one line (e.g., 8&9 means that
the second pair part occupies lines 8 and 9). As shown in Table 5.11, not all
adjacency pairs consist only of two immediate utterances. The most
straightforward pair is found in lines 5 and 6, where the host (H) and the
guest (G) greet each other in an independent utterance. Table 5.11 summarizes the functions of the pairs according to our schema introduced in
section 5.3 above.

Table 5.11   *Initiation and response*

Pair	Lines	Initiation	Response
1	5/6	greeting	greeting
2	7/8&9	statement	disagreement
3	16/17	question	indirect
4	20&21/22	statement	acknowledgement
5	26/27&29&31&33	question	direct/proper
6	34&35/36&37&38	statement	acknowledgement
7	39&40/41&42	statement	acknowledgement/ comment

そう::ですね *so::desune* (line 8) with the prolongation of the first part
might indicate that G does not really agree with H who considers G's name

as uncommon. In fact, G claims (line 11) that his name is common in Nagoya. It was mentioned that in Talk I, そうですね is the marker of agreement (p. 189), but what the conversation here suggests is that the prolongation can also designate the speaker's gently expressed disagreement.

Like in Talk I, H sends many backchannels to G. The backchannels used in Text 5.23 are summarized in Table 5.12. Note that all the backchannels are sent from H.

Table 5.12 *List of backchannels*

Backchannel	Line	Speaker
はい	10	H
はあ:	12	H
そうですか	14	H
え	23	H
はい	28	H
ええ	30	H
はあ	32	H

G often uses hesitation. For example, まあね *māne* (line 17), え *e* (line 24), まあ *mā* (line 25) are used before G starts explaining. G often prolongs the final vowel of a word but he pronounces it as if it were an independent sound. These are exemplified by two instances: (i) 銀行さんのお:: *ginkōsan-noo::* 'Bank's' (line 27) and (ii) システム主にい:: *shisutemu omonii::* 'System, especially' (line 31). This type of prolongation may be salient in official talk. Although the talk G participates in is unrelated to his profession, the topic he is talking about is concerned with his routine job. This way of prolonging the vowel may be a common style among Japanese business professionals. You may recall that Ms Sakuraki in Talk I does not prolong the vowel the way Mr Kanemori in Talk II does. It might be an interesting topic to investigate whether the types of prolongation are gender-specific.

Activity 2

Each individual speaker has some special features when he or she talks. Mr Kanemori's special feature is a frequent use of そうですね *sōdesune*. Text 5.24 displays three instances of そうですね used with subtly different nuances. Look at the text carefully and consider what interpersonal meaning(s) this expression imparts in the talk. Also consider our brief discussion on the same expression in Activity 1 above.

Text 5.24

140 H:	乗り越えなければ 100 の壁 90 の壁 80 の壁がありますね	
141 G:	ええ	
142 H:	ゴルフなんて誰がその (***) おるとかね (1.0) ハーフキューと	
	かね (1.0)	
143	誰が考えたかと思えるぐらいねほんとに (.) さすがイギリス人	
144 G:	(laugh)	
145 G: →	そうですね	
146 H:	思う (.) ゴルフですね	
147 G:	ええ	
148 H:	次回じゃまた一回 (2.0) お相手をさせていただいて =	
149 G: →	= そうですね: あのう (2.0) まあ: 社交辞令もなんですから今	
150	じゃこの後決めましょう	
151 H:	(laugh)	
152 G:	(laugh)	
153 H:	奥さんは何かお仕事お持ちですか	
154 G: →	そうですね 家の奥さんは最近はベリーダンスをですね始めて	
	まして:	
155 H:	ベリーダンスあのあの中近東の =	
156 G:	= え もうあのお腹だすやつですよ	
157 H:	へえ おへそ出す	

© 2006 17 April FM96.3

Commentary

In these units of Talk II, そうですね is only used by G. The first one is an agreement (line 145); H highlights the complex rules of golf, admiring the English people, who invented them. The second one (line 149) is also an agreement such that G accepts H's suggestion to play golf with him. The short prolongation of the word-final vowel is due to the fact that G's response may not only be an agreement but also a preparation for a humorous and possibly unrealistic proposal articulated within the same utterance. The final one (line 154) is not an agreement but serves as a hedge that reveals G's polite negative reply to H's question of whether G's wife has a job (line 153). This use of そうですね may resemble that of そうですね in Text 5.23 (line 8) in the sense that G's response to H's utterance is not positive.

5.6 Transcribed Talk I

In order to transcribe the talk, we have followed the general conventions in conversation analysis relevant to this chapter. For this purpose, we have avoided detailed phonetic transcriptions.

1. The speaker's utterances are demonstrated in lines.
2. Utterances are not marked by commas, question marks or full stops.
3. Utterances are separated after exclamations and hesitations, and at clause boundaries.
4. (.) indicates micro pauses that last less than one second.
5. (1.0) or (2.0) indicates pauses for one second or two seconds.
6. : or :: indicates the prolongation of a sound; the former is shorter than the latter.
7. (laugh) indicates laughs (e.g., hahaha or huhuhu)
8. (***) indicates inaudible sounds that cannot be transcribed.
9. [indicates overlaps; speakers talk simultaneously.
10. (*h) indicates audible in- or out-breaths.
11. = indicates a latched utterance that immediately follows the preceding utterance without an audible gap. This sign is placed at two places: at the end of the preceding utterance and at the beginning of a new utterance.
12. ___ indicates a word that receives particular stress, emphasizing its meaning in an utterance.
13. → marks an utterance that the main text discusses

Text 5.25 The whole text of Talk I

Talk I 13 April 2006 (Monday)

1 H: ウェルカム ツゥ スツゥディオの時間がやってまいりました

2 　 今朝は桜木桃子さんにスタジオに来ていただいております

3 　 おはようございます

4 G: おはようございます::

5 H: リスナーの方桜木桃子さん (.) といわれても (.) よう分かんない

6 　 と思うんですが　ちょっともうちょっと (1.0) しゃべっていただけ

```
7        ますか

8 G:     そうですね だれだおまえはですよね

9        ええと あのう 実は (1.0) え 4月から毎週月曜日のモーニングナビゲー

10       ションの担当をさせていただくことになりました

11       えっと 声の仕事は (1.0) ええ::五年前からやっているんです

12       けれども=

13 H:    =そうですね あのう私も::リスナーの方もどっかで聞いた

14       ような声だと思われると思いますけれども (laugh)

15       実は (.) ある某

16 G:    某

17 H:    (***) ねシンガポールエアラインズの

18 G:    あらららら

19 H:    [機内で::え::番組をお持ちということなんですね

20 G:    [(laugh)

21 G:    はい

22 H:    あれも二時間 (1.0) 一時間番組ですか

23 G:    二時間 [です

24 H:         [二時間です [ね

25 G:                  [はい

26 H:    もう : ほんとにあの出発::シンガポール出たときにどっか出張

27       行ってですね

28 G:    え

29 H:    帰ってくるときに (1.0) 松本静さん (1.0)

30 G:    あら そこまで言ってしまう [んですね (laugh)

31 H:                        [というお名前をいただいたときに

32       あの声でですね私何回かあの::出張のつらさをですね (1.0)

33       癒されたことがあると思うんですけれども

34 G:    あっ ありがとうございます::

35 H:    前はどういうお仕事をされていたんですか
```

201

36 G: 前はですね 実はあのう 空飛ぶお姉さんでございました

37 H: あっ これも某同じ

38 G: 某

39 H: SQ で

40 G: ええと (*h) そうですね あのう SQ から始まりまし [て

41 H: [はい

42 G: え:: (1.0) ヨーロッパ系 その後アメリカ系と三社

43 H: あっ

44 G: (laugh)

45 H: もうそれこそあのう世界の (laugh) 空を (.) 渡り歩いているわけ

46   ですな

47 G: そうですね 個人的にはあんまり旅行していないんですけれども

48 H: う::ん

49 G: 仕事では行きました

50 H: そうするとヨーロッパアメリカアジアですから

51 G: はい

52 H: あと:::ほとんどないんじゃないんですか南米ぐらいじゃないで

53 :   すか

54 G: 南米中近東ですかね

55 H: 中近東

56 G: (laugh) いやでも (.) あのそんなに行ってないんですよ 外資系の会

57   社ばかりでしたので 日本人は同じような所しか飛ばないんです

58 H: やっぱりどうなんですか

59 G: ん

60 H: その (.) 機内でもね

61 G: え

62 H: いろんな:::放送するんじゃないんですか

63 G: 機内アナン [ス

64 H: [機内アナンス [ね

65 G: [そうですね

66 H: あの::::どういんですか ライフジャケットがどうの

67 G: (laugh)

68 H: あの: 乱気流に入りますから座ってくださいの::デューテイフリーが

69   どうやのこうやのと

70 G: え

71 H: ああいうのってやっぱ何か何となくその (1.0) しゃべるというか

72 G: う:ん

73 H: マイクロホーンを持つのに興味を持たれたんですか

74 G: (***) そうですね (.) やはり (.) 自分のその時の声の調子っていう

75   のも ありますけど

76 H: うん

77 G: あっちょっと今日はうまくいったかもしれないって思うときもある

78   んですね

79 H: ほ::

80 G: それと あ: ちょっと今日は: (1.0) 風邪気味だったからよくなかたなあ

81   とか

82 H: ほ::

83 G: でも (.) やはりあのうれしいのは

84 H: うん

85 G: あのうときどきこう (1.0) マイクのスイッチを切ったときに

86 H: うん

87 G: お客様がこう振り向いて

88 H: うん

89 G: あのどこで言っているのかなあっていって私を目で探して

90 H: はいはい

91 G: あのう::私を見つけてですね親指をこうやって立ててくれる

92 H: はあはあ

93 G: うん よかったよって 言ってくれる (1.0) 方なんかもたまにはいらっ

94 　　 しゃってですねそれが励みになりました::

95 H: なるほど

96 G: (laugh)

97 H: それじゃ::これからの番組も

98 G: ええ

99 H: そういう形でみんなねリスナーの人が癒される (.)

100 G: はい

101 H: 番組を作っていただきたいと思います

102 G: がんばっていきます はい (laugh)

103 H: 4月の3日

104 G: はい

105 H: まさしく今日でございますけど この後え::ソロデビューの前の

106 　　 プレ (.) デビューみたいな形になっております [え:::

107 G: 　　　　　　　　　　　　　　　　　　　　　　　[突然ですね

108 H: 3日からプレ (.) デビュー

109 G: はい

110 H: 10日にえ::本番と

111 G: はい

112 H: いうことですが (*h) 心構えはどうですか

113 G: えっとですね今までずっと収録::番組ばかりでしたので

114 H: ん::

115 G: 生放送は実は初めてなんです

116 H: はい

117 G: とても緊張しております (1.0) 失敗は許されないですからね

118 H: いいや たまには (laugh)

119 G: いいですか

120 H: いいですよ と思いますよ

121 G: もう::

204

122 H: ごめんといえばあれでしょうけれども

123 G: (laugh) ごめんちゃいですみますか

124 H: あのう::桜木桃子さんの趣味は

125 G: 趣味 (1.0) ええと (.) 実はですね

126 H: はい

127 G: 食べるのが好きなんで料理も好きなんです

128 H: ほ::

129 G: (laugh)

130 H: 食べるのも好き料理もすき

131 G: はい (laugh)

132 H: お酒の方はどうですか

133 G: はいもう (laugh) 大好きでございます

134 H: そうですか (laugh) たとえばそのワイン系とかいろんな::ジャンル

135　　問わず

136 G: ジャンル問わず (.) あのう::量はそんなに飲めないんですけども基

137　　本的に苦くなければ大丈夫です [にが

138 H: 　　　　　　　　　　　　　　　[ビールは駄目ということですか

139 G: ビールも (.) あのほんとに (2.0) かる:::いのがあるじゃないですか

140 H: はいはいはいはいはいはい

141 G: 名称いっていいんですか

142 H: いいですいいです

143 G: コロナとか

144 H: はいはいはいはい

145 G: ああいうのでしたら大丈夫です

146 H: あっなるほどね

147 G: ええ

148 H: だいぶそうるすと飛行機乗ってるときも

149 G: はい

150 H: あのうワインあまったやつをがあと

151 G: あのうですね (laugh)

152 H: そんなことない (laugh)

153 G: そういうことはしません

154 H: しませんでしたか (laugh)

155 H: しかし機内で (.) いうと酔いが回るの早いじゃないですか

156 G: さん::ぱいといわれていますね

157 H: ねそこで鍛えられたのかなと思いました

158 G: そんな不良みたいなことしませんよ (laugh)

159 H: そうですか (laugh)

160 H: 音楽はどんなもん音楽が好きなんですか

161 G: 音楽はですね (1.0) え::とジャンルに分けるのは難しいんですけれども

162 H: はい

163 G: アーティスト名でいいますと私は実は (2.0) ええと中西けいぞうとか

164 H: はいはい

165 G: 山下達郎とか

166 H: あっ何かメッセージをこう発信する人ですな

167 G: そうですねそうですね

168 H: うん

169 G: あのう::(1.0) 好きな (1.0) うん惚れた晴れたよりも

170 H: うん

171 G: まあメッセージを発信してくれるほうが好きかもしれません

172 H: それじゃ::まず今日はそのリクエスト曲にお答えしたいと思いますが

173 G: はいはいはい

174 H: 桜木桃子さんのリクエスト曲 (.) 何がよろしいですか

175 G: 山下達郎さんの君の声に恋してる

176 H: これはまた何で

177 G: これは(1.0) まあこれからまあリスナーの方にこういう風に (.)

178　　思っていただけたらなという (laugh)(*h)

179 H: なるほど

180 G: はい希望が [こもっています

181 H: 　　　　　　[なるほど

182 H: いいですね

183 G: はい

184 H: これじゃやるとしたらリスナーの人が::どんどんどん (laugh)

185 　　 リクエストを (laugh) かかってくるか分かんないですね

186 G: ねえ:

187 H: ねえ

188 G: そうなったらいいですね::=

189 H: =楽しみでございます

190 G: はい

191 H: それじゃ曲を (.) ご紹介してください

192 G: はい 山下達郎で君の声に恋してる

— interruption (song is played) —

193 H: 何か失敗談ちょんぼは

194 G: ちょんぼですか

195 H: ええ

196 G: はええもう明日になってしまいます::(laugh)

197 H: (*h) たと [えば　どんな

198 G: 　　　　　 [数え切れない

199 G: ええとですね 仕事::ええと学生上がりで一番初め::にもう

200 　　 あのう::(1.0) え 航空会社の

201 H: あ::

202 G: え

203 H: そそそれで社会経験なく学生からそく入られた

204 G: そうです

205 H: うん

206 G: なったんですが

207 H: はい

208 G: もうはじめの何回かのフライトでですね

209 H: ん

210 G: え::と制服を着て (.) タクシーに乗って (.)

211 H: はい

212 G: 家からでるんですけれども

213 H: う

214 G: あのう::その頃家の中で (.) あのシンガポールですからね

215 H: うん

216 G: ビーチサンダルを履いてたんですね

217 H: ああ まあ[ね

218 G: 　　　　　　[家の中でリ[ビング家の中でです　外ではなくて

219 H: 　　　　　　　　　　　　[はいはいはいはい

220 H: まあ素肌　素足というと

221 G: え

222 H: 大理石で寒いし

223 G: そうです

224 H: といってといってなんやいうてやっぱ: そういう

225 　　　サンダルっぽいとか

226 G: ええ

227 H: スリッパ系 [シンガポール履きますよね

228 G: 　　　　　　[スリッパ

229 G: スリッパ代わりですよね　スリッパ代わりに家では (1.0)

230 　　　あのうビーチサンダルを履いてたんですけども

231 H: え

232 G: あのう (***) を着て

233 H: うん

234 G: バックを持ってお化粧ばっちりして

235 H: うん

236 G: タクシーに乗って

237 H: うん

238 G: 空港に着いたらですねビーチサンダル履いてたんですねえ

239 H: (laugh)

240 G: (laugh)

241 H: ああ

242 G: もう<u>真っ青</u>になりました =

243 H: =靴忘れてるんですか

244 G: 履き替えるのを忘れちゃったんです

245 H: 履き替えるのを忘れちゃった

246 G: そのままビーチサンダルで行ってしまいましてもう:そのすぐ

247　　タクシーで引き帰して

248 H: うん

249 G: また (laugh) ユータンして空港に戻りましたけど

250 H: (***) よかったんでしょうね

251 G: そのままで (laugh)

252 H: (laugh)

253 G: そういうわけにはいかないと思いますけど (laugh)

254 H: 他には

255 G: 他にですか:

256 H: う

257 G: 後は よく あのう (1.0) あ (*h) これさっきの不良じゃないっていう

258　　ふうに私反論しましたけれども

259 H: うう

260 G: あのう:新人の時に

261 H: う

262 G: 先輩に

263 H: う

264 G: ええと ゲレンデに戻った時にですね

265 H: う

266 G: サービスが終って あっ 桃子ちゃんあのう飲み物用意したから

267　飲んでのど渇いたでしょうっていって

268 H: はい

269 G: いただいたんですよ

270 H: え

271 G: アップルジュースだと思ってありがとうございますって

272 H: え

273 G: があって一気飲み (.) 一気に一杯飲んだら

274 H: う

275 G: 水割りだったんですね

276 H: ウイスキーかなんか

277 G: ウイスキーかなんか

278 H: はい

279 G: そのころ私飲めなかったんですよ うぶでしたから

280 H: <u>おお</u>

281 G: はい

282 H: 一切

283 G: 一切

284 H: どうなったんですか

285 G: 顔にはでません (.) でした　私<u>顔に出ないんです</u>　どんなに

286　飲んでも

287 H: 強い

288 G: 強い　え　いや

289 H: それで

290 G: でもあのう一杯行けましたら (.) その先輩の方があせってい

291　ましたね

292 H: あっ　(***)

293 G: (laugh)

294 H: (***)

295 G: 全部飲むとは思わなかったと

296 H: うう::ちょっと嫌がらせやないけど

297 G: (laugh)

298 H: ちょっと面白半分でしたのにっ

299 G: え　決して嫌がらせじゃないですよ　面白半分であのう:笑っ

300 　　てました:

301 　　(laugh)

302 H: その後全然 (.) 業務には差 [し支えなかった

303 G: 　　　　　　　　　　　　　[差し支えなかったです (.) それは

304 　　プロですからね (laugh) プロですから

305 H: なるほど

306 G: あとはですね (.) あのう: (1.0) ええとですね桃子何十何番の (.)

307 　　Aのお客様に

308 H: はい　シートの番号

309 G: そうです

310 H: はいはい

311 G: オレンジシュース持ってって (.) と言われて

312 H: はい

313 G: あのう分かった分かったってオレンジシュース持ってたら (.)

314 　　くまのぬいぐるみがシートベルトして座ってたりとかですね

315 H: (laugh)

316 G: だまされることが多かったですね

317 H: ああ　くまさんが:みんなやっぱね 仕事厳しいですしストレス

318 　　たまるから

319 G: そうですね

320 H: ちょっと楽しく愉快に

321 G: 新人をからかおうっていうのがあるんでしょうね

322 H: ジョークで (.) でそのくまさんどうしたんですか

323 G: くまさんですか あ まあ実はなでて帰ってきましたけれど (laugh)

324 H:　(laugh) なるほど

325 G:　<u>あとは</u>ですね

326 H:　ええ

327 G:　あのう (1.0) アミニティセットでこう (1.0) くしとか [歯ブラシとか

328 H:　　　　　　　　　　　　　　　　　　　　　　　　　　　　[ありますねあります

329 G:　おいてるんですけれども

330 H:　あのうこう (1.0) え (.) なんちゅうですかこう (.) 睡眠の

331 G:　アイマスクですか

332 H:　アイマスク　えええ

333 G:　あのう (1.0) そうですアムニティキットのそのくしをですね (.) これをまた

334　　　何十何番のえと何番のお客様に持ってってて言われて分かりましたって

335　　　トレーに載せてお待たせ致しましたって持ってったらですね

336 H　はい

337 G:　なんとつんつるてんのお客様だったんです (laugh)

338 H:　(laugh)

339 G:　それは失礼 [な::::::話ですよね

340 H:　　　　　　　[<u>それは:::</u>怒りますよ お客さん

341 G:　まあ 映画上映中でしたので暗かったから

342 H:　う

343 G:　あのう (.) ま 見えなかったので

344 H:　え

345 G:　あのう (.) 間違えましたシート間違えましたって言って戻って

346　　　来ましたけど

347 H:　<u>それでも</u>

348 G:　はあ

349 H:　僕やったら:::あれですよ

350 G:　つかみかかりますか

351 H:　つかみかかりませんけど (laugh) あののの::どうしようね

352　　　(laugh) ものすごいですね (.) いやこんな話ばかり聞いていると何

353 　かくしがぬけてくような話になると思うんで (laugh) あれですが

354 　あのう 今凝ってることってどんなことですか

355 G: 凝ってることですか (1.0) <u>そうですね</u> (2.0) 健康 (***) かな

356 H: はっ (***) どんなに

357 G: (laugh) いや (.) たいしたことないんですけれどもあのう 人からどんな

358 　健康法をやってる かという情報だけ試して

359 H: はい

360 G: 頭でっかちになるだけなって自分では試さないという

361 H: はあ (***) 健康のためには死んでもええと思うタイプですね

362 G: はあ (*h) つうはんとか

363 H: つうはんから始まって<u>あり</u>とあらゆるものを

364 G: そうですか

365 H: ええ信じられないこと

366 G: 信じられないことというますと

367 H: つい最近は (2.0) <u>くまの</u> (1.0) <u>たん汁</u>を飲むんですよ

368 G: <u>えっ</u> =

369 H: =くまの胆のうを食べて (***) 漢方薬で何百万するやつですよ (.)

370 　生きたくまから たんのうを (***) 抜いて (.) それで飲むんですよ

371 G: まあ

372 H: そうすっとね胆のうっていうのはね (.) 生命のいろんな腎臓

373 　肝臓ね要は 五臓六法

374 G: え

375 H: これをうまく機能させるための あのう 機能

376 G: <u>みやばん</u>

377 H: うん そういわれるんです

378 G: (laugh) そうですか

379 H: しかしこれがねものすごいんですよ生命の あのう (.) 末期ガンの

380 　飲んだらですね (1.0) だいたいそれで1か月ぐらい (.) 生命を維持し

381 　ちゃう (2.0) モルヒネを打たなくていいっていうちょうえん作用

213

382 G: すごい (1.0) 効果がちりなんですね

383 H: だから本来ならくまさんは殺されて (.) くまの手::とかねあれを

384 全部でチャイニーズにクッキングされたりとか

385 G: え

386 H: 肉やとか胆のうを取られたりしまうんですけれども そのく

387 まさん生きている 生かされてるんですよ (1.0) 六ヶ月に一ぺんしか

388 胆のうを (.) 取られないいんですよ

389 G: [(***)

390 H: [だからくまさん率は (***)

391 G: 胆 胆汁用に買われている [くまさんですね

392 H: [そうそう

393 六ヶ月にいっぺんだけあとは半年は睡眠してますから冬眠して

394 ますから まあかまへん

395 G: なんと気の毒ななんと気の毒な (laugh)

396 H: いやそういうくまのプーさん本当にありがとうございます

397 G: ありがとうございます ねえ

398 H: まっいろんなあ話を (.) してますけれども

399 G: はい

400 H: さっえ:: (1.0) 今週 (.) 来週と (.) え: 本格 (.) デビューするんですが

401 最後にリスナーの皆さんに桜木桃子さんから (.) こんな番組に

402 したい (.) こんな形で (.) というのがありましたらぜひお聞かせ願い

403 たいんですが

404 G: そうですねえ: (1.0) あのう今日は (.) かなり (1.0) くだけました

405 けれども (.) わりと A 括弧 C なんです実は

406 H: うん

407 G: ですから (.) あまりオブラードにくるまずに

408 H: はい

409 G: 素の (.) 桜木桃子が出せたらいいなと思っております

410 H: ん

411 G: 一方通行でなくてね

412 H: そうですねえ

413 G: あのう (.) リスナーの方もあのう隣で聞いてくださっているよう

414　　な (1.0) ものにできたらいいなと思います

415 H: どしどしねメールとか[ファックスで

416 G:　　　　　　　　　　　　[はい

417 H: リクエスト曲もそうですし

418 G: え

419 H: あのういろんなコメントとか

420 G: え

421 H: どんどん送っていただいて

422 G: はい

423 H: え 桜木桃子を<u>サポート</u>していただけるかと思います

424 G: よろしくお願いいたします

425 H: じゃまずは え:振れ振れ桜木桃子

426 G: はい

427 G: 来週からがんばってください

428 G: ありがとうございます　ど[うぞよろしく

429 H:　　　　　　　　　　　　　[今朝はお忙しいというかあ (laugh)

430　　ええ 大変 な時でございますけれども

431 G: はい (laugh)

432 H: 来週楽しみにしてます　今朝はありがとうございました

433 G: どうもありがとうございました　よろしくお願いいたします

434 H: これからがんばってください

435 G: はい

Notes

1　Refer to Chapter 3, section 3.5.1 for the concept of 'information'. This section deals with the concepts of new and old information from different discursive perspectives in written text.

2   The article comes to be omitted when the original word enters the Japanese lexicon. We looked at a similar phenomenon under the sub-heading 'Grammatical reduction' in Chapter 3, section 3.3.2.3 in JL.

3   The personal and company names used in the talks are pseudonyms.

4   Pseudonyms different from the real names appear in the text cited.

5   All three tables (5.2 to 5.5) only demonstrate the cases of prototypical adjacency pairs in in-studio radio talks; that is, H is an initiator and G is a respondent. They do not consider cases in which H responds to G's answer or G is an initiator and H is a respondent. Interested readers should consult the whole text of Talk I in section 5.6.

6   See example (23) in Gibbs (1999: 67). It illustrates the relationship between conversational implicature and metonymy.

7   The concept 'context of the situation' was, to the best of my knowledge, first introduced by Malinowski (1972 [1923]: 146), referring to the ethnographic view of the discourse.

8   There are a number of studies that have examined backchannels or *aizuchi* in Japanese. Based on the finding that Japanese backchannel more often than Americans, some scholars distinguish backchannels from *aizuchi* (e.g., Kita 1996). In this book, we do not go into this distinction.

9   Thornbury (2005a: 9) points out that *really?* or *no!* does not only signal the listener's attention to what the speaker says but also indicates the listener's interest or shock.

10 In Chapter 4, we have considered 'politeness' as a non-intrusive behaviour that arises from the social distance that exists between two people. In this chapter, politeness associated with the use of hedges refers to the means to express an interpersonal relationship between two people who are concerned with each other's 'face' or social needs.

11 Regardless of the morphological conditions under which they are prolonged, the length of the prolonged vowels corresponds to one mora (Chapter 2, section 2.4 in JL).

12 Some scholars assign the notion 'filler' to what we call backchannel, hedge or hesitation in this chapter (see Yamane 2002 for Japanese and Pridham 2001 for English). Whether a certain conversation strategy is given one name or another depends on how certain linguistic forms behave in a given context and how they are categorized by a linguist.

References

The references listed here include works quoted in the book and consulted during the writing of it.

Akiba-Reynolds, K. (1998) 'Female speakers of Japanese in Transition', in J. Coates (ed.), *Language and Gender: A Reader*. Oxford/Malden, MA: Blackwell, pp. 299–308.

An Encyclopedia of Contemporary Words [Gendai Yōgo no Kiso-chishiki] (2003) Tokyo: Jiyū Kokuminsha.

Atkinson, J. M. and Heritage, J. (eds) (1984) *Structures of Social Action: Studies in Conversation Analysis*. Cambridge: Cambridge University Press.

Austin, J. L. (1962) *How To Do Things With Words. The William James Lectures Delivered at Harvard University in 1955*, J. O. Urmson (ed.). Cambridge, MA: Harvard University Press.

Backhouse, A. E. (1993) *The Japanese Language: An Introduction*. South Melbourne: Oxford University Press.

Bales, R. F., Strodtbeck, F. L., Mills, T. M. and Roseborough, M. E. (1951) 'Channels of communication in small group interaction', *American Sociological Review*, 16, 461–468.

Bloomer, A., Griffiths, P. and Merriston, A. J. (2005) *Introducing Language in Use: A Coursebook*. London: Routledge.

Cameron, D. (2000) 'Styling the worker: gender and the commodification of language in the globalized service economy', *Journal of Sociolinguistics*, 4(3) 323–347.

Cameron, D. (2001) *Working with Spoken Discourse*. London/Thousand Oaks, CA/New Delhi: Sage.

Carter, R., Goddard, A., Reah, D., Sanger, K. and Bowring, M. (2001) *Working with Texts: A Core Introduction to Language Analysis* (2nd edn). London: Routledge.

Chafe, W. L. (1994) *Discourse, Consciousness, and Time: The Flow and Displacement of Conscious Experience in Speaking and Writing*. Chicago: Chicago University Press.

Chandler, D. (2002) *Semiotics: The Basics*. London: Routledge.

Chino, N. (1991) *All about Particles: A Handbook of Japanese Function Words*. Tokyo: Kodansha International.

Dooley, R. A. and Levinsohn, S. H. (2001) *Analyzing Discourse. A Manual of Basic Concepts*. Dallas, TX: SIL International.

Gibbs, R. W., Jr. (1994) *The Poetics of Mind: Figurative Thought, Language, and Understanding*. Cambridge: Cambridge University Press.

Gibbs, R. W., Jr. (1999) 'Speaking and thinking with metonymy', in K.-U. Panther and G. Radden (eds) *Metonymy in Language and Thought*. Amsterdam/Philadelphia: John Benjamins, pp. 61–76.

217

Goffman, E. (1981) *Forms of Talk*. Philadelphia: University of Pennsylvania Press.

Grice, P. (1989) *Studies in the Way of Words*. Cambridge, MA/London: Harvard University Press.

Grundy, P. (2000) *Doing Pragmatics* (2nd edn). London: Arnold.

Gudykunst, W. B. (2004) *Bridging Differences* (4th edn). Thousand Oaks, CA/London/New Delhi: Sage.

Halliday, M. A. K. (1985) *Spoken and Written Language*. Victoria, Australia: Deakin University.

Halliday, M. A. K. and Hasan, R. (1976) *Cohesion in English*. London: Longman.

Halliday, M. A. K. and Hasan, R. (1985) *Language, Context, and Text: Aspects of Language in a Social-Semiotic Perspective*. Victoria, Australia: Deakin University.

Hancher, M. (1979) 'The classification of cooperative illocutionary acts', *Language in Society*, 8, 1–14.

Hebron, M. (2004) *Mastering the Language of Literature*. Basingstoke, England/New York: Palgrave Macmillan.

Hinata, S. (2000) *Exercise Book for Honorifics: You Will Learn It Swiftly* [Omoshiroi hodo Minitsuku Keigo no Renshūcho]. Tokyo: Chūkei.

Hinds, J. (1986) *Japanese*. Dover, NH: Croom Helm.

Hinds, J. (1987) 'Thematization, assumed familiarity, stating, and syntactic binding in Japanese', in J. Hinds, S. K. Maynard and S. Iwasaki (eds) *Perspectives on Topicalization: The Case of Japanese Wa*. Amsterdam/Philadelphia: John Benjamins, pp. 83–106.

Holmes, J. (1995) *Women, Men and Politeness*. London: Longman.

Holmes, J. (2001) *An Introduction to Sociolinguistics* (2nd edn). Harlow, England: Longman.

Hopper, P. J. (1979) 'Aspect and foregrounding in discourse', in T. Givón (ed.) *Syntax and Semantics, Vol. 12: Discourse and Syntax*. New York: Academic Press, pp. 213–241.

Huddleston, R. D. (2002) 'Clause type and illocutionary force', in R. D. Huddleston and G. K. Pullum (eds) *The Cambridge Grammar of the English Language*. Cambridge: Cambridge University Press, pp. 851–946.

Hutchby, I. (1991) 'The organization of talk on talk radio', in P. Scannell (ed.) *Broadcast Talk*. London/Newbury Park, CA/New Delhi: Sage. pp. 119–137.

Hutchby, I. (2006) *Media Talk: Conversation Analysis and the Study of Broadcasting*. Maidenhead, England: Open University Press.

Ishiguro, K. (2005) *Explaining Techniques for Composing Sentences* III (Yoku Wakaru Bunshō-hyōgen no Gijutsu]. Tokyo: Meijishoin.

Iwasaki, S. (2002) *Japanese*. Amsterdam/Philadelphia: John Benjamins.

Jespersen, O. (1992 [1924]) *The Philosophy of Grammar*. Chicago/London: The University of Chicago Press.

Johnstone, B. (2002) *Discourse Analysis*. Oxford/Malden, MA: Blackwell.

Jugaku, A. (1979) *Japanese Language and Woman* [Nihongo to On-na]. Tokyo: Iwanami.

Kaiser, S., Ichikawa, Y., Kobayashi, N. and Yamamoto, H. (2001) *Japanese: A Comprehensive Grammar*. London/New York: Routledge.

218

Kamei, H. (2003) *Dictionary of Young People's Language* [Wakamono-kotoba Jiten]. Tokyo: NHK Shuppan.

Kawashima, S. A. (1999) *A Dictionary of Japanese Particles*. Tokyo/New York/ London: Kodansha International.

Kikuchi, Y. (1994) *Honorifics* [Kēgo]. Tokyo: Kadokawa.

Kita, S. (1996) 'Japanese confronted communication viewed from backchannels and nodding' [Aizuchi to unazuki kara mita nihonjin no taimen komyunikēshon]. *Nihongogaku*, 15, 58–66.

Knowles, M. and Moon, R. (2006) *Introducing Metaphor*. Abington: Routledge.

Koide, K. (1983) 'Hesitations' [Īyodomi], in O. Mizutani (ed) *Expressions of Spoken Language* [Hanashi-kotoba no Hyōgen]. Tokyo: Chikuma.

Kuno, S. (1973) *The Structure of the Japanese Language*. Cambridge, MA: The MIT Press.

Lakoff, R. (1975) *Language and Women's Place*. New York: Harper & Row.

Leech, G. N. (1983) *Principles of Pragmatics*. London: Longman.

Makino, S. (1996) *Inside and Outside Cultural Linguistics: Cutting through Grammar with Culture* [Uchi to Soto no Gengo-bunkagaku: Bunpō o Bunka de Kiru]. Tokyo: ALC.

Makino, S. and Tsutsui, M. (1986) *A Dictionary of Basic Japanese Grammar*. Tokyo: The Japan Times.

Makino, S. and Tsutsui, M. (1995) *A Dictionary of Intermediate Japanese Grammar*. Tokyo: The Japan Times.

Malinowski, B. (1972 [1923]) 'Phatic communion', in J. Laver and S. Hutcheson (eds) *Communication in Face to Face Interaction*. Harmondsworth: Penguin, pp. 146–152.

Mangajin's Basic Japanese through Comics (1998 [1993]) Vol. 1. New York/Tokyo: Weatherhill.

Matthews, P. H. (1997) *The Concise Oxford Dictionary of Linguistics*. Oxford/New York: Oxford University Press.

Maynard, S. K. (1998) *Principles of Japanese Discourse: A Handbook*. Cambridge: Cambridge University Press.

McClure, W. T. (2000) *Using Japanese. A Guide to Contemporary Usage*. Cambridge: Cambridge University Press.

Mey, J. L. (2001) *Pragmatics: An Introduction* (2nd edn). Oxford: Blackwell.

Nagano, M. (1986) *An Introduction to the Study of Syntax* [Bunshōron-sōsetsu]. Tokyo: Asakura.

Nakamura, A. (1977) *An Overview of Metaphor* [Hiyu no Aramashi]. Tokyo: Kadokawa.

Neuliep, J. W. (2003) *Intercultural Communication: A Contextual Approach* (2nd edn). Boston, MA: Houghton Mifflin.

Okamoto, S. and Shibamoto Smith, J. S. (eds) (2004) *Japanese Language, Gender, and Ideology: Cultural models and real people*. Oxford/New York: Oxford University Press.

Ōno, S. (1966) *Japanese: The Wisdom of Age* [Nihongo no Nenrin]. Tokyo: Shinchosha.

Ono, T. (1990) 'Te, I, and Ru clauses in Japanese recipes: a quantitative study', *Studies in Language*, 14(1) 73–92.

219

Oxford Dictionary of English (2005) (2nd edn., revised). Oxford: Oxford University Press.

Palmer, F. R. (2001) *Mood and Modality* (2nd edn). Cambridge: Cambridge University Press.

Pridham, F. (2001) *The Language of Conversation*. London: Routledge.

Quirk, R., Greenbaum, S. and Leech, G. (1972) *A Grammar of Contemporary English*. London: Longman.

Radden, G. and Kövecses, Z. (1999) 'Towards a theory of metonymy', in K.-U. Panther and G. Radden (eds) *Metonymy in Language and Thought*. Amsterdam/ Philadelphia: John Benjamins, pp. 17–59.

Rubin, J. (1998) *Making Sense of Japanese: What the Textbooks Don't Tell You*. Tokyo/New York/London: Kodansha International.

Sack, H. (1992) *Lectures on Conversation*. Vol. II, G. Jefferson (ed.). Oxford: Blackwell.

Sack, H., Schegloff, E. A. and Jefferson, G. (1974) 'A simplest systematics for the organization of turn-taking for conversation'. *Language*, 50(4) 696–735.

Sakairi, I., Sato, Y., Sakuragi, N., Nakamura, K., Nakamura, H. and Yamada, A. (1991) *100 Questions Foreigners Frequently Ask to Japanese Teachers* [Gaikoku-jin ga Nihongo-kyōshi ni Yoku Suru 100 no Shitsumon]. Tokyo: Baberu Press.

Schegloff, E. (1972 [1968]) 'Sequencing in conversational openings', in J. Laver and S. Hutcheson (eds) *Communication in Face to Face Interaction*. Harmondsworth: Penguin, pp. 374–405.

Searle, J. R. (1969) *Speech Acts: An Essay in the Philosophy of Language*. Cambridge: Cambridge University Press.

Shibatani, M. (1990) *The Languages of Japan*. Cambridge: Cambridge University Press.

Shoji, K. (1997) *Basic Connections: Making Your Japanese Flow*. Tokyo/New York/ London: Kodansha International.

Soga, M. (1983) *Tense and Aspect in Modern Colloquial Japanese*. Vancouver: University of British Columbia Press.

Stenström, A.-B. (1994) *An Introduction to Spoken Interaction*. London/New York: Longman.

The Cambridge Advanced Learner's Dictionary (2005). Cambridge: Cambridge University Press.

Thomas, J. (1995) *Meaning in Interaction: An Introduction to Pragmatics*. London: Longman.

Thornbury, S. (2005a) *Teach Speaking*. Harlow, Essex: Longman.

Thornbury, S. (2005b) *Beyond the Sentence: Introducing Discourse Analysis*. Oxford: Macmillan.

Trask, R. L. (1996) *Historical Linguistics*. London/New York: Arnold.

Tsujimura, N. (1996) *An Introduction to Japanese Linguistics*. Malden, MA/ Oxford: Blackwell.

Tsujimura, T., Kasuga, K., Morino, M., Sakurai, M., Komatsu, H. and Miyaji, Y. (1971) *The History of Honorifics* [Kēgoshi]. Tokyo: Taishukan.

Tsujimura, T., Kuwayama, T., Hosokawa, H., Kawagishi, K. and Kikuchi, Y. (1991) *Usage of Honorifics* [Kēgo no Yōhō]. Tokyo: Kadokawa.

220

Van Dijk, T. (1982) 'Episodes as units of discourse analysis', in D. Tannen (ed.) *Analyzing Discourse: Text and Talk*. Georgetown University Round Table on Languages and Linguistics 1981. Washington, DC: Georgetown University Press, pp. 177–195.

Wales, K. (2001) A Dictionary of Stylistics (2nd edn.). Harlow: Longman.

Yamaguchi, T. (2007) *Japanese Linguistics: An Introduction*. London: Continuum.

Yamane, C. (2002) *Fillers in Japanese Discourse* [Nihongo no Danwa ni okeru firā]. Tokyo: Kuroshio.

Yngve, V. H. (1970) 'On getting a word in edgewise'. *Papers from the Sixth Regional Meeting of the Chicago Linguistics Society*, pp. 567–578.

Yule, G. (1996) *Pragmatics*. Oxford: Oxford University Press.

List of authentic texts

Academic texts

Tomioka, J. and Shima, K. (1991) *An Introduction to Intermediate Japanese Reading* [Nihongo Chūkyū Dokkai Nyūmon]. Tokyo: ALC.

Children's books

Aman, K. (1977) *The Colour of the Car Is the Colour of the Sky* [Kuruma no Iro wa Sora no Iro]. Tokyo: Poplar, pp. 6–17.

Kanzawa, T. (1977) *A Bear Cub Uf* [Kuma no Ko Ūfu]. Tokyo: Poplar, pp. 6–16.

Comics

Adachi, M. (1996) *Full of Sunshine* [Hiatari Ryōkō]. Tokyo: Shogakukan.

Adachi, M. (2001) *Always Misora* [Itsumo Misora]. Tokyo: Shogakukan.

Fujiko F., F. (1995) *Doraemon: Kandō-hen*. Tokyo: Shogakukan.

Fujiko F., F. (2002) *Doraemon: Nobita-Grafity*. Tokyo: Shogakukan.

Isshiki, M. (2003) *Do It Again!* [Denaoshitoide!] Tokyo: Kodansha.

Kasahara, K. (ed.) (1982a) *Japanese History* [Nihon no Rekishi] Vol. 13. Tokyo: Shueisha.

Kasahara, K. (ed.) (1982b) *Japanese History* [Nihon no Rekishi] Vol. 18. Tokyo: Shueisha.

Oda, T. (2005) *Tomoo in Public Housing Compound* [Danchi Tomō]. Tokyo: Shogakukan.

Plays

Yamada, T. (1991) *Uneven Apples* III [Fuzoroi no Ringo-tachi III]. Tokyo: Magazine House.

Internet

http://www.asahi.com/

Newspapers

Asahi Newspaper [Asahi Shinbun]. Tokyo.
Yomiuri Newspaper [Yomiuri Shinbun]. Tokyo.

Novels

Kuroyanagi, T. (1982) *Totto-chan: The Little Girl at the Window*. Translated by Dorothy Britton. Asian Edition. Tokyo: Kodansha International.

Kuroyanagi, T. (1984) *Totto-chan at the Window* [Madogiwa no Totto-chan]. Tokyo: Kodansha.

Yoshimoto, B. (2003) *Hagoromo*. Tokyo: Shinchosha.

Short stories

Ochiai, K. (1996a) 'Morning with Jasmine tea' [Jasumin tī no asa], in K. Ochiai, *Lovers* [Koibito-tachi]. Tokyo: Kodansha, pp. 55–68.

Ochiai, K. (1996b) 'Single play' [Hitori-asobi], in K. Ochiai, *Lovers* [Koibito-tachi]. Tokyo: Kodansha, pp. 7–21.

Otsu, I. (2003a) 'Calling You', in I. Otsu, *Lost Story* [Ushinawareta Monogatari]. Tokyo: Kadokawa, pp. 5–47.

Otsu, I. (2003b) 'A story about a thief who holds your hands' [Te o Nigiru Dorobō no Monogatari], in I. Otsu, *Lost Story* [Ushinawareta Monogatari]. Tokyo: Kadokawa, pp. 121–163.

Tōdō, S. (2002) 'Cold hands' [Tsumetai te], in S. Tōdō, *Feeling Lonely* [Sabishigari]. Tokyo: Kodansha, pp. 131–160.

Radio broadcast

The International Channel FM96.3. Singapore.

English Index

When the entries are indicated with (texts), they refer to authentic texts discussed in the main text.

address forms/terms 139–42, 145–6, 149–50
  see also in-group; out-group; reference forms/terms
  definition of 139
adjacency pairs 76, 172–3, 195, 197, 216n.5
  list of 173
adversative conjunction 103
  see also conjunction; contrast
affixation 160, **161–2**
  see also young people's language; affixation in JL
  definition of 161
  four types of 162
aspectual 33
  marker 162
  suffix 94, 162
  see also aspect in JL
assumption 16–17
  definition of 16
auxiliary verb 31

backchannels 169, **184–9**, 191, 195, 198, 216n.8
  see also conversational strategies
  definition of 184
  speaker support 184
  list of 188–9, 198
basic schema for exchange 175

children's story (texts) 5–6, 44, 95,
clause linkage 76, **87–93**
  definition of 87
  juxtaposition 89
  coordination 89
  subordination 90
  and style of the author 92–3
clipping **160–1**, 162, 165
  see also young people's language
  definition of 161
closing a talk 172–4
  see also opening a talk

co-text 39, **49–54**, 93, 94, 97
  definition of 49
  and pragmatic act 50
  and context 54
coherence **76–9**, 80, 87, 93, 106, 114,
  see also cohesion
  definition of 76
  incoherence 77
  and **temporal sequence** 79
cohesion 76, **80–4**
  see also coherence
  definition of 80
  cause-and-effect 80
  and **reference** 80–1, 84
    see also reference
  and **demonstrative** 81
    see also demonstratives
  and **conjunction** 81
    see also conjunction
  and lexical word 84
  author's logical thinking 81
comics (texts) 4, 8, 12, 15, 16, 17, 18, 19, 20, 21, 22, 23, 27, 28, 29, 30, 31, 32, 33, 34, 35, 36, 37, 42, 43, 46, 58, 59, 63, 123, 143–4, 152, 158–9, 166
compound 54
  see also compounds in JL
confirmation 14–15, 138, 181, 194
  see also judgement
  definition of 14
  and self-confidence 15
conjunction 76, 81, 83, **84–7**
  definition of 84
  connectives 84
  intention of the writer 86
  list of 87
context 39, **54–61**
  definition of 54
  and literal meaning 39, 55
  and register 57
  offensive ~ 57

and word-level expressions 59
and expressions longer than words 59
context of situation 26, 184, 189
contextualization 94, 97, 99
  see also usage of *wa* and *ga*
  definition of 94
  familiarity 94, 96, 97
contracted form 17–18, 35, 128, 138, 164
contrast 102–5, 117, 118
  see also usage of *wa* and *ga*
  definition of 102
  single occurrence 102, 105
  and ellipsis 103
conventional implicature 61, **62–3**, 65, 67, 68, 180
  see also implicature
  definition of 61
  primary force 61, 63, 180
conversation 169–70
  difference between talk and ~ 170
conversational discourse 76
  see also adjacency pairs
conversational implicature 61–2, **63–9**
  definition of 62
conversational strategies 183–95
  see also backchannels; hedges; hesitations;
    interruptions; repetitions; laughs
  definition of 183

deixis 41
demonstratives **40–1**, 43–9, 81, 125
  definition of 40
  proximate ~ 41, 45
  intermediate ~ 41
  distal ~ 41
diary (texts) 45, 80
difference between *te*-form and *renyō*-form 87
  see also clause linkage
diminutive form 141
discourse 76
  definition of 76
  and text 76
discourse theme 97
  see also usage of *wa* and *ga*
drama (texts) 55–6, 124–5, 125–6, 134–5, 135–6, 138, 146–9

editorial article (texts) 81–3
elaboration 106–9, **108**, 112–13
  see also sentence-final forms

ellipsis 113–17
  see also non-occurrence of ellipsis
  definition of 114
  and old/new information 114
  and **discourse topic** 114
  and episode 114
  discourse unit 114
emotion 2, 9, 10, 14, 21, 39, 48, 57, 58, 61, 67, 112–13, 138, 167, 193
epistemic modality 14
  see also modality
expectation 15
  definition of ~ 15
  and politeness 15
explanation 2–14
  definition of 2

femininity 193
figure of speech 39, **70–5**
  definition of 70
  see also metaphor; simile; personification;
    metonymy
  speaker's expressiveness 70
  and implicature 70
    see also implicatures
  and cultural attitudes 75
  and newspaper article 73–5
folktale (texts) 84–5, 93, 98,

gender 121–38
  definition of 121
  personal pronouns 121–6
    list of 122
    history of 125
  lexical and **prefixed** words 126–7
    kinship terms 126
    politeness suffix 126
    and **irony** 126–7

Heaven's Voice, Men's Words (texts) 97, 109
hedges 169, 184, **189–90**, 191, 195
  see also conversational strategies
  definition of 189
  and **politeness** 189
hesitations 190–1
  see also conversational strategies
  definition of 190
  difference between hesitations and hedges 191
  list of 191

honorific
  expression 32, 33, 125
  form 33, 34
  title 145
  verb 29
honorifics 121, **153–9**
  definition of 153
  levels of socialization 168n.8
  passive form 168n.9
  respect ~ 153–5
    examples of ~ 154
  humble ~ 155–7
    examples of ~ 156
illocutionary acts 2
implicature 39, **61–9**
  see also conventional and conversational ~
    co-existence of 63, 67, 68
  and naturalness 62
  and figure of speech 70
  and interrogative 68
  negative versus **positive interrogative**
    questions 65
in-group 17, 31, 56, 121, **139–50**
  see also out-group
  definition of 139
  family 139–44
  company 145–50
in-studio talk 170
  definition of 170
  normal procedure in 175
  Talk I 170–95
    transcription of 200–15
  Talk II 195–200
in-studio talk (texts) 171, 174, 176, 177, 178,
    179, 180, 181, 182, 182, 183, 185–6,
    188, 190, 192, 193, 194, 194–5,
    195–7, 199, 200–15
indirectness 163–4
  see also young people's language
  and metonymy 164
    see also metonymy
  and simile 164
insertion 172
insertion sequence 172
interactional particles 15, 36, 37, **127–38**,
    181
  see also case particles in JL
  examples of 130–3
  meanings of 129
  word-final versus sentence-final ~
    133

and prolongation 138
  emotion 138
interpersonal
  meaning 198
  relationship 123–4, 168n.8, 169, 189,
    216n.10
interruptions 191–2
  see also conversational strategies
  definition of 191
  overlap 191
  and power 192
  difference between backchannels and
    interruptions 191–2
intratextual reference 43–4, 45, 49
  see also reference
  definition of 43
  anaphoric ~ 43–4, 45–6, 48–9
  cataphoric ~ 43–4, 48–9, 83
irony 61, 126–7

judgement 14–25
  definition of 14
  see also assumption; confirmation;
    expectation; opinion; regret;
    speculation,
  uncertainty

kotoda 12–14
  see also explanation
  topic and account 12–13

language and culture 121–68
  definition of 121
language of beautification 167n.3
laugh 169, 184, **193–5**, 200
  see also conversational strategies
  definition of 193
  metapragmatic role 193
literal meaning 27, 39, 55, 57, 73

main protagonist 94–5
  see also usage of *wa* and *ga*
  definition of 94
maintaining a talk 175–83
  exchange between the host and the guest
    175
meaning extension 163
  see also young people's language
metaphor **70–1**, 73–5
  see also figure of speech
  definition of 70

metonymy 51, 70, **72**, 73, 75, 164, 180
  definition of 72
  contiguity 72
  and **synecdoche** 72
  sensation and economy 72
modality 1–2, 14, 19
  definition of 1
  see also epistemic modality
monoda 9–12
  see also explanation
  speaker's personal experience 9–10
  general opinion/fact 10, 11

narrative 8, 95, 103, 105
  text 4, 77
  world 110
naturally occurring conversation 169
new episode 97–8
  see also usage of *wa* and *ga*
new grammar 165
  see also young people's language
new information 93, 96, 97–8, 114, 116, 117
  definition of 93
newspaper article
  characteristics 105
newspaper article (texts) 9, 10–11, 13, 53,
     74, 81–3, 96, 97, 99, 104, 106–7,
     109
noda 2–8
  see also explanation
  rhetorical device 2, 3, 4
    see also rhetorical
  giving a reason 2–3
  emphasizing speaker's statement 2, 3
  and narrative texts 4
  shared information 7
non-occurrence of ellipsis 117–20
  see also ellipsis
  contrast 117–18
    see also contrast
  receiving emphasis 118–19
  and **cleft construction** 118
  target of action 119
  experiencer 119–20
  noun modification 119
    see also noun modification in JL
novel (texts) 44, 63–5, 66–7, 68–9

old information 93, 94, 102, 114
  see also usage of *wa* and *ga*
  definition of 93

opening a talk 170–2
  see also closing a talk
opinion 18–19
  see also judgement
  personal ~ 18
order and request 25–38
  definition of 25
  distinction between 25
  formation of order forms 25–6
    positive order form 25–6, 28
    negative order form 25–6, 29, 35
  formation of request forms 26
  didactic role 36
  the speaker's assertions/opinions 37
  without order forms 37
  summary of 38
out-group 121, 139–50
  see also in-groups

palatalization 18
  see also place of articulation in JL
personal pronouns 40, 121–6
  list of 122
personification 70, **71–2**, 73–4
  see also figure of speech
  definition of 71
phatic communion 173
physical reference 41–2, 49
  definition of 41
  see also reference
polarity question 180
  and conventional implicature 180
politeness 4, 15, 121, **150–2**, 216n.10
  definition of **150–1**
  polite forms versus dictionary forms
     150–1
  marker 139
  prefix 126–7, 142
  suffix 139, 145
  and exclamations 152
  and honorifics 153
  and hedges 189
    see also women's language
  and social distance 151
pragmatics 1–38, 39–75
  definition of 1, 39
procedural text 77–9
  definition of 77
prolongation 138, 190, 191, 197–8, 199,
    200
proper nouns 40, 96–7

psychological reference 45–6, 48–9
  definition of 45
  see also reference
  psychological closeness 45
  emotional commitment 45
  shared knowledge 45, 46

question and answer 177–83
  see also maintaining a talk
  direct versus **indirect** answers
    177
    proper answer 178–9
    supplementary answer
      179–80
    implicit answer 180–1
quotative 18, 108, 181

radio talk 169–216
  definition of 169
reduplication 162
  see also young people's language
reference 39, **40–9**
  definition of 40
    see also intratextual, physical,
      psychological ~
reference forms/terms 139–42, 145–6,
  149–50
  see also address forms/terms
  definition of 139
  self-reference 142, 146, 150
register 23, **26**, 57, 125
  definition of 26
  men's ~ 15, 21, 37, 123, 138
  women's ~ 21, 37, 134
  formal ~ 26
  informal ~ 124
  offensive ~ 57
  and social distance 26
regret 17–18
  see also judgement
  definition of ~ 17
repetitions 192
  see also conversational strategies
  definition of 192
  list of 192
request and answer 182–3
rhetorical
  device 2, 3, 4, 110
  effect 108
  question 37, 58
  strategy 105, 106

self-contained fact 98–9
  see also usage of *wa* and *ga*
  phenomenal sentence 120n.3
sentence-final forms 105–13
  see also elaboration; states and views; tied
    up with the protagonist
  definition of 105
  past and **present tense forms** 105
    alternation between 108, 110, 113
    and newspaper articles 106–10
    foregrounding and backgrounding
      105
    and short stories 110–13
short essay (texts) 99, 102, 103
short story
  characteristics 106
short story (texts) 24–5, 47–8, 51–2, 56,
    59–60, 88–9, 91, 94, 100–1, 110–12,
    115, 116, 117, 118, 119, 120,
similie 11, **71**, 73–5
  see also figure of speech
  definition of ~ 71
social relation 169
  see also conversation; talk
speaker meaning 39, 90
speculation 19–21
  see also judgment
  definition of ~ 19
  and **evidentiality** 19
  and deductive thoughts 19–20
  and five senses 20
speech act 1
  definition of ~ 1
  descriptive or constative 1–2
  peformative 2
spoken language 160, 169
statement and reply 175–7
  see also maintaining a talk
    acknowledgement 175–6
    comment 176
    disagreement 177
states and views 108–10
  see also sentence-final forms
  perpetuating states 109
  perpetuating views 109
suspense 99–102
  see also usage of *wa* and *ga*

talk 169–70
  difference between conversation and ~
    170

tied up with the protagonist 110–13
  see also sentence-final forms
  dynamism in the narration 110
transcribing talk
  general conventions 200
turn-taking 171
turns 171

uncertainty 21–3
  definition of 21
  and surprise or astonishment 22
  and expectation 23
usage of *wa* and *ga* 93–105
  see also contrast; discourse theme; main
     protagonist; new
  episode; self-contained fact; suspense; old/
    new information

wakeda 8–9
  logical explanation 8

logical consequence 8
cause and effect 8–9
WH-word 178
women's language/speech 137–8,
  189

young people's language 159–68
  see also affixation; clipping;
    indirectness; meaning extension;
    new
  grammar; reduplication
  definition of 159–60
  characteristics of 160
    socio-cultural 160
    linguistic 160
  emphatic use of 166, 167
    see also emotion
  and fashion 167
  and gemination 167
    see also gemination in JL

Japanese Index

The part of an entry discussed in the main text is in boldface.

あ
あいづち 184
あいつの足 46
遊んだ**もんだ** 12
遊びにいき**たがって**たね 17
あっち行ってて 42

い
いいよどみ 191
生き**な** 28
いけません 35
今何時だと思ってるの？63
隠喩 70

う
植えちゃ**いけません** 35
うかがおう 159
ウソォ 59
うち 139
うまれた**んだ** 8

お
おいし**そうだ** 21
おきてきちゃ**だめ** 36
おぼえ**てごらん** 33
おぼえ**てらっしゃい** 33
おまえ 56
お前 55
おまえもね！123
思い出した**らしい** 20

か
が 93, 97–102
帰す**んだ**よ 36
かし**て** 31
かしら 21–3
からです 3
がる 16–7
かわいがっている**みたい** 20
含意 61
間投助詞 133
がんば**れ** 28

換喩 72

き
きけない**の** 37
擬人法 71
きみ 57
禁じる 25

く
ください 34–5
くまの子ウーフ 5–6

け
敬語 153
元気だし**なさい** 30
謙譲語 155
現象文 120

こ
小泉首相 40, 49
こうふんし**ないで** 34
ことだ 12–14
この世にいない**と思う**わ 19
固有名詞 40
語用論 1
コンテクスト 54
こんなとこ 42

さ
さるかに合戦 84–5

し
しかし 86
時間を**ください** 35
指示詞 40
指示代名詞 40
死の星になって**しまう** 18
自発 168n.9
社説 10
終助詞 133
しらべ**なさい** 30
死んでくれる**はずだ** 16

す
すぐもどる**はずよ** 16
すぐれたジョークだ 60

せ
税金を払っているような**ものだ** 10–11

そ
そうだ 19, 21
総理どう**いたし**ましょうか 158
そだって**おくれ** 32
そと 139
そのキズ 42
尊敬語 153
そんな気 43

た
待遇表現 168n.7
旅だ**つんだよ** 8
だめ 35–6
団地になっ**ちゃう**んだよね 18
段落 114
談話 76

ち
ちゃう 17–18
昼食 52–4
直喩 71

つ
つきそっていた**んだろ** 15

て
て 31–4, 87
提喩 72
ておく 79
てください 34–5
てしまう 17
てつだって**てくれ** 32
天声人語 97, 106

と
という 108
と思う 18
どこへ行く**んだ** 4
としのせい**かしら** 23
とって**こい** 28
どなたでした**っけ**? 152
どんな子**かしら** 23

な
な 28–9
なさい 29–30

に
にげ**ろ** 27
人称代名詞 40

ね
熱でもあるんじゃない**かしら** 22
ねなさい 30

の
の 37
のだ 2–8

は
は 93–7, 102–3
ばか 58
バカ**みたい** 58
はずだ 15
バックれる 166–7

ひ
飛行機 50–2
比喩 70
病気になった**らしい** 20

ふ
ふってきた**みたい** 20

へ
勉強し**ろ** 27

ほ
本気**かしら** 22

ま
マジ 166–7
ます 150
まるで 71

み
みたい 19–21
みたいだ 71
みたいな 71

む
昔話 93
むちゃくちゃいう**な** 29

め
命じる 25

も
ものだ 9–12
桃太郎 93, 98
もんだ 9, 12

や
やめてください 34

よ
よ 37
ようだ 71
ような 71
よそ 139

ら
らしい 19–21
ランチ 52–4

れ
連用 87

わ
若者言葉 159
わたしが**お答えします** 158
若者用語 159
わけだ 8–9

ん
んだ 2–8
んです 3

Lightning Source UK Ltd.
Milton Keynes UK
UKOW05f0950220916

283564UK00006B/123/P